DUTCH REFERENCE GRAMMAR

The following books by the same author are also available from Martinus Nijhoff Leiden:
- B.C. Donaldson, *A Dutch Vocabulary*, Melbourne, 2nd ed. 1985
- B.C. Donaldson, *Dutch. A linguistic history of Holland and Belgium*. Leiden, 1983

DUTCH REFERENCE GRAMMAR

B.C. Donaldson
B.A. (Hons), Litt. drs., D. Litt.
Senior lecturer in Dutch
University of Melbourne

Third edition

Martinus Nijhoff / Leiden, 1987

CIP-gegevens Koninklijke Bibliotheek, Den Haag

Donaldson, B.C.

Dutch reference grammar / B.C. Donaldson. – Leiden: Nijhoff
Met index, lit. opg.
ISBN 90-247-2354-X
SISO *837.1 UDC 802.931-5
Trefw.: Nederlandse taalkunde/Nederlands als tweede taal; grammatica.

Contents

Preface

Behind this book lie years of frustration, firstly as a student of Dutch and later as a teacher of the language, at the lack of an advanced grammar for the English speaking student. Advanced textbooks of many of the world's languages that have fewer speakers than Dutch have been written for the Anglo-Saxon student. I have always considered it indicative of the Dutch lack of pride and interest in their language that none of them has endeavoured to fill this gap, and there have probably been too few non-native-speakers proficient enough in the language to do so – a result of there never having been a satisfactory grammar perhaps?

Nederländsk Grammatik by J. de Rooy and I. Wikén Bonde (Språkförlaget, 1971) is the only book I know which presents Dutch grammar in anything like the detail that I do here for the foreign student of the language. I am indebted to the said book which I used on numerous occasions to monitor the completeness of my own grammar.

This book, lacking any predecessor upon which to improve, will undoubtedly have many shortcomings, but a beginning had to be made somewhere at some time by someone. Any constructive criticism on any aspect of the book at all will be most welcome. Perhaps future editions will then contain fewer imperfections.

There is also a lack of an advanced course book for Dutch and when the present work was first conceived, I was at odds whether to make it a course book or a reference grammar. On reflection I decided that a reference grammar was more urgent, particularly because a reference work can, with a little effort, be used as an advanced course book, whereas the reverse is not possible. It is hoped, however, that in the future a supplement of exercises geared to specific paragraphs in the grammar will appear. The present work will then go a lot further in fulfilling the demand for an advanced course book as well.

This reference grammar is aimed at the tertiary and upper secondary student as well as at the private student who has a thorough knowledge of grammatical terminology and whose knowledge has already gone beyond what the existing grammars offer. It is not intended to replace the existing beginners' grammars, except perhaps in the case of a student with some prior knowledge who simply wishes to consolidate that knowledge, but it is intended to complement those grammars. There are several very good reference grammars of Dutch for native-speakers of the language (see p. 262) but these are not enough. Firstly the gap between the beginners' grammars and these Dutch grammars is enormous and secondly the approach is simply not the right one for anyone with an imperfect knowledge of Dutch. At that level certain contrasts with the mother tongue are still necessary; the student is still in need of a degree of prescription whereas the Dutch reference grammars are all descriptive.

The conflict between prescription and description necessitates a certain explanation. It was not possible, nor indeed desirable, to describe every detail of the spoken and written language. I have endeavoured to prescribe forms which I know to be generally acceptable in both the spoken and written languages of the Netherlands. If at any stage I have mentioned spoken forms which are not acceptable in writing, or written forms which are not usual in the spoken language, this has been either clearly stated in each instance or the abbreviations 'coll.' for colloquial, 'arch.' for archaic or 'lit.' for literary have been used. I make no apology for being quite strongly prescriptive at times, although I am aware that some will find forms I don't recommend quite acceptable; there comes a point where the foreign student is not helped by being offered a whole series of alternatives without any recommendation for one form or another. Historical explanation of grammatical forms has been kept to a bare minimum and has only been given where I deemed it necessary for the student's understanding of the particular point, eg. *gij* versus *jij*.

Belgian usage has been scarcely considered at all; to have done so would have rendered certain sections of the book rather unwieldy and in the interests of standardisation and prescription it seemed to me desirable to stick to current usage in the Netherlands, all the more so as the current trend in Belgium seems to be to follow the north in language issues.

My approach to grammar is a conventional one. Objective classification and consistency in lay-out are imperative for a book like this to be successful. I feel that by keeping to the categories the student is likely to be acquainted with from his other language studies, the information will be more readily accessible to the majority who make use of it. The contents of this book are only accessible to the student who has a thorough knowledge of the traditional categories of grammar; this is after all the only classification that is international enough to give the work currency wherever it may be used in the world.

Countries with mother tongues other than English, in particular Germany, now have numerous tertiary institutions teaching Dutch and they suffer from an even greater lack of suitable texts for learning the language. Although my approach has been entirely from the point of view of a native speaker of English, I feel and hope that most of the material will be of equal validity for native speakers of other languages, and that this book might find currency in those countries until such time as a similar work appears in those languages. The wide-spread knowledge of English among European youth these days should facilitate access to the information contained in the book.

It will be noticed that each new section of grammar gives the Dutch name for that particular grammatical category. My motivation was the following: if one of the functions of this book is to bridge the gap between the existing beginners' grammars and the reference grammars for native speakers, the student needs to know what the concept is called in Dutch in order to be able to go directly to the relevant section of such works.

The many examples used throughout the book to illustrate the grammatical points have purposely been kept as simple and everyday as possible, so much so that at times translation did not seem to be necessary.

Although the categories used are, on the whole, internationally recognised, there are inevitably some idiosyncracies in my classifications; for example, possessive adjectives will be found under pronouns and proper nouns appear in an appendix rather than in the chapter on nouns. For this reason I advise the reader to fully acquaint himself with the system by firstly paging through the entire book. Then, with the aid of the contents and the index, he should have little trouble in being able to refer quickly to any point of grammar.

I feel at this point a word of explanation is necessary about the numerous lists in the book. Some readers may feel that some of these lists are simply duplicating the dictionaries, but, having attempted to weed much of the information from dictionaries to compile these lists, I can assure them that the dictionairies are usually inadequate. For example, no Dutch reference work gives a satisfactory list of countries and nationalities and the Dutch themselves simply do not know, or are not sure, what an inhabitant of Zaïre is called, to mention but one instance. Many hours of frustrating interviewing and collating of varying opinions went into the compilation of that list alone.

Other lists contain information that is indeed to be found in dictionaries, but not of course in this format. For example, the adverbial expressions of time will nearly all be found as separate entries in any dictionary, but by attempting to bring them all together and listing them under key words, the student will learn so much more about the formation of such expressions by looking them up in this grammar than he will by seeking them in a dictionary.

Other lists are not intended so much for reference as for trying to illustrate certain concepts in Dutch. For example, prepositions could have been tackled in two ways: either I could have taken English prepositions one by one and illustrated the various ways they are rendered in Dutch, but this would in my opinion, have been unwieldy and of little practical use; or alternatively I could have taken and did indeed take Dutch prepositions one by one and listed as many everyday idiomatic uses of each I could think of. In this way I hope the student, while not being able to use the list for reference exactly, will however be able to acquire a feeling for the usage of each of these idiomatic little words.

My treatment of all non-regular verbs also requires a little explanation. I have classified all such verbs as either strong, mixed, modal or irregular. For facility's sake and to assist the student with an historical linguistic background, strong verbs have all been assigned to the original *Ablautreihe* to which they belong. On p. 118-120 there is an alphabetical list of every non-regular verb which tells the reader which *Ablautreihe* or other category the verb belongs to. Then on pages 121-127 the reader can look up the tenses of that verb under the category designated on p. 118-120.

Finally it will be noticed that there is no one chapter devoted to syntax (word order), for which I expect some criticism. All attempts to formalise the extremely complex issue of word order that I have seen in Dutch and German grammars fail miserably. I found myself unable to write a chapter on syntax that would be practical for reference and that would not involve unnecessary repetition of issues dealt with elsewhere in the book. For this reason I finally opted for an entry entitled 'syntax' in the index which refers the reader to all issues of word order as and where they occur in the description of the grammar.

University of Melbourne, Dec. 1980   Bruce C. Donaldson

To the third edition

Although a total revision of this book is not yet possible, mainly because of financial constraints, this edition does contain a very large number of additions and alterations, many of which have been incorporated on the advice of readers all around the world who have taken the trouble to write to me with their suggestions. It is always most gratifying to hear from one's readers and I hope the trend will continue so that the fourth edition will be even better. The invitation to all readers who feel they have something constructive to offer still stands. Please don't hesitate to write to me at the address below with your criticisms and suggestions.

Since this book first appeared, a very important Dutch language reference work for the foreign student has appeared, the *Algemene Nederlandse Spraakkunst*, by G. Geerts (ed.) e.a., Wolters-Noordhoff, Groningen, 1984 (1309 pages). The appearance of the *ANS* does not in any way render this book superfluous as the *ANS* often goes too far in its explanations, even for the relatively advanced student, and it is also not specifically tailored to the difficulties experienced by the English speaking student of Dutch. I mention the *ANS* here as a book to which the enthusiast can progress once he feels that he has mastered the contents of this book. It is also likely to contain descriptions of more esoteric structures not dealt with by me here.

I have also produced a companion volume to this grammar since the first edition appeared. It is entitled *Dutch: a linguistic history of Holland and Belgium*, Martinus Nijhoff, Leiden, 1983. I recommend it to the student who wishes to know more about the origins of the language, the dialects and the situation with regard to Dutch in Belgium for example.

In the preface to the first edition mention was made of a supplement of exercises to appear at some later date. That book is currently in preparation and may hopefully see the light of day by 1988.

April, 1986

Dr. B.C. Donaldson
Department of Germanic Studies
University of Melbourne
Parkville, Victoria
Australia 3052

Acknowledgements

My thanks are due to Prof. W.Z. Shetter of Indiana University, Bloomington and Dr. H.C. Wekker of Nijmegen University for their thorough reading of the manuscript and for the many valuable corrections and additions they suggested. I would similarly like to thank a post-graduate student of mine, Ms. J. Bennett, and Ms. R. van Eck from Martinus Nijhoff for their reading of the text.

Thanks are also due to my employer, the University of Melbourne, which provided me with six months study-leave in 1977 during which time a start was made on the writing of this book and without which time the initial ice may never have been broken. In addition the Faculty of Arts at Melbourne University made a considerable sum of money available for typing and assistance with the compilation of the index. This money was gratefully received.

The former secretaries of the Department of Germanic Studies, Mrs. V. Denman and Mrs. A. Heineke-Sieuwerts, must be thanked for the laborious hours they spent typing and retyping the manuscript.

Finally I wish to express my gratitude to Ms. C. McLiesh who, in her capacity as student research assistant, compiled the index, the backbone of any reference work.

Melbourne, July 1983

B.C.D.

Abbreviations

arch.	– archaic		lit.	– literary
c.	– common gender		n.	– neuter
coll.	– colloquial		pej.	– pejorative
fig.	– figurative		s.o.	– someone
inh.	– inhabitant		s.t.	– something

1 Pronunciation *(uitspraak)*

It is assumed that anyone using this book is acquainted with the basics of Dutch pronunciation and thus they are not dealt with here. Students requiring detailed information on assimilation, stress and other aspects of pronunciation are advised to consult R.H.B. De Coninck *Groot uitspraakwoordenboek van de Nederlandse Taal*, Uitgeverij De Nederlandsche Boekhandel, Antwerpen, 1970 and E. Blancquaert *Praktische uitspraakleer van de Nederlandse Taal*, De Sikkel, Antwerpen, 1969. Pages 141-9 in the latter book contain a very good description of Dutch stress patterns.

2 Spelling *(spelling)*

As with the pronunciation, it is assumed that the reader has grasped the essentials of the highly phonetic spelling of Dutch and that there is no need to repeat them here. In case of doubt on any point, the reader is referred to pages XXXV to LI of *Woordenlijst van de Nederlandse Taal – samengesteld in opdracht van de Nederlandse en de Belgische regering*, 's-Gravenhage, 1954.

The following complications of spelling are covered in great detail in the *Woordenlijst* on the pages given. Only those uses which differ from English and are thus not dealt with in the *Woordenlijst* are mentioned here.

Acute and grave accents

The numerous French loan words written with accents in that language usually retain those accents in Dutch.

> *café, à, Française*

Note, however, that diminutives of words ending in *-é* no longer require the accent.

> *café – cafeetje, logé(e) – logeetje*

Words of French origin ending in *-ée* drop the accent in Dutch:

> *orchidee, marechaussee* **but** *logée* (< fem. of *logé*)

Words beginning with *é* also drop the accent:

> *etage, etalage*

The acute (´) and grave (`) are otherwise used on Dutch words for emphasis where in an English text we would normally underline the word of print it in bold type. The grave is usually used only on the letter *e* but is occasionally found on other vowels. The acute also often replaces the grave in such cases; there seems to be little consistency here.

> *Een tè behoudende koers* – A **too** conservative approach
> *Werklozen èn studenten* – The unemployed **and** students or Both the unemployed and students
> *Dit woord wordt gewoonlijk zónder, maar ook wel mèt klemtoon gesproken* – This word is usually pronounced **without**, but sometimes **with** stress.

In the sentence *Je doet het, hè?* – 'You're doing it, aren't you?' the grave reflects the pronunciation and distinguishes the word *hè (niet waar)* from *hé* (hey).

The acute is used on all other vowels for emphasis. Notice the difference in meaning it gives to the following words:

een – a, *één* – one; *voor* – for, *vóór* – in front of, before

Even when these two words have the second meaning they are written with accents only when the meaning could be ambiguous, otherwise they are left off.

om een uur – at one o'clock
een van mijn vrienden – one of my friends
er staat een boom voor het huis – there is a tree in front of the house
but
er staat een boom vóór het huis, niet erachter – there is a tree in front of the house, not behind it.

Sometimes the accents are used on other words to avoid ambiguity:

vèrstrekkend – far-reaching
verstrekkend – issuing, supplying

Apostrophe *(het weglatingsteken) p. LXVII*

Unlike English, the apostrophe is not used to show possession.

Jans boek, mijn moeders auto

Only when the proper noun ends in *a, o, u, s* or *z* is the apostrophe used:

Hans' boek, Helma's woordenboek

The abbreviated forms of *ik, het, mijn, zijn* etc. using an apostrophe are best avoided in writing except in certain standard expressions:

met z'n drieën, op z'n Nederlands (always abbreviated in these two cases)
ik heb 't koud, over 't algemeen (commonly abbreviated)

Capital letters *(hoofdletters) pp. LXVIII-LXX*

The Dutchman regards the diphthong *ij* as one letter (it is a separate key on a typewriter, for example) and thus if a word starts with *ij* and has to be capitalised, both the *i* and the *j* are affected.

Het IJ, het IJsselmeer

In Dutch family names with *van, den, der, ten* and *ter* one usually writes such particles separately and small letters are used when a christian name or initials precede.

H. van der Molen

When the christian name or initials are not mentioned, a capital letter is used.

> *de brief van Van den Berg*
> *We hebben het over De Bruijn*
> *meneer Van der Plank*

Note: When looking up a name in a Dutch telephone book or bibliography, it is written as follows: *Berg, H. van den.*

'Mr.' and 'Mrs.' are always written with small letters in Dutch (see p. 24) for one notable exception):

> *meneer Smit, mevrouw Aantjes*

Note on *meneer/de heer:* (see also p. 24 and p. 231)

When a man is addressed directly, *meneer* precedes his name. If he is being talked about, however, *de heer* will usually precede his name rather than *meneer*; this is particularly the case in formal style.

It will be noticed that in some avant-garde publications (student newspapers, some modern literature etc.) adjectives of nationality are often written with small letters, eg. *nederlands, amsterdams*. The *voorkeurspelling*, as used in the *Woordenlijst*, does not support this, however.

Hyphen *(het koppelteken) pp. LXIV-LXV*

The hyphen is not as common in Dutch as in English because the rules for compound words are on the whole more clearly defined than in English. For example, hesitation about 'kitchen-door' or 'kitchen door', 'racing-car' or 'racing car' does not arise in Dutch, i.e. *keukendeur, raceauto* etc.
It is, however, commonly used when listing compound nouns that share a component of the compound.

> *maag-, hoofd- en kiespijn* – stomach, head and tooth-ache
> *voor- en namiddag* – morning and afternoon
> *matrozenuitdrukkingen en -vloeken* – seamen's expressions and curses

Dieresis *(het deelteken, het trema) p. LXVI*

Medial sounds in compounds words *(tussenklanken in samenstellingen) pp. LVI-LXIII*

i.e. *kippevel, kippenhok, kinderzegel, broekspijp*

Syllabic division *(verdeling van woorden in lettergrepen)* *pp. LII-LV*

New trends in spelling

Nowadays many foreign words are being written according to the rules of Dutch phonetics:

cadeau – kado/kadootje
niveau – nivo
historisch – histories

Until such time as the *Woordenlijst* had been revised and gives the seal of approval to such spellings one is advised to follow the *voorkeurspelling*, i.e. the traditional spelling as recommended in the *Woordenlijst*.

3 Punctuation *(interpunctie, leestekens)*

Generally speaking Dutch punctuation does not differ greatly from that of English. Only the comma is used somewhat differently – usually more sparingly than in English – and thus only the comma is dealt with here. For a complete account of Dutch punctuation see H.M. Hermkens, *Spelling en interpunctie*, Malmberg, Den Bosch.

The Comma *(de komma)*

Only those uses that differ from English are dealt with here.

3.1 It may be used between two adjectives before a noun when no conjunction is used (see p. 87), as in English, but is also often omitted in such cases; it is, however, always used when three or more adjectives precede the noun.

> *een koude(,) natte avond*
> **but**
> *een koude, natte en stormachtige avond*

3.2 When a subordinate clause precedes a main clause in a compound sentence, a comma is usually used to separate the verbs:

> *Als je het morgen doet, krijg je iets van me.*
> *Omdat hij zo laat thuisgekomen was, was zijn vrouw boos op hem.*
> *Ik blijf thuis en omdat ik me misselijk voel, ga ik onmiddellijk naar bed.*

When the main clause precedes a subordinate clause introduced by *dat*, the comma is often omitted; with other conjunctions the comma is always used.

> *Ik geloof dat hij morgen komt.*
> *Ik heb de pan aan mijn moeder gegeven, hoewel ik er zelf geen had.*

3.3 With relative clauses a comma is always used at the end of the clause but seldom before it (although it is sometimes found with longer relative clauses).

> *De man die in dat huis woont, is mijn oom.*
> *De universiteit(,) die graag later in het jaar een aantal nieuwe cursussen had willen invoeren, heeft besloten dat dat niet mogelijk zal zijn.*

The following subtle difference in meaning when the first comma is omitted or used should be noted: with a comma the relative clause relates back to the entire group whereas without a comma it refers to only a section of the group; strictly speaking this is the same in English.

> *De jongens die te laat waren, moesten schoolblijven*
> i.e. There were other boys and perhaps girls who were not late.

De jongens, die te laat waren, moesten schoolblijven
i.e. There were only boys and all had to stay behind.

3.4 Note that the following English commas, which merely indicate a reading pause within a clause, are not used in Dutch:
It is, however, very difficult.
Het is echter erg moeilijk.
He has, unfortunately, not done it.
Hij heeft het helaas niet gedaan.

3.5 See p. 209 (note) and 215.

4 Cases (naamvallen)

Case, once so prevalent in Dutch – especially in the written languange – is to all intents and purposes dead nowadays. Remnants of the cases will still be found chiefly in standard expressions, official titles and occasionally in very formal writing. Articles, demonstratives, possessives, adjectives and nouns can all be affected by case (see the relevant chapters).

It is traditional in English-speaking countries to refer to the four cases in the following order: nominative (subject case), accusative (direct object case), genitive (possessive case) and dative (indirect object). In Holland, however, the classical order used in the learning of Latin and Greek is more common, i.e. nominative, genitive, dative and accusative. This has resulted in the Dutch naming the cases after their number in the above sequence, i.e. nominative – de eerste naamval, genitive – de tweede naamval etc.

Some common expressions preserving archaic case endings are given below to illustrate the concept; the number is actually infinite. Only the genitive and the dative, apart from the nominative of course, are recognisable nowadays:

Expressions preserving the genitive:

wiens hoed, wier jurk	whose hat, whose dress
's middags	in the afternoon
blootshoofds	bare-headed
desnoods	in case of need
het teken des kruises	the sign of the cross
's lands wijs, 's lands eer	when in Rome, ...
het Leger des Heils	the Salvation Army
in naam der wet	in the name of the law
Koninkrijk der Nederlanden	Kingdom of the Netherlands

Expressions preserving the dative:

ter wille van (see p. 204)	for the sake of
ten einde raad	at one's wits' end
tenslotte	finally
op heterdaad	red-handed
op den duur	in the long run
van ganser harte	from the bottom of one's heart
om den brode	for a living

5 Articles *(lidwoorden)*

The indefinite article *(het onbepaalde lidwoord)*

The indefinite article 'a, an' in English is *een* in Dutch which is pronounced *'n* and sometimes written as such in direct speech. The numeral 'one' is also *een*, pronounced with a long *e* and written *één* when ambiguity can arise (see p. 15 and 208).
Occasionally in standard expressions and archaic style older case forms of *een* are found.

> *enerzijds* – on the one hand
> *het leed ener moeder* – the sorrow of a mother

Omission of the indefinite article

The indefinite article is sometimes omitted in Dutch where it is used in English.

a it is often omitted after the preposition *als* (see p. 187):

> *Hij gebruikt zijn schoteltje als asbak.*
> He's using his saucer as an ashtray.
> *Ik doe Duits als bijvak.*
> I'm doing German as a secondary subject.

b it is commonly omitted after the preposition *zonder*:

> *Ik zag een man zonder hoofd.*
> I saw a man without a head.
> *Hij ging uit zonder hoed.*
> He went out without a hat.

c it is usually omitted before professions (when the verb is *zijn, worden* or *blijven*), but always inserted when the profession is preceded by an adjective:

> *Ik ben leraar* – I am a teacher.
> *Ik ben een zeer goede leraar* – I am a very good teacher.
> Also: *Hij is vader geworden* – He has become a father.

d it is commonly omitted before nationalities (when the verb is *zijn, worden* or *blijven*), but always inserted when the nationality is preceded by an adjective:

> *Hij is (een) Nederlander* – He is a Dutchman.
> *Hij is een rasechte Nederlander* – He is a genuine Dutchman.

e it is omitted in various standard expressions:

Het was jammer – It was a pity
maag-, kiespijn hebben/krijgen – to have/get a stomach-ache, tooth-ache
oog om oog, tand om tand – an eye for an eye, a tooth for a tooth
kwart voor/over drie – a quarter to/past three

The definite article *(het bepaald lidwoord)*

The definite article used before singular common gender nouns is *de*, and *het* is used before neuter nouns. Both genders employ *de* in the plural.

de man, de deur, het kind, het gat – de mannen, de deuren, de kinderen, de gaten

There are many remnants of former cases in the definite article (see p. 204). The most common are *der* (genitive singular feminine and plural), *des* or *'s* (genitive masculine and neuter singular) and *den* (dative masculine and neuter singular). Many case forms of the definite article have been preserved in standard expressions:

in de loop der tijd – in the course of time
Beatrix, Koningin der Nederlanden – Beatrix, Queen of the Netherlands
's morgens – in the morning
in naam des konings – in the name of the king
het Leger des Heils – the Salvation Army
desondanks – in spite of it/that
op den duur – in the course of time

The genitive feminine singular and plural *der* in particular is still productive; it is, however, rather formal.

Omission of the definite article

In certain idioms the definite article is omitted where it **is** used in English:

aan tafel – at the table
op tafel – on the table
op kantoor – at the office
naar kantoor – to the office
op straat – in the street
op zolder – in the attic
in bad – in the bath
in huis – in the house
naar zee – to the seaside
aan zee – at the seaside
met mes en vork – with a knife and fork
in staat van oorlog – in a state of war
op antwoord wachten – to wait for an answer

piano/gitaar enz. spelen – to play the piano/guitar etc.
koningin en prins – the queen and (the) prince
in eerste instantie – in the first place
ik ben van mening dat – I am of the opinion that
in naam van de koning – in the name of the king

It is also commonly omitted before nouns in apposition

Reagan, president van de V.S., is op het ogenblik op staatsbezoek in Japan.

Inclusion of the definite article

There are many more cases in which the definite article is used where it is not in English.
Some cases are situations where its use can be defined, others are individual idioms.

a it is always used before **certain abstract nouns**.

de mens – mankind
de natuur – nature
de liefde – love
de moderne kunst – modern art
de (Nederlandse) geschiedenis – (Dutch) history
de dood – death
het leven – life
de hemel – heaven
de hel – hell
het paradijs – paradise

De natuur is mysterieus.
Nature is mysterious.
De belangrijkste gebeurtenis in de geschiedenis.
The most important event in history.
Zo is het leven.
Such is life.

b it is always used before **names of towns and countries** when they are preceded by
adjectives.

het mooie Amsterdam – beautiful Amsterdam
het toenmalige Duitsland – Germany in those days

c it is always used before **seasons**.

in de lente – in spring
De winter in Australië is erg zacht.
Winter in Australia is very mild.

d it is always used with **meals** after the prepositions *na* and *vóór*.

na/vóór het avondeten – after/before dinner
tijdens de lunch – during lunch

e it is always used before the **names of streets, parks and squares.**

Ik woon in de Hoofdstraat.
I live in Main Street.
Hij woont op de Erasmusweg.
He lives in Erasmus Road.
Ze sliep in het Vondelpark.
She slept in Vondel Park.
Op het Waterlooplein.
At Waterloo Square.

f **religions and names of airlines** are always preceded by the definite article.

Hij vloog met de KLM.
He flew with KLM.
Waar is het hoofdkantoor van de TWA?
Where is TWA's main office?
De islam is een godsdienst uit het Midden-Oosten.
Islam is a Middle Eastern religion.
Het christendom door de eeuwen heen.
Christianity through the ages.

g it is used after *Meneer* and *Mevrouw* when the **profession** (not the personal name)
follows – usually a form of direct address.

Meneer de Voorzitter – Mr. Chairman
Mevrouw de President – Madame President
Meneer de Kat – Mr. Cat (in a fairy-tale)
Sprookjes van Moeder de Gans – Mother Goose's fairy-tales

h it is used in **various idioms.**

in de stad – in town
naar de stad – to town
in de kerk – in church
in de gevangenis – in jail
aan de universiteit – at university
in de praktijk – in pratice
onder de zeespiegel – below sea level
in het Duits – in German
uit het Frans vertalen – to translate from French
op het tweede net – on channel two (T.V.)
de school begint om… – school begins at…
in de tweede versnelling – in second gear
tussen de 12 en de 15 – between 12 and 15 (items or age)
over/onder de 50 – over/under 50 (items or age)
voor de lol – for fun
in het rood gekleed – dressed in red
de een na de ander – one after another, one by one
met de auto/tram etc. – by car, tram etc.
met de hand – by hand

de volgende keer – next time
op het eerste gezicht – at first sight

i In Dutch it is not possible for one definite article to do service for two nouns that follow if they are of different gender; the article should be repeated for each noun. If the same article is required by both nouns, the article can be omitted.

de melk en het brood waren duur – the milk and bread were expensive
om de hals en (de) handen – around the neck and hands

6 Demonstratives (aanwijzende voornaamwoorden)

6.1 The demonstrative, like the definite article, varies according to the gender of the noun it precedes:

common gender:	*deze* – this	*die* – that
neuter gender:	*dit* – this	*dat* – that
plural (both genders):	*deze* – these	*die* – those

> *deze man* – this man, *deze deuren* – these doors, *die leraar* – that teacher, *dat huis* – that house, *die huizen* – those houses

Note: *de*
  deze   common gender and plural
  die

het
  dit   neuter singular
  dat

6.2 Other case forms of the demonstratives are found in standard expressions

> *een dezer dagen* – one of these days
> *op de 18de dezer* – on the 18th of this month (in letters)
> *destijds* – at that time
> *dientengevolge* – as a result of that

The genitive form *diens* sometimes replaces the English possessive adjective 'his', see p. 56.

6.3 'The former' and 'the latter' are rendered in Dutch by *deze* and an archaic demonstrative *gene* which is also used in other contexts

> *Wij wonen aan deze zijde van de rivier, onze vrienden aan gene.*
> We live on this side of the river, our friends on that (side).

6.4 The pronominal use of demonstratives is dealt with under pronouns, see p. 59.

7 Nouns (*zelfstandige naamwoorden*)

Gender *(geslacht)*

Dutch nouns know only two genders: common gender and neuter. The former is an amalgamation of what were formerly masculine and feminine. Only in some archaic case forms is any distinction between the two still made (see Definite article p. 22). In the south of Holland and in Belgium the difference between masculine and feminine is still heeded in the use of pronouns (see p. 52).

Dutch dictionaries usually indicate gender by placing an *m (mannelijk)*, a *v (vrouwelijk)* or an *o (onzijdig)* after the noun.

Every new Dutch noun must be learnt together with the appropriate definite article. There are a few reasonably reliable rules for learning the gender of nouns but there are nevertheless many words which do not fit the rules and for which the gender simply has to be learnt by heart. The following is a list of rules, some hard and fast, others a little vague, to assist in learning genders.

7.1 Rules for the gender of Dutch nouns

7.1.1 COMMON GENDER NOUNS

The names of men and women:

> *de burgemeester* (mayor), *de dochter* (daughter), *de moeder* (mother), *de penning-meesteres* (female treasurer), *de vader* (father), *de verpleger* (male nurse), *de ver-pleegster* (nurse), *de zoon* (son).
> Exceptions: *het mens* (woman), *het wijf* (woman).

The names of most animals, including birds and fish:

> *de haring* (herring), *de leeuw* (lion), *de mus* (sparrow)
> (for exceptions see Neuter nouns, names of young animals)

The names of trees, flowers and fruit:

> *de anjer* (carnation), *de eik* (oak), *de perzik* (peach)

The names of stones, considered as objects (see Neuter nouns, minerals):

> *de baksteen* (brick), *de diamant* (diamond), *de robijn* (ruby)

The names of days, months and seasons (except compounds with *jaar*)

The names of mountains and large rivers:

de Mont Blanc, de Nijl (Nile), *de Rijn* (Rhine), *de Vesuvius*

The names of objects whose names end in *-aard, -aar, -erd:*

de standaard (standard), *de lessenaar* (desk), *de mosterd* (mustard)

The names of tools or instruments, derived from verbs, and ending in *-el* **and** *-er:*

de beitel (chisel), *de sleutel* (key), *de gieter* (watering-can)

Words ending in *-em, -lm* **and** *-rm:*

de bezem (broom), *de helm* (helmet), *de term* (term), *de storm* (storm)
Exception: *het scherm* (screen)

Words ending in *-ing* **and** *-ling:*

de regering (government), *de leerling* (school student)

Most monosyllabic words derived from verbs:

de lach (laugh), *de loop* (walk, gait), *de val* (trap, fall), *de zucht* (sigh)

The names of letters of the alphabet:

de a, de b, de c

The names of figures (numerical symbols):

de een, de zeven, de honderd

The names of musical instruments:

de hobo (oboe), *de piano* (piano), *de viool* (violin)
Exceptions: *het spinet, het clavecimbel* (harpsichord)

The names of virtues and vices:

de nijd (anger, envy), *de woede* (rage), *de genade* (mercy), *de liefde* (love)

Words with the suffix *-e:*

de kou(de) (cold), *de vrede* (peace), *de zonde* (sin)
Exception: *het einde* (end)

Words derived from adjectives, and with the suffix *-te:*

de duurte (expensiveness), *de hoogte* (height), *de lengte* (length)

Words ending in *-heid* **and** *-nis:*

de vrijheid (freedom), *de waarheid* (truth), *de gebeurtenis* (event), *de geschiedenis* (history)

Words ending in *-age, -ij, -ei, -ie, -iek, -teit* **and** *-theek:*

de plantage (plantation), *de batterij* (battery), *de pastei* (pie), *de harmonie* (harmony), *de fabriek* (factory), *de elektriciteit* (electricity), *de bibliotheek* (library) Exceptions: *het publiek* (public), *het schilderij* (painting)

Words ending in an unaccented *-(t)ie* **and** *-uw:*

de produktie, de *schaduw* (shadow, shade) Exceptions: *het concilie* (council), *het evangelie* (gospel), *het genie* (genius)

Adjectives uses as nouns and referring to a person:

de rijke (rich one), *de verminkte* (crippled one), *de zieke* (sick one)

Words ending in *-schap* **signifying a condition** (see Neuter nouns, *-schap*):

de dronkenschap (drunkenness), *de verwantschap* (relationship), *de vriendschap* (friendship), *de zwangerschap* (pregnancy)

but also the following:

de boodschap (message), *de broederschap* (brotherhood), *de eigenschap* (quality), *de nalatenschap* (inheritance), *de wetenschap* (science)

7.1.2 NEUTER NOUNS

All diminutives:

het kindje (child), *het koekje* (biscuit)

All infinitives used as nouns:

het eten (food, eating), *het geven* (giving), *het werken* (working)

The names of young animals (except *de big* – piglet)

het kalfje (calf), *het kuiken* (chicken), *het veulen* (foal)

A great number of **minerals**. This group includes

a Stones, where the name denotes the matter in general, or is a collective noun (see Common gender nouns, names of stones)

het diamant (diamond), *het steen* (stone), *het kwarts* (quartz) b All well-known **metals**

> *het blik* (tin), *het goud* (gold), *het koper* (copper), *het nikkel* (nickle), *het radium* (radium), *het staal* (steel), *het tin* (pewter), *het ijzer* (iron), *het zilver* (silver)

c **Other minerals**

> *het asbest* (asbestos), *het barium* (barium), *het erts* (ore), *het gips* (gypsum, plaster)
> Exception: *de kalk* (calcium)

The names of countries and provinces (the article is only used when the name is qualified):

> *het mooie Australië, het België van toen, het oude Friesland*

The names of cities and villages (including those which have *den* included in the name):

> *het fraaie Den Haag, het mooie Amsterdam* (although *de Dam*)

Words ending in *-sel* (except nouns whose *-sel* is not a true suffix, e.g. *de mossel* – mussel, *oksel* – armpit, *wissel* – postal note):

> *deksel* (lid), *stelsel* (system), *verschijnsel* (phenomenon), *voedsel* (food)

All collective nouns with the prefix *ge-* **and suffix** *-te:*

> *het gebergte* (mountain range), *het gebladerte* (foliage), *het geboomte* (trees)

Collective nouns with the prefix *ge-* **and no suffix:**

> *het gebroed* (brood), *het gepeupel* (populace, rabble)

Nouns formed from verbal stems beginning with the prefixes *be-, ge-, ont-, ver-:*

> *het belang* (importance), *het gesprek* (conversation), *het ontbijt* (breakfast), *het verbod* (prohibition)
> Exceptions: *de verkoop* (sale), *de uitverkoop* (sale), *de verhuur* (hiring out, letting)

Adjectives ending in *-e* **used as abstract nouns:**

> *het goede* (that which is good)
> *het kwade* (that which is evil)
> *het genotene* (that which has been enjoyed)

All colours:

> *het blauw* (blue), *het groen* (green)

All words ending in *-um:*

> *het album* (album), *het gymnasium* (grammar school)
> Exception: *de datum* (date)

Most words ending in -*dom*:

het eigendom (property), *het christendom* (Christianity), *het mensdom* (humanity)
Exceptions: *de adeldom* (nobility), *de ouderdom* (old age), *de rijkdom* (riches, wealth)

Words ending in -*schap* signifying a function (see Common gender nouns):

het priesterschap (priesthood), *het burgemeesterschap* (mayoralty), *het vaderschap* (fatherhood)

but also the following:

het graafschap (county), *het gezelschap* (company), *het gereedschap* (tools), *het landschap* (landscape), *het genootschap* (society)

All words ending in -*isme*:

het communisme, het socialisme, het germanisme

All words ending in -*aat*:

het internaat (boarding school), *het secretariaat* (secretariat), *het consulaat* (consulate), *het resultaat* (result)

Points of the compass:

het noorden (north), *het noordoosten* (north-east)

7.1.3 COMPOUND NOUNS

Compound nouns always take the gender of the last noun in the compound:

het ontbijt, de tafel – thus, *de ontbijttafel*

The following are exceptions to this rule:

de blik (glance)	*het ogenblik* (moment)
de draad (wire)	*het prikkeldraad* (barbed wire)
de hof (courtyard)	*het kerkhof* (grave-yard)
de kant (side)	*het vierkant* (square)
de stip (dot, point)	*het tijdstip* (point in time, period)
het stuk (piece)	*de biefstuk*[1] (steak)
het weer (weather)	*de brandweer*[2] (fire-brigade)
het zegel (seal)	*de postzegel* (stamp)

1 In fact this is a corruption of the English word 'steak'.
2 Actually of different origin; derived from the verb *weren* = to avert; compare also *het paard* (horse) and *de luipaard* (leopard).

7.1.4 NOUNS WITH TWO GENDERS

There are many nouns that can have two genders: there are those that have two genders with no difference in meaning and those that do have a difference in meaning:

Nouns with two genders with no difference in meaning, the more common gender is given first (there are more nouns in this category):

de/het aanrecht (sink)
het/de affiche (poster)
het/de deksel (lid)
het/de draad (wire)
de/het kaneel (cinnamon)
de/het kauwgom (chewing gum)
het/de knoflook (garlic)
de/het matras (mattress)
de/het omslag (envelope)
het/de poeder (powder)
de/het rooster (toaster, time-table)
de/het schort (apron)
de/het sloop (pillow case)
de/het soort (sort)

Note: *de keer* (time) but *deze/dit keer*

Note the peculiarities of gender in the following expressions:

het been **but** *hij is weer op de been*
he is on his legs again (actually an old plural form)
het weer **but** *hij is in de weer*
he is up and about, busy
het meer **but** *de Bijlmermeer, de Haarlemmermeer*
het hout **but** *de Haarlemmerhout*

Nouns with two genders with a difference in meaning:

de bal (ball) pl. *ballen*	*het bal* (ball, dance) pl. *bals*
de band (ribbon, tape, i.e. object)	*het band* (ribbon, tape, i.e. material)
de blik (glance)	*het blik* (tin, i.e. metal and tin can)
de bos (bouquet)	*het bos* (forest)
de bot (flounder)	*het bot* (bone)
de doek (cloth, i.e. object)	*het doek* (canvas, curtain, film screen)
de hof (courtyard)	*het hof* (court of a king)
de hoorn (horn, object)	*het hoorn* (horn, material)
de idee (philosophical idea)	*het idee* (plan, thought)
de jacht (hunting)	*het jacht* (yacht)
de eerste maal (first time, occasion)	*het maal* (meal)
de mens – (man, mankind)	*het mens* (woman)
de pad (toad) pl. *padden*	*het pad* (path) pl. *paden*
de patroon (patron, sponsor)	*het patroon* (pattern)

de portier (porter)	*het portier* (door of a vehicle)
de punt (point, i.e. of a needle)	*het punt* (point, mark, place)
de Heilige Schrift (Bible)	*het schrift* (exercise book)
de soort (species)	*het soort* (kind, sort)
de stof (material)	*het stof* (dust)
de veer (feather, spring)	*het veer* (ferry)

Note that the names of all precious stones have two genders: they are common gender when the noun refers to the individual stones and neuter when it refers to the stone as a material:

de smaragd – the emerald (jewel)
het smaragd – emerald (material)

7.2 Plural of Nouns *(meervoudsvorming)*

Dutch nouns form their plural by addition of either *-s* or *-en* to the singular, the latter ending being more common. The basic rule for plural formation is always to add *-en* unless the word belongs to one of the following *-s* plural categories.

7.2.1 -S PLURALS (i.e.: *-s* or *-'s*)

1 **All nouns ending in unstressed** *-el*, *-em*, *-en* **and** *-er*. This is a very large group, e.g. *tafels, bezems, jongens, spijkers*.
Exceptions: *aderen* (veins), *artikelen* (articles), *christenen* (Christians), *engelen* (angels), *maatregelen* (measures), *middelen* (means), *mosselen* (mussels), *redenen* (reasons), *wonderen* (wonders).

Also nouns with the suffix *-sel* and compounds with *-stel*, e.g. *verschijnselen* (phenomena), *beginselen* (principles); *opstellen* (essays), *toestellen* (appliances).

In older writings and more formal style nouns in this group are often found with an *-en* ending, eg. *appelen, wapenen*.
The following nouns take on a new meaning when given an *-en* plural:

hemelen	– heavens		*tafelen*	– tablets (of the law, biblical)
hemels	– canopies		*tafels*	– tables (for food)
hersenen	– brains (organ, food)		*vaderen*	– forefathers[4]
hersens	– brains (food)		*vaders*	– fathers
letteren	– literature[3]		*wateren*	– waterways
letters	– letters (of the alphabet)		*waters*	– waters
middelen	– means		*wortelen*	– carrots
middels	– waists		*wortels*	– roots, carrots

---

3 *Faculteit der Letteren* – Arts Faculty.
4 *de vroede vaderen* – the City Fathers.

Note: Words like *wiel* (wheel), *schoen* (shoe) and *mier* (ant) do not contain *-el, -en* and *-er* as endings and thus add *-en*; similarly *modél* has a stressed *-el* ending and goes *modellen*.
The plural of *stuk* (piece) is *stukken*, but *stuks* occurs too the with meaning of items, eg. *Ik heb tien stuks gekocht* I bought ten (pencils, balls etc.).

2   **Nouns ending in *-erd* and *-aard* and designating masculine beings,**
eg. *sufferds* (idiots), *grijsaards* (old men).
Exceptions: *Spanjaarden* (Spaniards).

3   **All diminutives ending in *-je*,**
eg. *koekjes* (biscuits), *huisjes* (houses).

Note:*kindertjes* (kiddies), *kleertjes* (clothes) (derived from the plural of the non-diminutive form).

4   **Nouns ending in *-a, -o* and *-u* (all are of foreign origin),**
eg. *firma's* (firms), *auto's* (cars), *paraplu's* (umbrellas).
The apostrophe is inserted because *auto's*, for example, would be pronounced with a short *o*; a long *o* sound can be preserved in a closed syllable only by doubling the letter. The Dutchman finds the spelling *autoos* strange and thus replaces the second *o* with an apostrophe. Thus it is not necessary in *cadeaus, cafés* and *Hindoes*, for example, but it **is** used in *baby's* and *ski's* although nothing has been omitted.

5   **Many foreign words ending in *-e*,**
eg. *actrices* (actresses), *dames* (ladies), *garages, secretaresses* (secretaries), *studentes* (female students).
For Dutch words ending in *-e* see p. 37.

6   **Foreign words ending in unstressed *-ie*,**
eg. *families, petities, provincies, studies*

In higher style the words in this group are found with *-ën*,
eg. *de elf provinciën van Nederland*.

7   **Many loan words** (mostly of English and French origin) **that are still regarded as foreign words,**
eg. *clubs, films, perrons* (platforms), *restaurants, tanks, telefoons, trottoirs* (footpaths).
Nouns of French origin ending in *-eur* and *-trice* belong here too,
eg. *auteurs* (authors), *automonteurs* (mechanics), *ingenieurs* (engineers), *kapiteins* (captains); *actrices, directrices*
Exception: *directeuren* (also with *-s*).

8   **Words ending in *-ier* and *-oor* take *-s* when referring to people and *-en* when referring to things,**
eg. *kruideniers* (grocers), *winkeliers* (shop-keepers), *portiers* (doormen), *pastoors* (R.C. priests); *formulieren* (forms), *scharnieren* (hinges), *portieren* (doors), *kantoren* (offices).
Exceptions: *officieren* (officers), *scholieren* (school-children).

9 A few native Dutch words denoting male beings,

eg. *broers* (brothers), *bruidegoms* (bridegrooms), *knechts* (manservant, also *-en*), *koks* (cooks), *maats* (mates), *ooms* (uncles), *zoons* (sons).

Note: *zoons* also has a plural *zonen* which is often found in names of firms, eg. *Van Goor en Zonen*.

The military ranks, *generaal, kolonel, korporaal* and *luitenant* also take *-s* (All take th stress on the final syllable).

7.2.2 -EN PLURALS (i.e.: *-n* and *-en*)

1 When the *-en* suffix is added to nouns to form the plural the following spelling changes apply:

a Nouns with *aa, ee, oo* or *uu* drop one vowel in the open syllable produced by the suffixing of *-en*,

> *maan* (moon) – *manen, peer* (pear) – *peren, brood* (bread) – *broden, muur* (wall) – *muren.*

b Nouns with long vowels or diphthongs ending in *-s* change to *z* (i.e. voicing of *s* in intervocalic position),

> *Chinees* (Chinese) – *Chinezen, huis* (house) – *huizen, kies* (molar) – *kiezen, prijs* (price, prize) – *prijzen, reis* (journey) – *reizen, roos* (rose) – *rozen.*
> Exceptions: *eis* (demand) – *eisen, kous,* (stocking) – *kousen, kruis* (cross) – *kruisen* or *kruizen, paus* (Pope) – *pausen, Pruis* (Prussian) – *Pruisen, saus* (sauce) – *sausen, zeis* (scythe) – *zeisen.*

c Nouns ending in *-ms, -ns* and *-rs* change *s* to *z*,

> *gems* (chamois) – *gemzen, gans* (goose) – *ganzen, grens* (border) – *grenzen, lens* (lense) – *lenzen, vers* (poem, stanza) – *verzen.*
> Exceptions: *dans* (dance) – *dansen, kikvors* (frog) – *kikvorsen, koers* (rate, course) – *koersen, krans* (wreath) – *kransen, lans* (lance) – *lansen, mars* (march) – *marsen, mens* (person) – mensen, *pers* (press) – *persen,* but *Pers* (Persian) – *Perzen, prins* (prince) – *prinsen, tendens* (tendency) – *tendensen, wals* (waltz) – *walsen, wens* (wish) – *wensen.*

d Nouns with long vowels or diphthongs ending in *-f* change to *v* (i.e. voicing of *f* in intervocalic position),

> *brief* (letter) – *brieven, graaf* (count) – *graven, kloof* (gap) – *kloven, neef* (nephew, male cousin) – *neven.*
> Exceptions: nouns of Greek origin ending in *-graaf*, eg. *fotograaf* (photographer) – *fotografen, paragraaf* – *paragrafen.*
> Also *filosoof* (philosopher) – *filosofen.*

e Nouns ending in *-lf* and *-rf* change to *v*,

> *golf* (wave) – *golven, wolf* – *wolven, werf* (wharf) – *werven.*
> Exception: *elf* – *elfen.*

f **Nouns containing a short vowel and ending in a consonant double the consonant to preserve the short vowel,**

bok (billy-goat) – bokken, fles (bottle) – flessen, hor (wire-screen) – horren, mus (sparrow) – mussen, pot – potten, straf (punishment) – straffen.

Note: The two stressed feminine endings -es and -in belong here, eg. boerin (farmer's wife) – boerinnen, lerares (female teacher) – leraressen.

g **Nouns ending in -ee add -ën,**

orchidee (orchid) – orchideeën, zee (sea) – zeeën.
Exceptions: words still regarded as French: eg. logée (female visitor) – logées, soiree (party) – soirees.
Also the Latin word dominee (reverend) – dominees.

2 **There is a group of very common nouns that have a short vowel in the singular but a long vowel in the plural,** i.e. nouns which one would expect to find under f. above which do not double the consonant and thus cause the vowel to be pronounced long.

Common gender:

dag	day	dagen
god	God	goden
hertog	duke	hertogen
hof	court, yard	hoven
oorlog	war	oorlogen
slag	blow, battle	slagen
staf	staff	staven[1]
weg	road	wegen

Neuter:

bad	bath	baden
bedrag	amount	bedragen
bevel	order	bevelen
blad	leaf of a book, magazine	bladen[2]
dak	roof	daken
dal	valley	dalen
gat	hole	gaten
gebed	prayer	gebeden
gebod	commandment	geboden
gebrek	failing	gebreken
glas	glass	glazen
graf	grave	graven[3]
hol	cave	holen
lot	lottery ticket	loten
pad	path	paden[4]
schot	shot	schoten[4]

1 Staven is also the plural of staaf (stick).
2 Blad (leaf of a tree) becomes bladeren.
3 Graven is also the plural of graaf (count).

slot	lock, castle	*sloten*
spel	game	*spelen*
vat	barrel	*vaten*[4]
verbod	prohibition	*verboden*
verdrag	treaty	*verdragen*

3   **There is a small group of nouns with a short vowel in the singular that both lengthen and change their vowel in the plural,**

gelid (joint) – *gelederen, lid* (member, limb) – *leden* (members), **but** *ledematen* (limbs), *schip* (ship) – *schepen, smid* (smith) – *smeden, stad* (city) – *steden*.

4   **Nouns ending in** -*aar* **usually take** -*en* **but are found with** -*s,*

adelaar (eagle) – *adelaren, ambtenaren* (official) – *ambtenaren, leraar* (teacher) – *leraren*.

5   **Nouns ending in stressed** -*ie* **add** -*ën,*

melodie (tune) – *melodieën, symfonie* (symphony) – *symfonieën*.
Exception: *bougie* (spark-plug) – *bougies*.

Those ending in unstressed -*ie* usually take -*s* (see -*s* plurals, point 7.2.1.6) but some are found with -*n* in higher style.

provinciën, koloniën, studiën (compare *melodieën* etc.).
financiën (finances) always takes -*n*.

6   **Foreign nouns ending in** -*or* **usually take** -*en* **with a change in stress to the penultimate syllable,**

proféssor – *professóren, léctor* (lecturer, reader) – *lectóren, mótor* – *motóren* (motors, engines, but *mótors* means motorcycles), *organisátor* – *organisatóren* but *tráctor* – *tráctors* or *tractóren* (usually the former)

The spelling *doctor* is used for the academic title and has a plural *doctóren* or *doctóres*; the physician is usually spelt *dokter* and has a plural in -*s*.

7   **Nouns ending in** -*e* **cause difficulty:** there are those that always take -*s* (see -*s* plurals, point 7.2.1.5); there are a few that always take -*n,*

seconde (second), *echtgenote* (female spouse);

There are also those that take either, both endings being very common – this is particularly the case for nouns formed from adjectives by the addition of -*te,*

ziekte (sickness, disease), *hoogte* (height), *vlakte* (plain); *type* (type).

---

4   *Pad* (toad) becomes *padden*.   *Spel* (game of cards) becomes *spellen*.
   Schot (Scot) becomes *Schotten*.   *Handvat* (handle) becomes *handvatten*.

8 **Many Dutch nouns that originally ended in -*de* in the singular** (and still do in formal style) **add -*n* to the -*de* in the plural,**

bladzij (de) (page) – bladzijden, la(de) (drawer) – laden, tree (step) – treden.

9 **The nouns *koe* (cow) and *vlo* (flea) insert an -*i*- before -*en*,**

koeien, vlooien (colloquially one also hears vlooi in the singular)

10 **Nouns (usually abstracts) ending in -*heid* (i.e. -ness) form their plural in -*heden*,**

moeilijkheid (difficulty) – moeilijkheden, schoonheid (beauty) – schoonheden.

7.2.3 -EREN PLURALS

There is a small group of neuter nouns that preserve an old plural ending in -*eren* (compare Eng. child*ren*):

been	(bone)	beenderen[5]
blad	(leaf)	bladeren[6]
ei	(egg)	eieren
gelid	(joint)	gelederen[7]
gemoed	(mind)	gemoederen
goed	(goods, wares)	goederen
hoen	(fowl)	hoenderen[8]
kalf	(calf)	kalveren
kind	(child)	kinderen
lam	(lamb)	lammeren
lied	(song)	liederen
rad	(wheel)	raderen
rund	(cow, ox)	runderen
volk	(nation, people)	volkeren[9]

Kleren (clothes) is a contracted form of *klederen* (from *kleed*, an archaic form).

---

5 *Been* (leg) becomes *benen*.
6 *Blad* (leaf of a book; magazine) becomes *bladen*.
   eg. *dagbladen* – daily newspapers.
7 See -*en* plurals, point 7.2.2.3.
8 Also *hoenders*, which is more common than *hoenderen*.
9 Also *volken*.

7.2.4 IRREGULAR PLURAL FORMATIONS

7.2.4.1 **Words ending in** *-man* **have a plural in** *-lieden* **or** *-lui*, the former being more formal,

zeeman (sailor) – *zeelieden, zeelui; koopman* (merchant) – *kooplieden, kooplui.*

Some words which are only used in formal contexts never employ *-lui*,
edelman (nobleman), *raadsman* (councillor).

Exceptions: *muzelmannen* (Muslims), *Noormannen* (Normans), *vuilnismannen* (rubbishmen); *Engelsman* (Englishman) – *Engelsen, Fransman* (Frenchman) – *Fransen; buurman, -vrouw* (neighbour) – *buren.*

7.2.4.2 **Words of Greek and Latin origin:**

a Nouns ending in *-um* can take *-s* or *-a*, the former being more common,

albums (never *alba*), *atheneums* (high schools), *datums* (dates), *decennium* (decade) – *decennia* (never *decenniums*), *museums* or *musea.*

b Nouns ending in *-us* referring to people take *-i*,

doctorandus (Dutch academic title) – *doctorandi, historicus** (historian) – *historici, musicus** (musician) – *musici, neerlandicus** (graduate in Dutch) – *neerlandici;* also *catálogus* – *catalogi* (the accent is only to show stress).

* **Note:** The letter *c* of the singular is pronounced *k* and that of the plural is pronounced *s* (see note on p. 42). The words *cactus* and *circus* add *-sen.*

c The nouns *exámen* (examination) and *tentámen* (preliminary exam) can take *-s* or *-ina*, i.e. *tentàmens* or *tentàmina*, the former being more common.

7.2.5 ENGLISH PLURALS WHICH ARE SINGULAR IN DUTCH

The following nouns are singular in Dutch and are followed by a verb in the singular when one item is referred to; those with an asterisk can of course be used in the plural when more than one item is referred to.

ashes – *de as*　　　　　　　　　　politics – *de politiek*
binoculars – *de verrekijker** 　　pyjamas – *de pyjama**
economics – *de economie*　　　　scissors – *de schaar**
holidays – *de vakantie** 　　　　spectacles – *de bril**
the Netherlands – *Nederland*　　tongs – *de tang**
pants – *de broek** 　　　　　　　vegetables – *de groente** [10]

10　*Groente:* also pl. *groentes* or *groenten.*

7.3   Feminising masculine agents

Dutch has a variety of endings used to denote the female of certain professions, nationalities and animals. There are actually very few rules for their use and on the whole one can best simply learn the feminine equivalents by heart. The following will, however, serve to illustrate the endings in question.

7.3.1   *-e*:
a This ending is commonly used with foreign words with a stressed ending.

> *studente, docente, sociologe* (plural in *-n* or *-s*)
> *telefoniste* (plural in *-n* or *-s*), *typiste* (plural in *-s* or *-n*)

b Also indigenous words ending in *-genoot* (plural in *-n* or *-s*)

> *echtgenote, tijdgenote*

c The female inhabitant of most countries is designated by the adjective of nationality plus *-e* (see p. 240).

> *Australische, Engelse, Nederlandse*

7.3.2   *-es* (stressed):
(plural in *-sen*)

> *lerares, onderwijzeres, zangeres, barones, prinses*

7.3.3   *-esse* (stressed):
This ending is used to feminise masculine professions ending in *-aris* (plural in *-s*)

> *secretaresse, bibliothecaresse*

7.3.4   *-euse* (stressed):
This ending is only found in words of French origin of which the masculine ends in *-eur* (plural in *-s*).

> *ouvreuse, masseuse, coupeuse*

7.3.5   *-in* (stressed):
a Just a few nationalities take this ending (plural in *-nen*).

> *Friezin, Jodin, Russin*

b A few animals take this ending (plural in *-nen*).

> *berin, leeuwin, wolvin*

c Several other nouns (plural in *-nen*).

> *gravin, keizerin, vorstin; boerin, kokkin, godin, vriendin, negerin*

7.3.6   *-ster*:
a Nouns derived from verb stems take this ending (plural in *-s*).

> *kapster, schrijfster, toneelspeelster, verkoopster, verpleegster, werkster*

b Nouns ending in *-stander* and *-ganger* take this ending (plural in *-s*).

voorstandster, voorgangster

7.3.7 *-trice*:
Nouns of French origin ending in *-teur* take this ending (plural in *-s*).

actrice, directrice

Note: Some nouns of Latin origin ending in *-us* formerly took an *-a* ending to denote the female; nowadays, however, the masculine form is usually used (plural in *-i*, former plural of feminine forms in *-a* was *-ae* or *'s*).

musicus (formerly *musica*), *neerlandicus* (formerly *neerlandica*)
The *-a* ending is still occasionally used.

7.4 Possession

The English possessive 's' is known to Dutch also but is not used as extensively in Dutch. Generally it is only commonly used after proper nouns:

Annekes boek, Vaders auto

Close relatives preceded by a possessive can employ this *s* too:

mijn moeders keuken, zijn broers brommer

All other nouns can better employ a *van* construction, however:

de auto van mijn oom, de hoofdstad van Frankrijk

Note: a friend of my brother's – *een vriend van mijn broer*
The above is a safe guide to correct spoken and written forms; in practice, however, the *s* forms are commonly heard in instances not recommended here.

The apostrophe is only used to denote possession when the proper noun ends in a vowel, *s* or *z*:

Otto's boek, Rubens' schilderijen, Liz' fiets.

Colloquially one will often hear *Hans z'n vriend, mijn oom z'n auto, Anneke d'r vriend* (see p. 57).

Note: *de komeet van Halley* (Halley's comet), *de wet van Grimm* (Grimm's law).

7.5 Diminutives *(verkleinwoorden)*

The diminutive is used extensively in Dutch with many connotations of meaning. The mechanics of diminutising a noun are dealt with here first and then the semantic implications of the diminutive. The various forms of the diminutive are a question of phonetics.

7.5.1 FORMATION

-je
The basic form is the addition of *-je* to the end of the noun:

aap	*– aapje*	*huis*	*– huisje*[11]
boek	*– boekje*	*oog*	*– oogje*
fornuis	*– fornuisje*[11]	*pet*	*– petje*
hand	*– handje*	*zak*	*– zakje*

-tje
a Words containing a long vowel or diphthong, either final or followed by *l*, *n* or *r* add *-tje* to the noun:

ei	*– eitje*	*stoel*	*– stoeltje*
ui	*– uitje*	*schoen*	*– schoentje*
vrouw	*– vrouwtje*	*deur*	*– deurtje*

b Words ending in *-el*, *-en* and *-er* also take *-tje*:

tafel	*– tafeltje*	*kamer*	*– kamertje*
deken	*– dekentje*	*jongen*	*– jongetje*

-etje
a Words containing a short vowel and ending in *l*, *r*, *m*, *n* and *ng* (but not *-ing*, see below) add *-etje*:

bel	*– belletje*	*kam*	*– kammetje*
ster	*– sterretje*	*pan*	*– pannetje*
bloem	*– bloemetje*[12]	*ding*	*– dingetje*

b A few nouns containing a short vowel ending in *b*, *g* and *p* add *-etje* (but most will be found in the first group):

krab	*– krabbetje*	*big*	*– biggetje*
rib	*– ribbetje*	*vlag*	*– vlaggetje*
slab	*– slabbetje*	*kip*	*– kippetje*

Some nouns with these characteristics have two diminutive forms (one as described in the first group and one as described here):

brug	*– brugje, bruggetje*
rug	*– rugje, ruggetje*
weg	*– wegje, weggetje*
pop	*– popje, poppetje*

-pje
Words ending in *m* add *-pje*:

boom	*– boompje*	*arm*	*– armpje*
duim	*– duimpje*	*bezem*	*– bezempje*

11 *sj* is pronounced [ʃ].
12 A little flower is either *bloemetje* or *bloempje* but the former can also mean 'a bunch of flowers', eg. *Ik heb een bloemetje voor haar meegenomen.*

Many of those monosyllabic neuter nouns which have a short vowel in the singular but a long vowel in the plural also have a long vowel in the diminutive form:

blad (pl. *bladeren*)	– *blaadje*	*pad* (pl. *paden*)	– *paadje*[14]
gat (pl. *gaten*)	– *gaatje*[13]	*schip* (pl. *schepen*)	– *scheepje*
glas (pl. *glazen*)	– *glaasje*	*vat* (pl. *vaten*)	– *vaatje*

but

dak (pl. *daken*)	– *dakje*	*spel* (pl. *spelen*)	– *spelletje* etc.

Three nouns in this category have two forms:

dag (pl. *dagen*) — *dagje, daagje(s)*
lot (pl. *loten*) — *lotje, lootje*
rad(pl. *raderen*) — *radje, raadje* (also:*radertje*)

The nouns *kind* and *kleren* (a plural) have a special form:

kindje — little child (can also take a plural -*s*)
kindertjes — little children (always plural)
kleertjes — little clothes (always plural)

-kje
Nouns ending in -*ing* change the *g* to *k* before adding -*je*: nouns ending in -*ling*, however, take -*etje*:

koning — *koninkje*
regering — *regerinkje*

but

wandeling — *wandelingetje*
leerling — *leerlingetje*

also

tekening — *tekeningetje*

Spelling peculiarities

Nouns ending in long vowels (i.e. an open syllable) need to double the vowel when the diminutive ending is added (i.e. making a closed syllable) to preserve the long sound:

oma — *omaatje*
auto — *autootje*
paraplu — *parapluutje*
café — *cafeetje*
Margot[15] — *Margootje*

---

13 *Gatje* = backside.
14 *Padje* = little toad.
15 't' not pronounced.

Variant forms of the diminutive

In the west of the Netherlands a colloquial variant of the diminutive exists which is sometimes also used in cultured speech for humorous effect; the ending is -ie, eg. *huisie, jochie, koekie, lichie* (from *licht*), *meisie*.

In the south of the Netherlands and in Belgium the -je form is often colloquially replaced by -ke, with the phonetic variant -ske:

huiske, meiske, slakske

This ending is common in female christian names, even in the north:

Anneke, Aafke

An archaic variant often found in names and titles is -ken:

Manneken Pis, Duyfken

7.5.2   SEMANTIC IMPLICATIONS OF THE DIMINUTIVE

It is particularly the nuances of meaning expressed by the diminutive which make it so peculiarly unique in Dutch but also so difficult for non-native speakers to master. The following can only serve as a guide to its main uses; its potential is infinite as it is very much a productive ending and is not restricted to nouns (see p. 46). On the whole the connotation of a diminutive form is a positive one, but sometimes it fulfills a derogatory function (see point 6).

1   The diminutive's basic function is to make things small:

huis – house; *huisje* – little house, cottage
Roodkapje – Little Red Riding Hood

Even with this meaning, however, the diminutive is commonly preceded by the adjective *klein*.

De kat zit onder een klein struikje.
The cat is sitting under a little shrub.
Hij woont op een heel klein kamertje.
He's living in a teeny weeny room.

2   The diminutive is also used as a form of endearment; christian names (and not just of children but particularly women's names) are often diminutised, eg. *Jantje, Frankje; Marietje, Annetje*.

3   Often the diminutive form of a noun renders a completely separate lexical item in English:

brood	– loaf of bread	*broodje*	– bread roll
kaart	– map	*kaartje*	– ticket
koek	– cake	*koekje*	– biscuit

koop	– buy	*koopje*	– bargain
lepel	– spoon	*lepeltje*	– teaspoon
Mongool	– Mongol	*mongooltje*	– mongoloid child
scheermes	– razor	*scheermesje*	– razor blade
schotel	– dish	*schoteltje*	– saucer
viool	– violin	*viooltje*	– violet, pansy

The diminutives of *broer* and *zuster* are *broertje* and *zusje* (not *zustertje*) respectively; these forms often render younger brother or sister, but this is not necessarily always the case.

> *Mijn broertje heeft er een.*
> My younger brother has one.

The diminutive forms of *man* and *wijf* are used for male and female with reference to animals.

> *Is het een mannetje of wijfje?*
> Is it a male or female?
> *Het is een wijfjesaap, geen mannetjesaap.*
> It is a female monkey, not a male monkey.

The latter forms are used chiefly for animals for which there is no separate word for male and female.

4 The diminutive is used to itemise some quantitative nouns, i.e. nouns that stand for a collective quantity (particularly varieties of food and drink) which take on the meaning of one item of that quantity when they bear the diminutive ending:

advocaat	– advocaat	*een advocaatje*	– a glass of advocaat
bier	– beer	*een biertje*	– a glass of beer
chocola	– chocolate	*een chocolaatje*	– a chocolate
gebak	– pastry, cakes	*een gebakje*	– a pastry, little cake
hout	– wood	*een houtje*	– a bit of wood
ijs	– icecream	*een ijsje*	– an icecream
kauwgom	– chewing gum	*een kauwgommetje*	– a piece of gum
krijt	– chalk	*een krijtje*	– a piece of chalk
likeur	– liqueur	*een likeurtje*	– a glass of liqueur
muziek	– music	*een muziekje*	– a piece of music (coll.)
snoep	– confectionery	*een snoepje*	– a sweet
worst	– sausage	*een worstje*	– a sausage

These endings can have other connotations, however:

> *een lekker wijntje* – a very nice wine (not a glass of wine)

5 A few nouns only exist as diminutives:

> *meisje* – girl (formerly from *meid*)
> *lachertje* – ridiculous suggestion, situation, etc.
> *dubbeltje* – 10 cents
> *kwartje* – 25 cents
> *op het nippertje* – in the nick of time

The names of children's games contain the diminutive (a productive ending):

krijgertje spelen – to play tag
verstoppertje spelen – to play hide and seek
touwtje springen – to skip
vadertje en moedertje spelen – to play mummies and daddies

6   Occasionally the diminutive can give a derogatory connotation to a noun:

burgermannetje – petit bourgeois
een raar taaltje – a strange lingo
boertje van buten[16] – yokel

7.5.3   DIMINUTIVES OF OTHER PARTS OF SPEECH

It is possible for words other than nouns to take a diminutive ending, thus giving a new connotation to the words concerned or even a completely new meaning.

1   **Adverbs** are the most notable example of words other than nouns that have this potential; the ending used is *-jes* (with phonetic variants *-tjes* and *-pjes*). Its function is one of toning down the intensity of meaning. In the spoken language it is still productive (see p. 104).

eventjes	– just a minute	*stilletjes*	– quietly, secretively
gezelligjes	– cosily	*stiekempjes*	– secretively
knusjes	– cosily	*strakjes*	– in a moment
losjes	– loosely	*warmpjes*	– warmly
netjes	– neatly	*zachtjes*	– quietly, softly

Wij zaten lekker warmpjes binnen.
We were sitting inside nice and warm.
Het is hier erg knusjes, hè?
It is very cosy here, isn't is?

2   **Adjectives** used as nouns can have a diminutive ending; this form of the adjective is particularly commonly used where we say in English 'a white one', 'a little one' where the 'one' cannot be translated literally:

een witje, een kleintje

also

de kleintjes – the little ones (children or things)
een nieuwtje – a piece of news

3   **Numerals** can also take the ending in certain expressions; 'on my/your/his own etc.' is always *in mijn/je/zijn eentje*. A more familiar form of *met z'n tweeën/drieën* etc. is *met z'n tweetjes/drietjes* etc. Also: *geef me (er) nog eentje* – Give me another one.

16   A colloquial form of *buiten*.

4 The expressions *een onderonsje* – 'a tête-à-tete' and *ietsje* – 'a little' show the diminutive being suffixed to **pronouns**,

Mag het ietsje meer zijn? (shopkeeper to customer).
Is a little bit more alright?

The adverb *iets* (somewhat) can also take it,

Ik ben ietsje moe.
I am somewhat tired.

5 *Een moetje* – 'a shotgun marriage' is a quaint example of a noun formed from **a verbal particle** by addition of the diminutive.

6 There are a few expressions derived from **prepositions** incorporating the diminutive:

toetje – dessert
uitje (from *uitstapje*) – excursion
een ommetje maken – to go for a short walk
rondje – round (of drinks)

8 Pronouns *(voornaamwoorden)*

8.1 Personal pronouns *(persoonlijke voornaamwoorden)*

There are two series of personal pronouns: subject and object pronouns. The forms in the right-hand columns are the unemphatic forms; those that are not normally written are given in brackets. Some pronouns do not have unemphatic forms.

		Subject		**Object**	
Sing.	1.	*ik* [1]	*('k)*	*mij*	*me*
	2.	*jij*	*je*	*jou*	*je*
		u		*u*	
	3.	*hij* [2]	*(ie)*	*hem* [2]	*('m)*
		zij [2]	*ze*	*haar* [2,5]	*(d'r)*
		het [2,3]	*('t)*	*het* [2]	*('t)*
Pl.	1.	*wij*	*we*	*ons*	
	2.	*jullie*	*je*	*jullie*	*je*
		u		*u*	
	3.	*zij* [3,4]	*ze*	*hen/hun* [4]	*ze* (people)
				die	*ze* (things and people)

8.1.1 UNEMPHATIC PRONOUNS

The distinction between emphatic and unemphatic pronouns, which also exists in English in the spoken language (but not in the written), is very important in Dutch.
One important difference from English is that many, but not all the unemphatic forms, are written. If no particular stress is required, it is of no consequence whether one writes the emphatic or unemphatic form of the subject pronoun.

---

1 An extra emphatic form *ikke* also exists in the spoken language only, eg. *Jij hebt mijn boek gestolen, niet waar? Wat, ikke?*
2 Neuter words referring to male or female beings (eg. *het jongetje, het meisje, het wijf*) are replaced by masculine or feminine pronouns (see also footnote 13 on p. 60) eg. *Het jongetje is ziek geworden maar hij wordt zeker wel beter.*
3 *Het* can also be used to translate English 'they' (see p. 53).
4 In colloquial Dutch *hun* also occurs as a subject pronoun meaning 'they' but it can only refer to people. This practice, which is becoming very common these days, is better avoided. eg. *Hun liggen op het bed.*
5 Colloquially one will often hear *ze* as the unemphatic object form of *haar*. It may also be written.

Heb je je vrouw gesproken?   **or**   *Heb jij je vrouw gesproken?*

but not

Heb je jouw vrouw gesproken?

Even the second example can be read aloud substituting orally *je* for *jij*.

a The unemphatic form of the possessive *zijn* is written only in such expressions as *met z'n tweeën, op z'n best, hoogst/minst* where it must be used (see p. 90). Also the colloquial forms *mijn broer z'n auto* and *mijn zuster d'r man*, if written, require the unemphatic form (see p. 57).

b The unemphatic form of *jullie* can be used when *jullie* has already been used as the subject of the sentence; *jullie* can then be followed by an unemphatic possessive or reflexive form.

Jullie kunnen je onmogelijk vergissen.
Jullie moeten je snoepjes in je zak stoppen.

The unemphatic subject form *je* can only be used when a previous sentence has indicated that this *je* stands for *jullie* and not for *jij*. In this case a singular verb is used even though *je* is standing for *jullie*.

Jullie mogen morgen komen en als je gegeten hebt, kunnen we naar de bioscoop gaan.

It is very common in spoken Dutch to begin a sentence with *jullie* to indicate that one means you plural and then to continue the conversation with *je* + singular verb; more than one *jullie* in a sentence sounds clumsy.

c *U* is officially both a singular and a plural pronoun. However, often *jullie* is used as an unemphatic or rather neutral form of plural *u*. Because *u* demands a singular verb it is felt to refer to one person and for this reason is often replaced by *jullie*, but not in contexts where one must mind ones p's and q's with regard to the form of address.

d Unemphatic *hij* is pronounced *ie* usually only when it follows the verb and the *-t* ending can act as a glide, eg. *Heeft-ie dat gedaan?, Vandaag gaat-ie naar huis.* The difference between this and the referential *die* (see *die*) is often not heard.

Heeft-ie, heeft die.

ie will also be heard after other words ending in *-t* eg. *Weet ie wat ie vandaag moet doen.* It sometimes occurs after sounds other than *-t*, eg. *Vertel me waar ie woont.* Only in avant-garde publications will one find *ie* sometimes written.

e Just as in English where the somewhat stilted pronoun 'one' is usually replaced by unemphatic 'you', so in Dutch *men* is replaced by *je* (never *jij*) in general speech and can also be said in this meaning to people one otherwise says *u* to. The emphatic form *jij* can only mean 'you', the person one is talking to. Similarly *ze* can replace *men* just as in English 'they' replaces 'one'; the difference between *je* and *ze* in such contexts is the same as between 'you' and 'they', i.e. the speaker and the person being addressed cannot be included in the action.

Men heeft gisteren de DDR erkend. Ze hebben gisteren de DDR erkend.

The pronoun *we* is often used in an impersonal sense too just as in English.

Hier hebben we het Paleis op de Dam
(see also p. 155)

f   Common in speech but rare in writing is the form *ze* for unemphatic *haar* meaning 'her'. Usually the context will indicate whether 'her' or 'them' is meant.

8.1.2   REMARKS ON SUBJECT AND OBJECT PRONOUNS

1   **Second person forms of address:** *jij, u, gij, jullie*

Anyone who has attempted to learn another language will be acquianted with the existence of two forms of second person address. In the ABN of the northern Netherlands the two forms are *jij* and *u*. Broadly speaking one can compare the usage of the two with similar couplets in other languages, i.e. French tu/vous, German du/Sie. In detail, however, usage sometimes differs quite dramatically from those languages.

The verb *tutoyeren*, borrowed from French, means to be on *jij* terms:

Hoe goed ken je de directeur? We tutoyeren elkaar al.

The verb *jijen* is also used.

a   **Use of** *u*

In addition to the usual usage of the polite form of address for strangers, elders etc., *u* is also employed in the following cases where it would not be used in German, for instance.

1 A minority of people, but quite a sizeable one, still say *u* to their parents. This was very common prior to the war and is still quite commonly found.
2 It is commonly used for grandparents and aunts and uncles, and is always used for God.

U/uw are often still written with capital letters in very formal letters, but this tradition is waning.

b   **Use of** *jij*

Generally speaking *jij* is used for friends, relatives (with the above exceptions), children and animals. Its usage differs from that of du in German, for example, in the following ways:

1 Teachers use *jij* for schoolchildren of all ages, but the student must say *u* to his teachers.
2 Young people of comparable age often call each other *jij* even if they are unacquaint-ed. University students always automatically say *jij* to each other.

c **Use of** *gij*

In Belgium *gij* (unemphatic *ge*) commonly replaces *jij* but the latter is becoming increasing popular as the south begins to follow the north more and more in linguistic matters. Dialectally *gij* is also used in the plural. The object and possessive forms of *gij* are *u* and *uw* respectively.

Note: Historically this form is older than *jij* and *u* and for this reason it was the standard written form for centuries, even in the northern Netherlands. It is this form that was used in the seventeenth century States Translation of the Bible and thus, if it is used in the north at all nowadays, it usually has a biblical connotation. *Gij* has the same ring about it to the Dutchman as 'thou' to the Englishman. *Gij* often has its own specific form of the verb: *ge zijt, ge waart, ge zoudt* (see p. 107).

d **Use of** *jullie*

For the use of *jullie* as the plural of *u* see p. 49. The origin of this form is *jelie(den)* (i.e. you people) and is often found as *jelui* in some older literary works.

2 **The object pronouns** *hen* **and** *hun* (see *'Woordenlijst'*, p. XVIII)

Historically there is no distinction between *hen* and *hun*. The two were originally simply phonetic variants of the one word. The distinction is an artificial one imposed upon the language by eighteenth century philologists. The artificiality of the distinction is reflected in Dutch speech today where hardly anybody uses the two according to the rules prescribed. It should be noted, however, that the Dutchman always usesd *hun* where grammar strictly speaking demands *hen*, a form which is actually seldom used in the spoken language. In writing, one should attempt to use them correctly.
The rule is:
hen is the direct object and is also used after prepositions.
hun is the indirect object, the only personal pronoun to have a separate dative form.

> *Ik heb hen gisteren in de stad gezien.*
> *Toen heb ik de informatie aan hen gegeven.*

> **but**

> *Ik heb hun de informatie gegeven.*

The distinction is similar to the following in English:

> I gave the information to them. *(aan hen)*
> I gave them the information. *(hun)*

One is well advised in all the above cases to use *ze* if one is in doubt, but *ze* can of course be used as an unemphatic pronoun only.

> *Ik heb de informatie aan ze gegeven.*
> *Ik heb ze de informatie gegeven.*

It is particularly difficult to distinguish whether *hen* or *hun* is required in cases like the following:

> *Wij wensten hun geluk.*
> *Het lukte hun de top van de berg te bereiken.*
> *Ik beloofde hun dat ik zou komen.*
> *Hun werd toen verboden bij deze verkiezingen te stemmen.*
> *Ik heb het hun beloofd.*
> *Ik zei hun dat ik morgen zou komen.*

In all these cases *hun* is used because the indirect object is required; this is clearly illustrated by the last two examples where the sentence can be rephrased with prepositions:

i.e *Ik heb het aan hen beloofd.*
Ik zei tegen hen dat ik morgen zou komen.

3 **'It'** **as a subject pronoun** (see *'Woordenlijst – geslacht en voornaamwoordelijke aanduiding'*, p. IX-XXIX)

a It should be noted that singular common gender nouns (whether persons or things) are regarded as being masculine when a pronoun replaces them:

> *Die stoel heb ik gisteren gekocht. Hij is erg mooi, vind je niet?*

b In Belgium the old distinction between masculine and feminine is still very much alive.

> *Doe de deur dicht. Nee, zij blijft open.*

Even in Holland abstract nouns are replaced in formal style by *zij*, but in colloquial language *hij* is often heard.
This applies to abstract common gender nouns ending in:

-heid	*waarheid, eenheid* etc.
-ie	*commissie, politie* etc.
-erij	*uitgeverij, bakkerij* etc.
-nis	*kennis, erfenis* etc.
-ing	*regering, regeling* etc.
-st	*kunst, winst* etc.
-schap	*wetenschap, verwantschap* etc.[6]
-de, -te	*begeerte, liefde* etc.

> *De regering heeft vandaag haar besluiten bekendgemaakt.*

Female animals, eg. *koe, merrie* etc., can be replaced by *zij* but one does commonly hear the Dutch using *hij* with reference to such animals.

> *Zie je die kat? Hij heeft net gejongd.*

---

6 Note that some nouns ending in *-schap* are neuter: *landschap, lidmaatschap* (see p. 29 and p. 31).

c   There is an added complication in the translation of an 'it' referring to common gender nouns. There are instances where an 'it' which one would expect to be *hij* is in fact *het*. The rule is as follows:
As subject of the verb *zijn* (and less frequently of *blijken, lijken schijnen* and *worden*) the pronoun *het* is used to refer to all nouns and persons (singular and plural) when
  a the predicate is a noun
  b the predicate is an adjective used as a noun
but not when the predicate is an adjective; then *het* is used only for singular neuter nouns.[7]
This is similar to the use of *ce* in French.

Deze stoel heb ik gisteren gekocht. Het is een heel dure.
but
Deze stoel heb ik gisteren gekocht. Hij was erg duur.

De stem van mijn zuster is erg zacht, maar het is wel een mooie.
but
De stem van mijn zuster is erg zacht, maar hij is wel erg mooi.

Het zijn Duitsers die naast ons wonen.
but
Ze zijn Duits, de mensen die naast ons wonen.

Ik heb twee glazen gebroken. Het waren antieke glazen.
but
Ik heb twee glazen gebroken. Ze waren antiek.

d   In addition to the cases mentioned under c where an 'it' which one would expect to be *hij* is *het*, there are also other instances where *het* is used instead of *hij* but for which no concrete rules can be given (see also 4, c below). It would seem that the pronoun in such cases refers to an action or state rather than to a noun in the first clause, or sometimes the antecedent is an abstract concept.

Je moet de oostkust bezoeken. Het is (er) prachtig.
Hij liet de auto langs de weg staan, want hij wist dat het daar veilig zou zijn.
(but *hij* if *staan* were used instead of *zijn*)
De boerderij van mijn oom is vlakbij Zwolle. Het is ongeveer een kwartier met de auto van Zwolle vandaan.
Is de tandpasta op? Ja, het is op. (uncountable material noun)
Is de tube tandpasta leeg? Ja, hij is leeg. (countable object)

---

7   When the subject is personal, *hij/zij* are possible, eg. *Ik weet dat hij/het een vriendelijke man is.*

4 'It' as an object pronoun *

a When an object pronoun 'it' refers to a common gender noun, *hem* is used in Dutch, not *het*.

> *Ik heb een antieke kast gekocht. Wil je hem zien?*
> *Ik kocht een tafel voor mijn moeder maar ze wilde hem niet hebben.*

b There are a few instances (see 3, b above) where *haar/ze* are used instead of *hem*.

> *Wat heb je met de oude tafel gedaan? Ik heb ze verkocht.* (Southern Dutch)

c On occasions one will hear *het* as an object pronoun where one would expect *hem* (see 3, d above).

> *Wat een rare lucht! Nou, ik vind het lekker.* (i.e. *Ik vind het lekker ruiken.*)
> *Er klonk een vlugge stap op de trap, maar zij hoorde het niet.* (i.e. *het stappen*)
> *Ik ga morgen een lezing houden, maar ik weet nog niet of ik het in het Engels of in het Nederlands ga doen.*

d 'It' as a prepositional object (i.e. in it, on it etc.) is neither *het* nor *hem* but *er* + preposition. The form is analogous to English therein, thereon etc.

> I put my money in it – *Ik heb er mijn geld in gestopt.*

The division of the prepositional object is generally more common in colloquial Dutch than the following:

> *Ik heb mijn geld erin gestopt.*

When separate, the *er* must go immediately after the finite verb and the preposition to the end of the clause, but **before** infinitives and past participles.

> *De studenten hebben er de hele dag aan gedacht.*

Negatives precede the preposition:

> *Wij willen er de bladeren niet in doen.*

It should be noted that a form such as *erop* etc. can also be translated by 'on them'. Whenever 'them' preceded by a preposition refers to things, it must be translated in this way.

> Here are three knives. Will you peel the oranges with them?
> *Hier hebben jullie drie messen. Willen jullie er de sinaasappels mee schillen?*

For further functions of *er* see p. 221.

---

* Note the use of an object *het* in the following expressions where no object is required in English:
Ik geloof/hoop/weet het wel (niet)
I think/hope so, I know (don't)

5 *Die* as a referential pronoun

a   The demonstrative *die* is very commonly used in Dutch as a substitute for *hij/hem*, *zij/haar*, *zij/hen/hun* with varying connotations of meaning. Except in questions, the clause always begins with *die*; sometimes it is stressed and thus serves as an emphatic pronoun, and in other cases it acts as an unemphatic pronoun.

Is Bob er nog niet? Nee, die komt niet. (unstressed) = *hij*
Ik weet het niet maar die weten het wel. (stressed) = *zij* (they)
Heb je Marie gesproken? Nee, die heb ik helemaal niet gezien.
(stressed or unstressed) = *haar*
Hebben die dat gedaan? (stressed or unstressed) = *zij* (they)

b   It should be noticed that *die* appears in the list of object pronouns on p. 48 as the stressed form of *ze* (them) referring to things: the emphatic forms *hen/hun* can refer only to people and *ze*, which can be used for people or things, is by definition unemphatic: when stressing 'them' refering to inanimate objects, one must use *die*.

Hebben jullie de appels opgegeten die ik vanochtend gekocht heb?
Nee, die hebben we niet opgegeten.

c   *Die* can also be a handy means of avoiding the difficulties caused by pronominal substitution of *hij/hem* or *het* mentioned under 8.1.2.3, d and 8.1.2.4, c.

Hij heeft zijn auto aan de kant van de weg laten staan want hij wist dat die daar veilig zou staan.
(here *die* replaces *hij* which could be ambiguous)

6   English difficulties with subject and object pronouns

a   Due to the subject and object forms of 'you' being the same in English, confusion as to whether to use *jij* of *jou* in Dutch can arise in instances like the following:

He is bigger than you.
Hij is groter dan jij.
I like him more than you.
Ik vind hem aardiger dan jou.
If I were you.
Als ik jou was.

b   Because of the confusion in the usage of 'I' and 'me' in colloquial English, a confusion which does not often occur in Dutch, the following mistakes are sometimes made:

He is bigger than me (= I).
Hij is groter dan ik. (never *mij*)
Robert gave some money to Jan and I (= me).
Robert gaf wat geld aan Jan en mij.

7 The use of 'to' in English before pronominal indirect objects.

Note the use or lack of *aan* in the following examples:

She gave it to the man	*Zij gaf het aan de man.*
She gave him the book	*Ze gaf hem het boek (de man het boek)*
She gave it to him	*Zij gaf het hem*
	Zij gaf het aan hem.
	(when emphasised)

Note : She gave it to them.   *Zij gaf het hun.*
Zij gaf het aan hen.
(when emphasised)

8.2   Possessive pronouns *(bezittelijke voornaamwoorden)*

mijn	*(m'n)*	
jouw	*je*	
uw		
zijn[8]	*(z'n)*	
haar[9]	*(d'r)*	See also p. 48 for unemphatic forms
zijn	*(z'n)*	
ons/onze		
jullie	*je*	
uw		
hun[10]		

8   In formal style *diens* may replace the masculine possessive *zijn* (see p. 26)

> *De gouverneur-generaal van Nederlands-Indië en diens echtgenote.*
> The governor-general of the Dutch East Indies and his wife.

Diens must be used when ambiguity can arise:

> *Hij ging wandelen met zijn vriend en zijn zoon* (= his son)
> *Hij ging wandelen met zijn vriend en diens zoon* (= the friend's son).

9   Neuter words referring to female beings (eg. *het meisje, het wijf*) take feminine possessive pronouns (see p. 60).

> *Het meisje heeft haar grootmoeder lekkere dingen gebracht.*

10   In formal (usually archaic) style *haar* can replace the possessive form *hun* when it refers to feminine plural.

> *Engelands Australische koloniën in haar ontstaan en tegenwoordige toestand.* (title of a book)

This explains why the unemphatic form of possessive *hun* is *d'r*, even with reference to masculine antecedents.

8.2.1 INFLECTION OF POSSESSIVES

a Only *ons* is inflected (i.e. becomes *onze*) before singular common gender nouns and before all plurals,

onze vriend, onze boeken **but** *ons boek.*

b In very formal style all possessives can take *-e* before feminine singular nouns and plural nouns,

Uwe Excellentie	Your Excellency
Hare Majesteit	Her Majesty
Mijne Heren	Dear Sirs

c Possessives sometimes take case endings in formal style or in standard expressions that have preserved such archaisms.

een uwer afgevaardigden	one of your representatives (genitive plural)
mijns inziens	in my opinion (masculine genitive singular)
te zijner tijd	in the course of time (feminine dative singular)

8.2.2 COLLOQUIAL POSSESSIVES

Expressions such as *de auto van mijn broer/mijn broers auto, het huis van mijn moeder/ mijn moeders huis, de kleren van die mensen,* have an alternative form which one often hears but usually avoids in writing.

mijn broer z'n auto
mijn moeder d'r huis
die mensen d'r kleren/die mensen hun kleren

Masculine antecedents use *z'n* (i.e. *zijn*) and *d'r* is used for feminine singular and plural antecedents while *hun* is used for masculine and feminine plural antecedents. (see p. 41).

8.2.3 In conversational style *die z'n* and *die d'r* can replace *zijn* and *haar*.

Die z'n vriend is een vreemd figuur.
His friend is a strange person.
Die d'r man studeert in Leiden.
Her husband is studying in Leiden.

(see also relative pronouns on p. 63)

8.2.4 REPLACEMENT OF POSSESSIVES BY REFLEXIVE PRONOUNS

Occasionally the possessive is replaced by a reflexive pronoun or object pronoun where parts of the body are concerned; the part of the body is then replaced by the definite article.

Hij heeft zich in de vinger gesneden
or
Hij heeft in zijn vinger gesneden.

De slang heeft hem in het been gebeten
or
De slang heeft in zijn been gebeten.

It is not, however, incorrect to use the reflexive and the possessive pronoun together, eg. *Hij heeft zich in zijn vinger gesneden. De slang heeft hem in zijn been gebeten.*

8.2.5   INDEPENDENT POSSESSIVE PRONOUNS

	Formal	Usual
mine	*de/het mijne*	*(die/dat) van mij*
yours	*de/het jouwe*	*(die/dat) van jou*
yours	*de/het uwe*	*(die/dat) van u*
his	*de/het zijne*	*(die/dat) van hem*
hers	*de/het hare*	*(die/dat) van haar*
its	*de/het zijne*	
ours	*de/het onze*	*(die/dat) van ons*
yours		*(die/dat) van jullie*[11]
theirs	*de/het hunne*	*(die/dat) van hen*

a   The formal forms can be used is conversation too although *de/het hunne* sounds particularly stilted.

Here is my car. Where is yours?
Hier staat mijn auto. Waar staat de jouwe?
or
Waar staat die van jou?

Your house is very nice but have you seen mine?
Jouw huis is erg mooi maar heb je het mijne gezien?
or
Heb je dat van mij gezien?

This is hers and that is theirs.
Dit is de hare en dat is de hunne
or
Dit is van haar en dat is van hen.

b   Note that 'a friend of yours/ours/theirs etc.' is rendered in Dutch by using this construction:

een vriend van jou/van ons/van hen.

11   *Jullie* has only the one form.

Compare: a friend of my mother's – *een vriend van mijn moeder*.

c   The formal forms are sometimes found with -*n* in the sense of 'you and yours' (i.e. your family) etc.

Hij en de zijnen kwamen de avond bij ons doorbrengen.

8.3   Reflexive pronouns *(wederkerende voornaamwoorden)*

Reflexive pronouns, both with and without verbs, plus the use of *zelf* and *eigen* are dealt with under reflexive verbs. (see p. 161)

8.4   Demonstrative pronouns *(aanwijzende voornaamwoorden)*

8.4.1   The demonstratives *deze/dit* and *die/dat* (see p. 26) can also be used pronominally just as 'this/these' and 'that/those' can be in English (usually this one, these ones etc., however).

> *Die stoel was duur maar deze was erg goedkoop.*
> That chair was expensive but this one was very cheap.
> *Dat* (referring to *huis*) *heb ik gisteren gekocht.*
> I bought that (one) yesterday.

8.4.2   There is also a pronominal usage of *dit* and *dat* (compare also *het* p. 53) which differs greatly from English: *dit* and *dat* (and *het*) can be followed by a plural form of *zijn* (as well as *blijken, blijven, lijken, schijnen* and *worden*) and can refer to a plural quantity in which case they replace English 'they, these and those'.

> *Dat zijn Duitsers.*
> They are Germans.
> *Dat (dit) zijn de enige die ik heb kunnen vinden.*
> Those (these) are the only ones I was able to find.

As with *het* (see p. 53), *dit* and *dat* can only be used in this way if the complement following *zijn* etc. is a noun or adjective used as a noun, otherwise *zij* or *die* are used.

> *Zij (die) zijn erg duur* – They are very expensive.
> *Zij (die) zijn nu op* – They have all gone now.

Note: In very formal style an archaic genitive form of the demonstrative still occurs, eg. *schrijver dezes* – the author (of this document). The adverbs *nadien* (afterwards) and *voordien* (before) preserve archaic dative forms (see p. 98, 99).

8.4.3 Independent demonstrative pronouns are not usually[12] preceded by prepositions; *hier* + preposition replaces *dit*, and *daar* + preposition replaces *dat*.

> *Stop het hierin* – Put it in this.
> *Ik heb het daarmee (= daar + met) geschreven* – I wrote it with that.

These forms are also separable.

> *Daar heb ik het mee geschreven.*
> I wrote it with that. (emphasised)

The adverbial expressions of time *daarna* (after that, afterwards), *daarop* (after that, thereupon) and *daarvoor* (before that) are not separated.

> *Kort daarna vertrokken wij.*
> Shortly after that we left.

8.5 Relative pronouns *(betrekkelijke voornaamwoorden)*

8.5.1 DIFFICULTIES WITH ENGLISH RELATIVES

English very often omits relative pronouns (actually only when they are objects, never when subject pronouns) but they must always be used in Dutch. In addition there is often a choice of relative in English.

> The man I saw yesterday is sick.
> The man whom/that/which (for non-personal antecedents) I saw yesterday is sick.
> *De man die ik gisteren zag, is ziek.*

> The person I gave the letter to has left.
> The person that/whom I gave the letter to has left.
> The person to whom I gave the letter has left.
> *De persoon aan wie ik de brief gaf, is weg.*

8.5.2 THE SIMPLE RELATIVE IN DUTCH

Die is the relative pronoun used for common gender nouns in the singular, and for both common gender and neuter nouns in the plural.
Dat is used for neuter nouns in the singular.[13] (see p. 62, footnote 14)

---

12 Occasionally they are preceded by prepositions when qualified, and in speech when extra emphasis is required.

> *Wat jij voorstelt past niet bij dit alles* – What you are suggesting doesn't fit in with all of this.
> *Vergeleken met dat van mij...* – Compared with mine...
> *Ik heb het met dit (= hiermee) gedaan* (emphatic) – I did it with this.

13 It is not uncommon for a personal neuter antecedent, eg. *meisje*, to be followed by *die* rather than *dat* as grammar demands:

> *Ik ken een meisje die in het vak zit* – I know a girl in the trade.

De man die hier woont, is ziek.
De mannen die hier wonen, zijn ziek.   Common gender

Het boek dat ik nu lees, is oud.
De boeken die ik nu lees, zijn oud.   Neuter

Note: 1 *Die/dat* are pronouns because within their own clause they stand for a noun. In English they are 'who/which/that'.
2 They are relative because they relate back to the preceding word.
3 The finite verb in relative clauses is sent to the end of that clause.
4 If a comma is used at all, it follows the relative clause. In shorter sentences like the above it is usually omitted.

8.5.3 RELATIVE PRONOUNS PRECEDED BY PREPOSITIONS

a   When a preposition occurs before a relative pronoun of common gender, the pronoun *wie* is used instead of *die* when it refers to a **person.**

De man met wie ik in de winkel stond te praten, is mijn oom.

This sentence can be translated as follows:

1 The man to whom I was talking in the shop is my uncle.
2 The man whom I was talking to in the shop is my uncle.
3 The man I was talking to in the shop is my uncle.

In archaic style a dative form *wie* (older *wien*) without a preposition can occur. This form was used until quite recently.

De man wie het gegeven werd, is verdwenen.
The man to whom it was given has disappeared.

b   When a preposition is used before a relative pronoun relating to a **thing**, whether it be a *de* of *het* word, *waar-* plus the preposition is used:

De tafel waarop het brood ligt, is van mij.

This can be translated as follows:

1 The table on which the bread is lying is mine.
2 The table which the bread is lying on is mine.
3 The table the bread is lying on is mine.

Note: There is, however, in this instance a second variation in word order in Dutch. This is in fact the more common of the two. In this case the preposition is sent to the end of the relative clause where it is placed before the verb which has also been relegated to the end of the clause.

De tafel waar het brood op ligt is van mij.

Further examples using a neuter noun and a plural where the construction is precisely the same:

Het brood waar ik van hou is niet verkrijgbaar – Neuter noun.
De bedden waar de katten onder slapen zijn oud – Plural noun.

c   In conversation it is also common to use the *waar* + preposition construction referred to in b for people.

> *De man waarmee (= met wie) ik in de winkel stond te praten, is mijn oom*
> or   *De man waar ik in de winkel mee stond te praten, is mijn oom.*

8.5.4   RELATIVES WITH INDEFINITE ANTECEDENTS – USE OF *WAT*

niets wat [14]	nothing (which/that) you say…
iets wat	something (which/that) you say…
veel wat	much (of what) you say…
alles wat	everything (which/that) you say…
dat wat [15]	that which you say… (see p. 64)
het enige wat,	the only thing (which/that) (see p. 68-69)
het laatste wat	the last thing (which/that)

Sometimes the antecedent of *wat* is an entire clause:

> *Hij heeft zijn auto total loss gereden, wat ik erg jammer vind.*
> He wrecked his car, which I think is a great shame.

8.5.5   WORD ORDER IN RELATIVE CLAUSES

Sending the verb to the end of the relative clause sometimes confuses English speakers who are used to the relative immediately following the noun to which it refers. One can keep the antecedent and the relative together in Dutch, as the following examples illustrate, but that is not usually the case.

a   *Ik heb hem het lijstje gestuurd dat je me gegeven hebt.*

This word order is preferable to the following although what follows is not incorrect (note the obligatory comma in such cases).

Ik heb hem het lijstje dat je me gegeven hebt, gestuurd.

b   *Laat me dat hondje eens zien dat je gekocht hebt.*

Here the distance between the relative and its antecedent is greater and the speaker may prefer:

Laat me dat hondje dat je gekocht hebt, eens zien.

Either is, however, still possible.

c   *Ik kan een kast toch moeilijk afsluiten waar jij de sleutel van hebt.*

Here the distance is so great that the following would be preferred:

Ik kan een kast waar jij de sleutel van hebt, toch moeilijk afsluiten.

---

14   In all cases *dat* is sometimes heard but *wat* is preferable. It is not uncommon in colloquial speech for relative *dat* (see p. 60) to be replaced by *wat*.
15   The *dat* can be omitted.

8.5.6 WHOSE

1	2	3
wiens (for masculine antecedents)	*van wie/waarvan*	*die z'n*
wier (for feminine & plural antecedents)	*van wie/waarvan*	*die d'r*
welks (for non-personal antecedents)	*waarvan*	*waarvan*

The forms given in column 1 are only found in the written language, *wiens* being somewhat more common than *wier* or *welks* which are regarded as particularly archaic.

Usually the forms in column 2 replace those in 1 in writing and speech and those in column 3 are restricted to the spoken language.

(written)	*De man wiens boek ik geleend heb, is ziek.*
(spoken & written)	*De man van wie ik het boek geleend heb, is ziek.*
	(note the new word order)
(spoken)	*De man die z'n boek ik geleend heb, is ziek.*
(written)	*Het huis welks dak ingestort is, is gisteren verkocht.*
(spoken & written)	*Het huis waarvan het dak ingestort is, is gisteren verkocht*
or	*Het huis waar het dak van ingestort is, is gisteren verkocht.*

8.5.7 PREPOSITION PLUS WHOSE

a As we have seen, 'whose' is normally expressed in Dutch by *van wie* or *waarvan*, but a complication arises when one is confronted with a sentence like the following:

The man in whose chair I am sitting is my uncle.

It is impossible to have *in* and *van* together. In such an instance *wiens*, although stilted when used as above, is somewhat more common when a preposition is involved.

De man in wiens stoel ik zit, is mijn oom.

But *wier*, as in *De vrouw in wier stoel ik zit, is mijn tante* is very rare.

In speech the following would be used:

De man in wie z'n stoel ik zit...
De vrouw in wie d'r stoel ik zit...
De mensen in wie d'r stoel ik zit...

In writing, if one wants to avoid *wiens* and *wier*, the following would be preferable:

De man/vrouw/mensen in de stoel van wie ik zit,...

b A preposition + whose, when the antecedent is a thing, i.e. not a person, also causes complications if one wishes to avoid using *welks*. Once again, as with *wiens, welks* is sometimes found in the formal written language when preceded by a preposition:

Het huis op welks dak de kat de hele nacht heeft gezeten, is ingestort.

This would not be said in the spoken language, however. Then the following would be more usual:

Het huis waar de kat de hele nacht op het dak gezeten heeft, is ingestort.

8.5.8 INDEPENDENT RELATIVES

These are relatives that begin sentences and thus have no antecedent: *die/wie*[16] – he who; *wat* – that which, what; *hetgeen* – that which, what. They could also be regarded as indefinite pronouns.

Wie (die) eens steelt, is voor altijd een dief.
He who steals is branded a thief forever.
Wie (die) komen wil, moet nu betalen.
Whoever[17] wants to come must pay now.
Wat je zegt is allemaal onzin.
What (that which) you're saying is simply nonsense.

Here the meaning is *dat wat*. This *wat* is commonly replaced in the written language by *hetgeen* (say: *'t geen*).

Hetgeen je doet is gevaarlijk.
What (that which) you are doing is dangerous.
Hetgeen ik zeggen wil is dit.
What (that which) I want to say is the following.

8.5.9 LESS COMMON RELATIVES

a The relative *hetgeen* commonly replaces in writing the *wat* which refers back to a whole clause: it is, however, an archaic form (see p. 62).

Hij heeft zijn auto total loss gereden, hetgeen ik erg jammer vind.

In this sense *hetwelk* (also written *'t welk*) can also be used; this form is also archaic.

De eendracht is in het land hersteld, hetwelk (hetgeen) de gehele bevolking met vreugde vervult.

b Historically related to *hetwelk* (and *welks* which was dealt with earlier) is the relative *welk(e)* which often replaces *die* in formal writing:

De regering welke (die) dat bekendgemaakt heeft, is gisteren afgetreden.
De idealen welke (die) eertijds de jeugd bezielden, doen ons soms glimlachen.

16 *Die* is rather literary.
17 *Degene(n) die* is common in this sense too (see Indefinite pronouns p. 67).

c   A further common usage of *welk(e)* which cannot be avoided, even in speech, is the following adjectival relative:

Hij zei dat hij alles begrepen had, welke opmerking ik niet de moeite waard vond tegen te spreken.
Max Havelaar, welk boek (welke roman) ik op mijn veertiende jaar leerde kennen, vind ik nog steeds prachtig.

8.5.10   ADJECTIVAL ADJUNCTS REPLACING RELATIVE CLAUSES

In formal style, and often in journalese, one finds on occasions an avoidance of relative clauses by placing the information usually contained in the relative clause before the noun it refers to, as one does an adjective. The adjunct always contains a present or past participle (or occasionally an infinitive – see last example).

Het boek **dat ik gisteren inbond,** *heb ik aan mijn beste vriend gegeven.*
Het **gisteren door mij ingebonden** *boek heb ik aan mijn beste vriend gegeven.*
Hij heeft een rijksdaalder gevonden in de boekenkast **die hij gemaakt heeft.**
Hij heeft een rijksdaalder gevonden in de **door hem gemaakte** *boekenkast.*
De bomen **die in dit park staan** *zijn allemaal eiken.*
De **in dit park staande** *bomen zijn allemaal eiken.*
Het bedrag **dat u nog betalen moet.**
Het **nog door u te betalen** *bedrag.*

Some adjectival adjuncts can be of unwieldy length as the following extreme example taken from a newspaper illustrates:

De in 1949 wegens collaboratie en roven van kunstschatten tot 8 maanden gevangenisstraf veroordeelde nu 77 jaar oude Blaricumse miljonair Pieter Menten, heeft het land weten te ontvluchten.

Relative clauses must be used in English when translating such adjectival adjuncts (see p. 154).

8.5.11   Under (8.5.10) examples of Dutch participial constructions which are rendered by relative clauses in English are given. There are, however, **participial** (both past and present) **constructions in English** which must be translated by relative clauses in Dutch.

The houses built in the fifties are noisy.
De huizen die in de jaren vijftig gebouwd zijn, zijn gehorig.

This could also be rendered by an adjectival adjunct:

De in de jaren vijftig gebouwde huizen zijn gehorig.

The man reading the paper in the corner of the room is seriously ill.
De man die in de hoek de krant zit te lezen, is ernstig ziek.

8.5.12   See note 3 on use of *dat*, p. 183.

8.6 Indefinite pronouns (onbepaalde voornaamwoorden)

One

The English pronoun 'one' has an exact equivalent in Dutch which is *men*. Like its English counterpart, *men* belongs more in formal speech and writing than in everyday language. In conversation it is commonly replaced by unstressed *je* or *ze* (i.e. they, see p. 155). It differs from English, however, in that *men* can only serve as a subject pronoun; when the object is needed, *je* (i.e. unstressed *jou*) or *iemand* is used in colloquial style; in formal style a passive is often used. (see p. 151)

If a teacher finds one in a classroom at lunchtime one is punished.
Als een leraar je tussen de middag in een klaslokaal vindt, word je gestraft.

The possessive pronoun 'one's' is rendered by *zijn* and the reflexive 'oneself' by *zich*.

One has to pay one's taxes every year.
Men moet jaarlijks zijn belasting betalen.

Everyone, -body

The most usual word is *iedereen*. Occasionally just *ieder* (also *ieders* – everyone's) is used. In more formal style *een ieder* and *elkeen* are also found, eg. *Dit is een 'must' voor een ieder die geïnteresseerd is in de kunst van de 17de eeuw.*

Someone, -body; anyone, -body; no-one, -body

The subtle distinction between 'someone' and 'anyone' does not exist in Dutch; both are rendered by *iemand*. When 'anyone' is used with a negative in English, Dutch simply uses *niemand* (nobody).

Heb je iemand gezien?
Did you see anyone?
Ja, ik heb iemand gezien.
Yes, I saw someone.
Nee, ik heb niemand gezien.
No, I didn't see anyone (i.e. I saw nobody).

Iemand and *niemand* also have a genitive form *iemands* and *niemands*, eg. *iemands pet* – somebody's cap.
'Somebody else' is *iemand anders*.
'Somebody else's cap' – *iemand anders z'n pet* (spoken)
                    de pet van iemand anders (written)
      also – *andermans pet* (written)

Something; anything; nothing

(see also *ergens, nergens* and *overal* p. 69)
The situation here is similar to that above: 'something/anything' are rendered by *iets* or more colloquially by *wat*; 'nothing' is *niets* or in the spoken language *niks*.

Heeft ze iets/wat gekocht?
Did she buy anything?
Ja, ze heeft iets/wat gekocht.
Yes, she bought something.
Nee, ze heeft niets gekocht.
No, she didn't buy anything. (i.e. she bought nothing)

For *iets/wat* and *niets* followed by an adjective see p. 74.

Note: *iets* and *wat* also render the adverb 'somewhat'.

Whoever; whatever (see p. 191)

Wie...ook and *wat...ook* translate the above.

Wie er ook komt, wij zullen voor hen kunnen zorgen
Whoever comes, we will be able to take care of them.

Alwie (whoever) and *alwat* (whatever) are sometimes used in the written language.

Note: *Wie dat zegt is een leugenaar.*
Whoever (= he who) says that is a liar. (see p. 64)
Die is used in formal style instead of *wie*.

Many, several, various, some, others, a few

veel, vele(n)	much, many
verscheidene(n) } *ettelijke(n)*	several
verschillende(n)	various
sommige(n)	some
andere(n)	others
enkele(n) } *een paar*	a few
degene(n) die,	the one who/which, those who/which
hetgene dat	that which; what

With the exception of *een paar*, all words in this category (plus also *alle* and *beide* – see below) add *-n* when they are used independently referring to people. All but the last two can also be used as adjectives before nouns, in which case they do not add *-n*, nor when used independently referring to things.

Verscheidene mensen willen niet komen.
Sommigen blijven thuis maar anderen gaan naar de bioscoop.
Ik heb vandaag een paar boeken gekocht. Ik heb er ook enkele gekocht.

Note that *vele* when used attributively before a plural noun can also be *veel*; eg. *veel kinderen, veel boeken.*
The form *veel* can also be used independently when referring to non-animate things.

Veel (winkels understood*) hebben moeten sluiten*
but
Velen (mensen understood*) hebben moeten gaan.*

Note: In literary style a genitive from *veler* is sometimes found, eg. *op veler verzoek* – at the request of many.

Both

a   The basic word for 'both' is *beide*. It is used in the same way as the expressions given above, i.e. *beide mensen; beide boeken; beide (boeken* understood*) waren duur; beiden (mensen* understood*) zijn vertrokken.*

b   In addition, there is a form *allebei* which is used to translate 'both of us/you/them' – also used with nominal subjects and objects.

>*Ze gaan allebei naar de markt.*
>They are both going/both of them are going to the market.
>*Ik heb ze allebei in de stad gezien.*
>I saw them both/both of them in town.

c   Expressions such as 'both the brothers' can be translated as follows: *de twee broers, beide broers* or *de broers gaan allebei naar de markt.*

All (see also, *ergens, nergens* and *overal* below)

The way in which 'all' is translated into Dutch is similar to the way in which 'both' is translated (see above).

a   The basic word is *alle* and is used like the expressions dealt with above, i.e. *alle mensen, alle boeken, alle (boeken* understood*) waren duur, allen (mensen* understood*) hebben moeten gaan.*

b   In addition, there is a form *allemaal* which is used to translate 'all of us/you/them'.

>*Ze gaan allemaal naar de markt.*
>They are all going to the market. (or All of them are going...)
>*Ik heb ze allemaal in de stad gezien.*
>I saw all of them in town. (or them all)

Note: the word *allemaal* is also used very idiomatically in spoken Dutch with a variety of meanings only vaguely related to the literal meaning.

>*Ik kan dat allemaal niet begrijpen.*
>I can't understand any of that.

c   Expressions such as 'all the men' can be translated in three ways: *al de mannen, alle mannen* or *de mannen zijn er allemaal geweest.*

d   Note the ambiguity of the following English 'all':

>That's all I can tell you, i.e. everything or the only thing.

The first meaning is translated as *dat is alles* (or even *al*) *wat ik je vertellen kan* and the second as *dat is het enige wat ik je vertellen kan.*
In practice, however, *alles* is used in both cases.

e Note that *alles* means 'everything' and *al* usually means 'already' (see c and d above for exceptions).

Pronominal use of *ergens, nergens* **and** *overal*

These three words which are usually used as adverbs rendering English 'somewhere/ somehow', 'nowhere' and 'everywhere' also have a pronominal function: when *iets* (something), *niets* (nothing) and *alles* (everything) are preceded by a preposition, they are often replaced (particularly in speech) by *ergens, nergens* and *overal* respectively and the preposition **follows** these words.

> *Hij kijkt ergens naar*[18]– He is looking at something.
> *Ik heb hem nergens over verteld* – I told him about nothing.
> *Je kunt het overal mee doen* – You can do it with anything.

Should the indefinite pronoun be followed by a relative clause, however, those alternative forms can't be used (see p. 62)

> *Hij kijkt naar iets wat ik gemaakt heb.*
> He is looking at someting I have made.
> *Je kunt het doen met alles wat je vinden kunt.*
> You can do it with anything you can find.

These forms also can't be used when *iets, niets* and *alles* are followed by an inflected adjective. (see p. 74)

> *Ik zoek iets leuks voor zijn verjaardag.*
> I'm looking for something nice for his birthday.

8.7 Interrogative pronouns *(vragende voornaamwoorden)*

(for Interrogative Adverbs see p. 190)

8.7.1 WHO; TO WHOM, FROM WHOM ETC.

The interrogative pronoun 'who' is *wie*, eg. *Wie is je leraar?* Questions involving 'who' plus prepositions are always posed as follows: *Aan wie heb je het schrift gegeven?* To whom did you give the exercise book? English usually employs the word order 'Who(m) did you give the book to?' This is not possible in Dutch.

> Who(m) did you get those scissors from?
> *Van wie heb je die schaar gekregen?*

---

18 Note the following adverbial use of *ergens: Ergens heeft hij wel gelijk* – Somehow he is right.

English speakers must be careful not to confuse the interrogative 'who' in indirect questions (i.e. *wie* in Dutch) with the relative pronoun 'who' (i.e. *die* or *waar* in Dutch, see p. 61)

> *Ik weet niet wie het gedaan heeft.* (indirect interrogative)
> *Hij is degene die het gedaan heeft.* (relative)

8.7.2   WHOSE

The possessive interrogative pronoun 'whose' is *wiens* or *van wie*.

> *Wiens boek is dit?* (lit.)
> *Van wie is dit boek?*   Whose book is this?
> *Wie z'n boek is dit?* (spoken language)

When the reference is obviously to a female being or plural beings, the written language also knows the form *wier*, and the spoken language *wie d'r* for feminine beings.

> *Wie d'r* (or *z'n*) *b.h. is dit?*
> Whose bra is this?

8.7.3   WHAT

a   'What' is *wat* but when used in combination with a preposition it is replaced by *waar* + preposition which can also be separated.

> *Wat heb je gedaan?*
> What have you done?
> *Waarmee heb je het gedaan?/Waar heb je het mee gedaan?*
> What did you do it with?

b   'What kind/sort of a' is rendered by the idiom *wat voor een*.

> *Wat voor een auto heb je?/Wat heb je voor een auto?*
> What sort of car do you have?

c   *Wat* is common in exclamations:

> *Wat jammer* – What a pity/shame.
> *Wat een mooi huis* – What a beautiful house.

Note: *Wat een dure boeken* – What expensive books.

d   Sometimes English 'what' is rendered by *hoe* in Dutch (see p. 103).

> What time is it? – *Hoe laat is het?*
> What is your name – *Hoe is uw naam?/Hoe heet u?*

e   Sometimes English 'what' means 'which'. (see 8.7.4 below)

8.7.4 WHICH

Dutch *welk(e)* can be used attributively before nouns or independently. English often uses 'what' in this sense too.

Welk boek (welke film, welke mensen) heb je gezien?
Which/what book (film, people) did you see?
Welke heb je gekocht?
Which/what ones did you buy?
Welk (boek understood) *heb je gekocht?*
Which/what one did you buy?

9 Adjectives *(bijvoeglijke naamwoorden)*

9.1 Rules for inflection *(verbuiging)*

An adjective used attributively (i.e. before the noun) will always take an *-e* ending except in the following cases:

a   Before a singular neuter noun preceded by *een, elk, geen, ieder, menig, veel, zo'n, zulk*. In addition one still finds omission of the *-e* inflection after possessive pronouns (i.e. *mijn, jouw, zijn, ons* etc.) but nowadays the ending is more commonly used than not, i.e. *ons kleine land* rather than *ons klein land* (lit.).
It should be noted that in expressions such as 'Jan's big house' Jan's acts as a possessive adjective and thus the adjective following it is inflected, i.e. *Jans grote huis*.

b   Before singular neuter nouns preceded by nothing, i.e. *oud brood, zoet water*.[1] Note that in **all** other cases an ending is required, eg. *het oude brood, zulke oude huizen, stoute kinderen, dat stomme ding* etc.

Predicative adjectives (i.e. those not used before nouns as in 'the book is green') never inflect in Dutch.

9.1.1   There are numerous cases where an adjective does **not** take an *-e* ending where you would expect one according to the rules above:

a   Adjectives ending in *-en*, which includes materials (eg. *houten, zilveren, open, eigen*) and strong past participles (eg. *gesloten, vertrokken, opgeblazen*).
Exception: *verscheidene* (several) always takes *-e*.
When adjectival past participles ending in *-en* are used as nouns they take *-e* (*-en* in plural), eg. *de betrokkene, volwassene* etc.

b   A limited number of adjectives do not take *-e* but are affixed to the following noun instead (see p. 87).

c   Some adjectives of foreign origin are indeclinable: *beige, crème, gratis, lila, nylon, oranje, plastic, platina, aluminium, rose*.

d   Place name adjectives in *-er*: *Groninger koek, Haarlemmer olie*.

---

1   In expressions such as *Witte Huis te koop* and *Engelse pond gedevalueerd* the meaning is definite even though the neuter article has been omitted; therefore the adjective is inflected.

e   Comparatives of more than three syllables: *interessanter, belangrijker*. One will often hear such comparatives being inflected in the spoken language, however (see p. 75).

f   A few adjectives take on a figurative meaning if uninflected: *oud-soldaat* = ex-soldier, *een groot man* = a great man (but *een grote vrouw*).

g   The adjectives *rechts* and *links* have their own peculiar form in *-er* and are often written as one word, particularly when referring to parts of the body and items of clothing: *de rechterhand, de linkerschoen;* also *de linkeroever, rechterkant, linkerzijde*. Preceding other nouns they behave as nominal adjectives: *rechts verkeer, de linkse partijen*.

h   It is very common for adjectives preceding nouns referring to human beings (particularly masculine beings) to be left uninflected after articles. One is advised only to copy those one has heard or read and otherwise to apply the ending, eg. *de waarnemend burgemeester* (the acting mayor), *de tijdelijk zaakgelastigde* (the temporary chargé d'affaires), *een bekwaam musicus* (a competent musician), *een vroom man* (a pious man), *een beroemd schrijfster* (a famous authoress), *Geyl is een bekend Nederlands historicus* (Geyl is a famous Dutch historian).

i   The adjective does not inflect after *een, geen, zo'n* etc. before the common gender noun *iemand*, eg. *een belangrijk iemand* – an important person.

Note: *een aardig mens* (a nice person) can only refer to a female.

j   There is a long list of nouns, particularly neuter nouns, which, even when preceded by the singular definite article, do not inflect the preceding adjective as one would expect according to the rules given above. The adjective and the noun are regarded as a compound in such cases. In the plural the adjective is, however, inflected, eg. *het academisch ziekenhuis, de academische ziekenhuizen*.

The following list is not complete but will serve to illustrate the concept:

het academisch ziekenhuis	*het menselijk lichaam*
het centraal station	*het noordelijk halfrond*
het cultureel akkoord	*het noordoostelijk deel*
het dagelijks leven	*het oostelijk deel*
het economisch herstel	*het openbaar vervoer*
het Engels Instituut	*het sociaal pakket*
het geestelijk leven	*het stedelijk museum*
het Gents Advertentieblad	*het stoffelijk overschot*
het heilig sacrament	*het uitvoerend orgaan*
het koninklijk gezin	*het verzameld werk*
het medisch onderzoek	*het zelfrijzend bakmeel*

The parts of speech also belong in this category, eg. *het bijvoeglijk naamwoord, het wederkerend werkwoord* etc.

The expression *hartelijk dank* also dispenses with inflection although *dank* is a common gender noun.

9.1.2 Inflection often causes spelling changes in accordance with the phonetic spelling rules of Dutch.

a Adjectives with *aa, ee, oo* and *uu*, drop one vowel, eg. *kaal – kale, geel – gele, groot – grote, duur – dure*. Those ending in *-ieel* add a dieresis, eg. *officieel – officiële*. Note also that past participles used adjectively are also subject to this rule, eg. *gehaat* (from *haten* – to hate) *– gehate, vergroot* (from *vergroten* – to enlarge) *– vergrote*.

b In adjectives with a long vowel or a diphthong and ending in *-f*, the *f* changes to *v* (i.e. the *f* becomes voiced between two vowels), eg. *lief – lieve, braaf – brave, doof – dove*.[2]. A word such as *laf* goes *laffe*, however, because it contains a short vowel (see rule d).

c Adjectives with a long vowel or diphthong and ending in *-s* change to *z* (i.e. voicing because of its intervocalic position), eg. *vies – vieze, dwaas – dwaze*. There are a few isolated exceptions to this rule, however, eg. *kies – kiese, overzees – overzeese, hees – hese, kuis – kuise, histories – historiese* (see p. 17), *Parijs* – Parijse.
Adjectives of nationality ending in *-ees* go *-ese*, eg. *Chinees – Chinese*, also *Fries – Friese* (as plural nouns they take *z*, eg. *Chinezen, Friezen*).

d Adjectives with a short vowel ending in a consonant double the consonant to keep the vowel short, eg. *dik – dikke, laf – laffe, wit – witte, tam – tamme, dun – dunne, fris – frisse*. Exceptions: *grof – grove, bros – broze* (often pronounced *groffe* and *brosse*, however).

e Adjectives with a long vowel or diphthong ending in *-d* are often pronounced with a vocalised *d*, eg. *rode – rooie, goed – goeie, oud – ouwe*. They are sometimes written like this too in less formal style.

f Note the adjective *bijdehand* (smart, bright) which goes *bijdehante*.

9.1.3 A limited number of adjectives usually denoting location take *-ste* instead of *-e*.

> *bovenste, middelste, benedenste; binnenste, buitenste; achterste, voorste, onderste*.
> (Note: *binnenstebuiten* = inside out, *ondersteboven* = upside down, *achterstevoren* = back to front).

In addition one often hears *enigste* instead of *enige* but the former is an analogical form and should be avoided, eg. *Dit is de enigste auto die wij nog hebben*. (This is the only car we still have.) The words *laatste, zoveelste, hoeveelste* belong here too (see p. 212, 217).

9.1.4 There is also an **-s inflection** of the adjective in Dutch. It is used nowadays in only a limited number of cases. It is always used after *iets/wat* (i.e. something), *niets* (see p. 66), *veel, allerlei, weinig, een heleboel, wat voor, genoeg*, eg. *iets nieuws* – something new. *niets sterkers* – nothing stronger (added here to the comparative), *een heleboel moois. Wat*

---

2 Both rules a and b applied.

heb je nou voor lekkers gekocht? – What sort of delicious things have you bought? *Er is nog genoeg fraais te bedenken.* – There are enough nice things to think of.
Adjectives that already end in -*s* (eg. *vies, Belgisch*) do not of course take another *s*.

Note: *wat* and *iets* can mean 'something' or 'somewhat'; with the latter meaning followed by an adjective, no -*s* is added, eg. *Het ziet er wat nieuw uit* – It looks somewhat new.

9.1.5   Formerly there was a complete paradigm of strong and weak adjectival endings for all four cases, as is still the case in German. The above rules for -*e* and -*s* inflection are in fact all that is left of these declensions except for those endings preserved in standard expressions and those found in older literary texts, eg. *op heterdaad* – red-handed (dative), *te allen tijde* – always (dative), *in koelen bloede* – in cold blood (dative); *blootsvoets* – bare-footed (genitive), *grotendeels* – on the whole (genitive), *vol zoeten wijns* (arch.) – full of sweet wine (genitive). The fact that these adjectives are often written together with the noun indicates that they are no longer regarded as inflected adjectives in the normal sense but more as compound nouns.

9.2   The comparative of the adjective *(de vergrotende trap)*

9.2.1   FORMATION OF THE COMPARATIVE:

The comparative is formed, as in English, by adding -*er* to the adjective whereby the same spelling changes apply as for -*e* inflection (see p. 76), eg. *groot* – *groter, doof* – *dover, vies* – *viezer, dik* – *dikker.*
Adjectives ending in -*r* take -*der*, eg. *puur* – *puurder, zuiver* – *zuiverder, ver* – *verder*. There are two adjectives that have an irregular comparative form, as in English:

  goed – *beter* (good – better),
  kwaad – *erger* (bad – worse)

Note: *kwaad* meaning 'angry' becomes *kwader*. *Moe* (tired) uses *vermoeider* as its comparative.

9.2.2   INFLECTION OF THE COMPARATIVE

When used attributively, comparatives follow the rules for the inflection of simple adjectives, eg. *een grotere jongen, een kleiner huis.*
Comparatives of more than three syllables cannot be inflected although the -*e* ending is commonly heard in such cases, eg. *een belangrijker man, een interessanter geschiedenis.*
It is also quite common for some comparatives of two syllables not to inflect; here one has the choice, however, eg. *na kortere of langere tijd.* The rules for -*s* inflection also apply to comparatives, eg. *iets groters* – something bigger.

9.2.3   USE OF *MEER* WITH THE COMPARATIVE

In English the comparative of longer adjectives is formed by placing 'more' before the word rather than by adding -er, eg. more important, more interesting. As a general rule one can say that this is not the case in Dutch, eg. *belangrijker, interessanter*. The comparative with *meer* is, however, known in Dutch but is seldom compulsory and should thus be avoided if in doubt, eg. *succesvoller* or *meer succesvol, typischer* or *meer typisch* (often used with adjectives ending in *-isch*). It is often used before adjectives of nationality too, eg. *meer Hollands* (= more Dutch, Dutcher, although the latter sounds somewhat peculiar in English too) and is also usually used before past participles used as adjectives eg. *meer geïnteresseerd* (also *geïnteresseerder*), *meer gewend aan, meer opgewonden* (also *opgewondener*). On occasions *-er* is possible in such cases, eg. *een vervallener huis dan dit is er nauwelijks, die acties waren nog uitgebreider.*

9.2.4 'MORE AND MORE' CONSTRUCTIONS

Dutch too has the potential to say *meer en meer, dieper en dieper*. It is, however, more common to use *steeds/alsmaar* + comparative, eg. *de hemel wordt steeds blauwer* – the sky is getting bluer and bluer. Another common alternative is *hoe langer hoe* + comparative, eg. *hoe langer hoe blauwer, hij werd hoe langer hoe brutaler* = he got more and more cheeky (as time passed).

9.2.5 ATTRIBUTIVE USE OF COMPARATIVE FORMS

Note the following difference between English and Dutch: the better of the two boys/the best of the three boys = *de beste van de twee jongens/de beste van de drie jongens*, i.e. no such distinction is made in Dutch. This is not the case after *een*, eg. *ik heb een betere oplossing gevonden* but *mijn oplossing was de beste van de twee* – the better of the two. The comparative is, however, found after articles and demonstratives in expressions like the following where no direct comparision is being made: *een oudere heer* – an elderly gentleman, *de jongere generatie* – the younger generation, *de hogere standen* – the upper classes.

9.2.6 'MORE THAN' AND 'AS BIG AS' CONSTRUCTIONS

He is bigger than I – *hij is groter* **dan** *ik*. Colloquially one often hears *als*[3] instead of *dan* but this should not be copied. The very English 'error' of saying 'she is richer than **me**' must be avoided in Dutch; a Dutchman would always say *ik*. Similarly in 'He is more important than you' the 'you' is *jij* not *jou*, i.e. subject pronoun. But: *ik vind hem aardiger dan jou*, i.e. object pronoun. (see p. 55).

Note: He is even bigger than I – *Hij is nog groter dan ik*.

---

3 *Als* **is** used in expressions such as '(just) as big as **I**' = *(net) zo groot als ik*. There is an alternative form: *even groot als*.

9.3   The superlative of the adjective *(de overtreffende trap)*

9.3.1   FORMATION OF THE SUPERLATIVE

The superlative of the adjective is formed by adding -*st* whereby no change in the spelling takes place, eg. *groot – grootst, doof – doofst, dik – dikst*.
Adjectives ending in -*s* simply add a -*t*, eg. *vies – viest, fris – frist*.
The two adjectives that have an irregular comparative also have an irregular superlative:

> *goed – beter – best* (good – better – best)
> *kwaad – erger – ergst* (bad/evil – worse – worst)

9.3.2   INFLECTION OF SUPERLATIVES

Superlatives used attributively are always inflected regardless of their length, unlike comparatives, eg. *de belangrijkste man, het interessantste verhaal*.

9.3.3   USE OF *MEEST* WITH SUPERLATIVES

There are certain parallels between the use of *meest* in superlatives and the use of *meer* in comparatives. Generally speaking all adjectives, however long, add -*st*, unlike English, eg. most interesting – *interessantst,* most exciting – *opwindendst*. The superlative with *meest* is, however, necessary in Dutch with adjectives ending in -*isch* and -*st*, eg. *typisch – meest typisch, juist – meest juist, robuust – meest robuust*.
For the same phonological reasons adjectives ending in -*s* also sometimes form their superlative in this way, eg. *los – meest los, fris – meest fris*.

As with comparatives some longer adjectives such as *succesvol* and *opwindend* will be heard in the superlative with *meest*, although an -*st* ending is also correct. One should, however, only copy examples one has heard or read except for adjectives of nationality and for past participles used as adjectives, eg. *meest Hollands* (most Dutch); *ik ben de meest geïnteresseerde, hij is de meest opgewondene van de groep*. There are in addition some adjectives of foreign origin which can't take an -*st* ending and thus use *meest*, eg. *meest sexy, meest beige*.

9.3.4   USE OF THE SUPERLATIVE

There is one usage of the superlative in Dutch which replaces an English comparative (see 9.2.5): otherwise it is used as in English.

9.3.5 ABSOLUTE SUPERLATIVES

Dutch has an adjectival intensifier formed from the superlative, eg. *een alleraardigste man* – a very nice man, *een allerbeste vriend* – a very good friend.
In addition *hoogst* and *uiterst* (actually adverbs) are used to intensify adjectives, eg. *Dat was hoogst interessant* – most interesting[4], *Dat was uiterst belangrijk* – extremely important.
Here *hoogst* and *uiterst* simply replace 'very'. (see p. 90)
The word *best* is used as an adjectival modifier, eg. *Ik vond het best leuk bij hem* = quite nice; *ik vind het best* – I have no objections; *het is best moeilijk* – it's quite difficult.
Best is also used in letters, eg. *Beste Wim* = Dear Wim.

9.3.6 NOTES ON SUPERLATIVES

a   Note the following compound adjectives incorporating superlatives:
dichtstbijzijnde (eg. *de dichtstbijzijnde brievenbus*) – closest, *dichtstbijgelegen* – closest.

b   There is a small group of adjectives of location which take an *-ste* inflection instead of *-e* and do not thus belong to the realm of superlatives, eg. *middelste, benedenste* etc. (see p. 74). See p. 212 for 'second best', third most important etc.

9.4   Adjectives used only predicatively or attributively

9.4.1   There is a small number of adjectives which can never precede a noun and thus are never inflected, eg. *anders* (different), *zoek* (lost). One says for example *Mijn pen is zoek*, but if one wanted to express this with an attributive adjective, one would need to use another word, eg. *mijn zoekgeraakte pen*. Similarly *verschillend* could replace *anders*. In addition the word *stuk* (broken), which is occasionally used before the noun and inflected, is however usually only used predicatively and is better replaced by *kapot* if an attributive adjective is required.

9.4.2   The material adjectives *betonnen, gouden, houten, ijzeren, marmeren* etc. can only be used attributively. Predicatively one says *van beton, van goud* etc., eg. this wooden house – *dit houten huis*, this house is wood(en); *dit huis is van hout*.

9.5   Predicative adjectives followed by prepositions

It is impossible to give a complete list of such adjectives, particularly of those derived from verbs but the following will serve as a guide. Many have the same preposition as in English. If in doubt, a good dictionary should give which preposition to use. * indicates those derived

---

4   Not to be confused with 'the most interesting story' which is *het interessantste verhaal*. (see p. 77).

from verbs (i.e. past participles); these adjectives can either precede or follow the object to which they refer, eg. *ik was zeer in hem geïnteresseerd* **or** *ik was zeer geïnteresseerd in hem; hij is met haar getrouwd* **or** *hij is getrouwd met haar.*
The other adjectives in this list can also follow the object they refer to but only for particular emphasis, eg. *Met jou ben ik tevreden, tegen mij was hij aardig.*

aardig voor ⎱	nice to
aardig tegen ⎰	
aannemelijk voor	acceptable to
(on)afhankelijk van	dependent on, (independent of)
afkomstig uit	originating from
allergisch voor	allergic to
analoog aan	analogous to
anders dan	different from
arm aan	poor in
bang voor	afraid of
* *bedekt met*	covered in, with
begerig naar	desirous of
* *begroeid met*	overgrown with
* *bekend met*	acquainted, familiar with
* *bekommerd over*	worried about
* *belast met*	in charge of
* *bemind om*	loved for
benieuwd naar	curious about
* *beroemd om*	famous for
* *bestemd voor*	intended for
* *bewust van*	aware of
* *bezeten van*	obsessed with
* *bezorgd over*	anxious about
blauw van	blue with
bleek van	pale with
blij met	pleased with
boos op	angry with
dankbaar voor	grateful for
dol op	mad about, keen on
enthousiast over	enthusiastic about
* *ervaren in*	experienced in
* *gedoemd tot*	doomed to
* *gehecht aan*	attached to (fig.)
* *gehuwd met*	married to
* *geïnteresseerd in*	interested in
gek op	mad about, keen on
gelijk aan	identical to
gelukkig met	happy with
* *geneigd tot*	inclined to
* *gepikeerd over*	sore at
* *getrouwd met*	married to
(on)gevoelig voor	(in)sensitive to

* *gewend aan*	used to
goed in	good at
goed voor	good to (s.o.)
identiek aan	identical to
* *ingenomen met*	pleased, taken with
* *ingesteld op*	oriented, geared to
karakteristiek voor	characteristic of
jaloers op	jealous, envious of [a]
kenmerkend voor	characteristic of
kwaad op	angry with
lelijk tegen	nasty to
links van	to the left of
medeplichtig aan	accessory to
nijdig op.	angry with, mad at
noodzakelijk voor	necessary for, to
* *omgeven door*	surrounded by
* *omringd door*	surrounded by
* *omsingeld door*	surrounded by
onderhevig aan	liable, subject to
* *ongerust over*	anxious, worried
onverschillig voor	indifferent to, regardless of
onzichtbaar voor	invisible to
* *opgewonden over*	excited about
optimistisch over	optimistic about
pessimistisch over	pessimistic about
rechts van	to the right of
rijk aan	rich in
schadelijk voor	harmful to
schuldig aan	guilty of
slecht in	bad at
* *teleurgesteld in*	disappointed in, with s.o.
* *teleurgesteld over*	disappointed in, with
ten noorden van	to the north of [b]
ten oosten van	to the east of [b]
tevreden met, over	pleased, satisfied with
toegankelijk voor	accessible to
trots op	proud of
trouw aan	faithful to
typisch voor, typerend voor	typical of
verantwoordelijk voor	responsible for
* *verbaasd over*	amazed at
* *verbannen uit*	banished from
* *vergeleken bij, met*	compared to, with
* *verliefd op*	in love with
* *verrast door*	surprised by
verschillend van	different from, to
* *verslaafd aan*	addicted to

* *vervangen door*	replaced by
* *verwant aan*	related to (languages, issues)
* *verwant met*	related to (people)
* *verwonderd over*	amazed at
vol	full of [c]
vriendelijk tegen	friendly towards
woedend op	furious with
zwak in	weak at

9.6 Adjectives used as nouns

9.6.1 Very often in English we use constructions such as 'large boats and little ones'. The 'ones' cannot be translated into Dutch and is rendered by the adjective, eg. *grote boten en kleine*. Whether the adjective is inflected or not in Dutch depends on whether it would be if the noun that is understood followed, eg. *een groot huis en een klein (huis)*.

9.6.2 *De rijke, de blinde* etc. can stand alone for *de rijke man, de blinde man*. Similarly in the plural *de rijken, de blinden* mean the rich and the blind.

9.6.3 *Het goede* – good, *het kwade* – evil, *het mooie* – the nice thing, *het stomme* – the stupid thing.
The inflected adjective preceded by the neuter definite article renders an abstract noun, eg.
Het leuke is dat ze een studiebeurs gekregen heeft.
The nice thing is she got a scholarship.
Het mooie van schaatsen is dat iedereen het doen kan.
The nice thing about skating is that everyone can do it.

9.6.4 Colours are *het groen, het geel* etc., eg.
Het groen van jouw trui bevalt me niet.
The green of your jumper doesn't appeal to me.

9.6.5. Note that adjectives of nationality are used in almost all cases to form the name of the feminine inhabitant, eg. *Chinees* = Chinese, *de Chinese* = the Chinese woman (see p. 234-240).

a *Jaloers* is ambiguous; if one specifically wants to express envy, the verb *benijden* must be used. *Ik benijd hem* – I envy him, I am envious of him.
b It is also possible to use *benoorden, beoosten* etc. as prepositions in themselves, eg. *benoorden de grote rivieren* = *ten noorden van de grote rivieren*. They are usually found only in written language.
c Dutch *vol* does not require any preposition, eg. *de emmer was vol water* – the bucket was full of water. *Moe* (tired of) and *zat* (fed up with) do not require a preposition either and they follow the noun to which they refer, eg. *Ik ben het alleenzijn moe/zat* – I am tired of/fed up with being alone. *Aan* is quite commonly omitted from *gewend aan* (used to) eg *'n Denemarken zijn we (aan) dit soort weer gewend* – In Denmark we're used to this sort of weather.

9.7 Formation of Adjectives

9.7.1 SUFFIXES

It should be noted that the endings *-aardig, -(kund)ig, -matig, -talig, -waardig* and *-zijdig* take the stress, eg. *plantáárdig, veelzíjdig.*

Note: Sometimes the same word can take a number of the endings given below, each new combination giving a new word, eg. *kinderachtig* – childish, puerile; *kinds* – senile; *kinderlijk* – child-like.

-(e)loos   is equivalent in every way to English '-less', eg.
doelloos – aimless, *ouderloos* – parentless, *hopeloos* – hopeless

> **Note:** *Werkloos* (unemployed) is often pronounced *werkeloos* and sometimes written as such.

-end(e)   actually the addition of *-d(e)* to the infinitive to form a present participle that can act as an adjective, eg. *werkend* – working, *de arbeidende klasse* – the working class

-achtig   a very common and useful ending and one that is still productive. It often renders English -like, eg. *katachtig* – cat-like, *doosachtig* – box-like. The possibilities are infinite, eg. *dat kind doet zo grote-mensen-achtig, oude-vrijsterachtig* – old-maidish. It can also be suffixed to colours to render -ish, eg. *groenachtig* – greenish. The literal meaning is, however, often no longer evident, eg. *twijfelachtig* – doubtful, *regenachtig* – rainy. In many cases the stress has even shifted to the ending, eg. *reusàchtig* – gigantic, *woonàchtig* – resident, *waaràchtig* – true(ly)

-baar   a common ending added to the stems of verbs often corresponding to English '-able', eg. *draagbaar* – portable, *onuitstaanbaar* – unbearable, *leesbaar* – readable, *dankbaar* – grateful, *zichtbaar* – visible

-en   this ending is suffixed to nouns denoting materials (see p. 78), eg. *houten* – wooden, *gouden* – golden, *kartonnen* – cardboard, *betonnen* – cement, *papieren* – paper, *stenen* – stone, *gipsen* – plaster

-rijk   'rich in', 'endowed with', eg. *fantasierijk* – imaginative, *belangrijk* – important, *schaduwrijk* – very shady, *glorierijk* – glorious

-talig   a handy ending for rendering '-speaking', eg. *Engelstalig* – English speaking, *Nederlandstaligen* – Dutch speaking people

-ig   a common ending often suffixed to nouns meaning 'having, characterized by', eg. *machtig* – mighty, *ijverig* – industrious, *buiig* – showery, *levendig* – lively. It is also used colloquially just like English -ish for approximation, eg. *groenig* – greenish, *viezig* – dirtyish, *nattig* – wettish

This ending is also commonly applied to school and university subjects ending in *-kunde* to form adjectives, eg. *taalkundig* – linguistic, *letter-kundig* – literary, *plantkundig* – botanical. From those adjectives are then formed the names of the people who practise the respective science, eg. *taalkundige* – linguist, *verloskundige* – obstetrician

-erig   not a very common ending which often has a pejorative meaning, eg. *petieterig* – tiny, *slaperig* – sleepy, *winderig* – windy, *zanderig* – sandy, *kitscherig* – kitschy, *hebberig* – greedy, *puisterig* – pimply, *paniekerig* – panicky

-isch   (sometimes spelt *-ies*) is chiefly found in foreign, often scientific words and is equivalent to English -ic, -ical, eg. *historisch, socialistisch, logisch*

-s   (formerly *-sch* and still found in pre-war books as such)
1 common ending for nationalities, eg. *Nederlands, Zweeds, Engels, Frans.*
2 for adjectives from place-names, eg. *Amsterdams, Leids, Londens, Gouds, Gronings.*
3 it is sometimes added to words other than proper nouns, eg. *kerks* – churchy, *hemels* – heavenly, *duivels* – devilish, *aards* – earthly, *kinds* – senile, *schools* – pedantic, *speels* – playful.
It is this ending which one employs in the very commonly used expressions *op z'n* adjective + *s* which are similar in meaning to the French 'à la + adjective', eg. *op z'n Frans* – à la française (i.e. as the French do, in the French way).
Colloquially invent such adjectives forming them from the names of people one knows, eg. *op z'n Pietersens* – as Pietersen would do it (i.e. sloppily, well etc.)

-(e)lijk   a very common suffix which has no adverbal qualities despite its historical connections with English -ly (compare lovely, homely). The '*e*' is usually included but not always, eg. *vriendelijk* – friendly, *maatschappelijk* – social, *menselijk* – human(e), *ongelofelijk*[5] – unbelievable, *vreeslijk* or *vreselijk*[5] – terrible (usually the latter), *gevaarlijk* – dangerous, *persoonlijk* – personal

-zaam   a common ending usually added to verbal stems, eg. *langzaam* – slow, *buigzaam* – flexible, *gehoorzaam* – obedient

-vol   similar to English '-ful', eg. *succesvol* – successful, *talentvol* – talented, *waardevol* – valuable

-vormig   corresponds to English '-shaped' and is still a very productive ending, eg. *trechtervormig* – funnel-shaped, *bolvormig* – spherical-shaped, *tegel-vormig* – tile-shaped

---

5   Notice that the final consonant of what was the verbal stem remains unvoiced.

-waardig   equivalent to English '-worthy', eg. *bezienswaardig* – worth seeing, *bewonderenswaardig* – praiseworthy, *betreurenswaardig* – lamentable, *zeewaardig* – sea-worthy, *merkwaardig* – remarkable

-aardig   not a very common ending and no longer productive, eg. *plantaardig* – vegetable, *kwaadaardig* – malignant, *goedaardig* – benign

-matig   this ending denotes a conformity to what is expressed in the noun it is suffixed to. It is quite a common ending, eg. *regelmatig* – regular, *kunstmatig* – artificial, *instinctmatig* – instinctively

-vrij   this corresponds to the English endings '-free' and '-less' and is still very productive, eg. *boomvrij* – treeless, *autovrij* – free of cars.

9.7.2   PREFIXES

on-   is the most common means of negating adjectives and is used in a similar way to English 'un-', eg. *onvriendelijk* – unfriendly, *ondankbaar* – ungrateful. *On-* is always unstressed.
There are a few compounds with *on-* whose principal component no longer exists, eg. *onnozel* – silly, *ondeugend* – naughty

in-   Some foreign words, as in English, are negated by the addition of *in- (im-)*, eg. *inconsequent* – inconsisten, *inefficiënt* – inefficient, *immoreel* – immoral, *intolerant* – intolerant

Dutch knows a number of adjectival intensifiers which are very commonly used:

aarts-   *aartsdom* – really stupid
aartslui – very lazy

dood-   (very common) *doodarm* – very poor, *doodgewoon* – quite ordinary, *doodeenvoudig* – simple, *doodstil* – very quiet, *doodmoe* – very tired
Note: *doodsbang* – very afraid, *doodsbleek* – very pale.

hartstikke-   (rather colloquial but very common and still productive), *hartstikkeleuk* – very nice, *hartstikkeduur* – very expensive, *hartstikkestom* – very stupid

hyper-   (usually with foreign words), *hyperintelligent, hypernerveus, hypermodern*

oer-   *oerdom* – very stupid, *oeroud* – very old, *oerlelijk* – very ugly, *oersaai* – terribly boring

poep-   (vulgar, more so is *stront-*), *poepduur* – very dear, *poepdeftig* – very posh; *stronteigenwijs* – as stubborn as a mule

reuze-	(still productive) *reuzeleuk* – really nice, *reuzepopulair* – very popular, *reuzevervelend* – very annoying
stapel-	(only used in combination with words for mad), *stapelgek, stapelidioot*
super-	*superfijn* – very fine, *superknap* – very clever, *superveilig* – very safe
ultra-	(usually with foreign words), *ultraradicaal, ultraconservatief*

In addition, the prefix *over-* has the same force as in English, eg. *overrijp* – over-ripe, *overgevoelig* – over-sensitive, *overgaar* – over-cooked.

The intensifiers given above are particularly common and are to a degree still productive. In addition to them are others, many of them nouns, which occur in only one compound adjective; sometimes these are translated almost literally, eg. *ijskoud* – ice-cold, *spotgoedkoop* – dirt-cheap, but very often in English they are rendered by an 'as - as -' phrase, eg. *stokdoof* – as deaf as a post. Beware when confronted with an English 'as - as -' expression because more often than not it will be a compound adjective in Dutch although *zo - als -* expressions do exist too, eg. *zo mager als een lat* – as thin as a rake; *zo blind als een mol* – as blind as a bat; *zo trots als een pauw* – as proud as a peacock.

The following list is by no means complete.

apetrots	as proud as a peacock
broodnuchter	as sober as a judge
drijf-, kletsnat	wet through
glashelder	as clear as a bell
gloedheet	as hot as hell
haarfijn	as fine as hair
hemelsbreed	very wide
hondsbrutaal	very cheeky, bold
ijskoud	ice-cold
keihard[6]	as hard as stone
kerngezond	as fit as a fiddle
kersvers	very fresh, new; hot from the press
kurkdroog	as dry as a bone
loodrecht	perpendicular, vertical
loodzwaar	as heavy as lead
morsdood	as dead as a doornail
peperduur	very expensive
piekfijn	very spruce, smart
piemelnaakt	as naked as the day was born
pikdonker	pitch-dark
poedelnaakt	as naked as the day was born
roodgloeiend	red-hot
rotsvast	as firm as a rock

6 *Keihard,* like the adjective *hard,* can mean hard, fast or loud and can thus be translated in various ways.

schatrijk	very wealthy
smoorverliefd	head-over-heels in love
snikheet	as hot as hell
spiegelglad	as smooth as silk
spotgoedkoop	as cheap as dirt
springlevend	alive and kicking
stampvol	chock-full
stikheet	as hot as hell
steenkoud	stone-cold
stokdoof	as deaf as a post
stokoud	as old as the hills
stomdronken	dead-drunk
straatarm	as poor as a church-mouse
tjok-, propvol	chock-full
vlijmscherp	as sharp as a razor
wagenwijd (open)	wide open
wildvreemd	completely strange.

9.7.3 COLOURS

beige	– beige	*oranje*	– orange.	
blauw	– blue	*purper*	} – purple	
bruin	– brown	*paars*		
geel	– yellow	*rood*	– red	
grijs	– grey	*rose*	– pink	
groen	– green	*wit*	– white	
lila	– lilac	*zwart*	– black	

-kleurig is often used to form new colours from nouns, especially from metals, eg. *goud-kleurig* – gold, *zilverkleurig* – silver.

licht- and **donker-** prefixed to any colour render light and dark, eg. *lichtgroen, donkerrood*. Note: *lichtpaars* – mauve.

-ig and **-achtig** (particularly the latter can be suffixed to the colours to render '-ish') eg. *groenachtig* – greenish.

All colours can be compounded with each other to render shades, eg. *grijsgroen* – greyish green, *geelbruin* – yellowish brown. Note: *zwartwit* – black and white[7], eg. *een zwartwit televisietoestel* – a black and white television set.
Sometimes nouns are prefixed to the colours as can be done in English, eg. *smaragdgroen* – emerald green, *kastanjebruin* – chestnut brown, *scharlakenrood* – scarlet, *okergeel* – ochre, *pikzwart* – black as pitch, *roetzwart* – as black as soot, *bloedrood* – blood red, *hemelsblauw* – sky blue, *grasgroen* – as green as grass, *spierwit* – as white as a sheet.

Note: *Wat voor kleur is het?* – What colour is it?

7　*Het zwart op wit hebben* – to have it (put) down in black and white.

9.8 Notes on some peculiarities of adjectives

9.8.1 The adjective *wijlen* = late (as of deceased persons) precedes the title as in English, eg. *wijlen Prof. T.H. Elsschot, wijlen Koning Karels zoon* = the late King Charles' son. **Note:** no definite article is required in Dutch in such expressions.

9.8.2 There are a number of standard expressions in which the adjective follows the noun. English has such cases too, eg. *moederlief, vaderlief, meisjelief* – mother dear etc., *God almáchtig* – God almighty, *gouverneur-generaal* – governor-general, *Staten-Generaal* – States-General, *moeder-overste* – mother-superior.

9.8.3 Some adjectives are now joined to the noun and are seen as forming a new concept, eg. *plattelánd* – country, *jongemán* – young man, *jongelúi* – young people, youth, *hogeschóol* – tertiary school, *hoogléraar* – professor, *vrijgezél* – bachelor. The shifted stress in such cases illustrates the degree to which such words are considered compound nouns. There are, however, some which retain the stress on the adjective, eg. *zuurkool* – sauerkraut, *rodekool* – red-cabbage. There does not seem to be any rule for inflection in such compounds; they must simply be learnt as they are met. Often one sees *halfdrie* etc. (i.e. time) written as one word as well as *een halfpond*.

9.8.4 Adjectives of nationality are always written with capitals although some modern writers ignore this. Note that although geographical regions are written as hyphenated nouns, the adjectives derived from them are not, eg. *West-Duitsland – Westduits, Midden-Europa –Middeneuropees*. Only those prefixes which are in themselves adjectives are hyphenated, eg. *Zeeuws-Vlaanderen – Zeeuws-Vlaams, Kaaps-Hollands, Brits-Amerikaans*.
Also many learned compounds made up of two adjectives, eg. *literair-kritisch*.

9.8.5 The adjectives *eerstejaars, eersterangs, tweedehands* and *volbloed* are prefixed to the noun without inflecting, eg. *een tweedehandspiano, een eerstejaarsstudent*.
The adjective *rot* (awful, horrible etc.), which is rather colloquial but very common nowadays, is also prefixed to the noun, eg. *een rothuis* – a horrible house, *een rotdag* – a ghastly day; there is, however, a predicative adjective with similar meaning, i.e. *rottig*.

9.8.6 *De* and *het* are prefixed to *-zelfde*, eg. *dezelfde man* – the same man, *dat is mij allemaal hetzelfde* – that is all the same to me.

9.8.7 On occasions when using more than one adjective before a noun in English we join the two by 'and' – this is never done in Dutch, eg. beautiful (and) unusual things – *prachtige, buitengewone dingen*.

9.8.8 The adjectives *heel, geheel* and *gans* – all of which mean 'whole' – although the last two are somewhat literary – can precede the definite article, eg. *heel de wereld* – the whole world, *gans het volk* (lit.) – the entire nation.

10 Adverbs *(bijwoorden)*

The difficulty associated with systematically describing and classifying adverbs is embodied in the Dutch word *bijwoord*, i.e. a word that is there, put in, tacked on. More specifically they are those words which describe when, where, why and how. They can be individual words or complete phrases. The approach adopted here is to look at the simplest adverbs, i.e. those derived from adjectives, and to list the most common adverbs of time and place (see TMP rule p. 91) as well as interrogative adverbs and finally to look briefly at the formation of adverbs. Adverbs from adjectives plus the diminutive ending *-(t)jes* are dealt with on p. 104.

The adverb and adjective are identical in Dutch, i.e. Dutch does not have any equivalent of the English -ly ending. (Exception: *gewoon* – usual; *gewoonlijk* – usually), eg. He is quick; he runs quickly – *Hij is snel; hij rent snel*. This rule is easily forgotten when the adverb precedes an inflected adjective,

an awfully nice bag	– *een ontzettend leuke tas*
a terribly old man	– *een verschrikkelijk oude man*

Compare:

a terrible old man	– *een verschrikkelijke oude man*

Also in:

that is a typically Dutch hat	– *dat is een typisch Nederlandse hoed*

10.1 Comparative and superlative of adverbs

As there is no distinction made between the adjective and the adverb in Dutch the rules for forming the comparative and superlative grades are basically as for adjectives, i.e. by the addition of *-er* and *-st* (see p. 75, 77).

The predicative superlative is preceded by the article *het* and may end in either *-st* or *-ste*, but the forms without *-e* are more common, eg. *het mooist(e), het grootst(e)*.

This use of *het* has a parallel in English:

When are the flowers (the) prettiest?	– *Wanneer zijn de bloemen het mooist?*
Who sang (the) longest?	– *Wie heeft het langst gezongen?*

At times it is difficult to decide whether it is the superlative of the adjective or the adverb that is required; in such cases usually both are correct but the use of the article varies (if 'the' can be left out, it is the adverb one is dealing with).

Which woman is (the) prettiest?
Welke vrouw is het mooist(e)?   – adverb
Welke vrouw is de mooiste?   – adjective

That road is (the) widest.
Die weg is het breedst(e).   – adverb
Die weg is de breedste.   – adjective

This girl is (the) nicest.
Dit meisje is het aardigst.   – adverb and adjective

Irregular comparative and superlatives:

goed	*beter*	*best*	– good, better, best
graag (see p. 140, 144)	*liever*	*liefst*	– willingly, more/most willingly
(*gaarne* lit.)			
veel	*meer*	*meest*	– much, more, most
weinig	*minder*	*minst*	– little, less, least

In addition one should note that although *dikwijls* and *vaak* (often) are interchangeable, only *vaak* has a comparative and a superlative form, i.e. *vaak – vaker – vaakst*. Also with *dichtbij* and *vlakbij* (nearby) only the former can be inflected, i.e. *dichterbij (het dichtste bij, het dichtstbij)* (see p. 78).

For the use of *meer/meest* to form the comparative and superlative grades of adjectives see p. 75, 77). The rules are the same for adverbs.

Zij is het meest geëmancipeerd van allemaal.
She is the most emancipated of all.

10.1.1 NOTES ON THE SUPERLATIVE OF ADVERBS

1 There is a difference in meaning between 'the most important meeting' and 'a most important meeting'; the former is the superlative of the adjective 'important' and is rendered in Dutch as *de belangrijkste vergadering*, whereas the latter is a superlative adverb qualifying the adjective 'important' and is rendered by *een hoogst belangrijke vergadering*.

2 *Minder/minst* are commonly used before adjectives in this way too.

Dit is een minder interessant boek dan dat.
This is a less interesting book than that.

Maar dit boek is het minst interessante.
But this is the least interesting.

3 at least – *minstens, tenminste, op z'n minst.*
not in the least – *niet in het minst*

4 A common alternative to the superlative formed from *het* + *st* is that formed from *op z'n/hun mooist* (see p. 49).

> *De bloemen zijn in de maand mei op hun mooist.*
> *Op z'n best* – at best; *Op z'n vroegst* – at the earliest.

Also: *laatst, op het laatst* – at last, in the end.

5 In the written language the following adverbial superlatives occur which are not translatable as such into English:

Ik zou dat ten zeerste betreuren.
I would regret that very much.
Dat is ten strengste verboden.
That is strictly forbidden.
Het moet ten spoedigste worden afgeleverd.
It must be delivered immediately.
Hij heeft het ten stelligste ontkend.
He flatly denied it.

10.2 Intensifying adverbs

Used to emphasize other adverbs and adjectives (see p. 78).

10.2.1 VERY: *HEEL, ERG, ZEER* (lit.)

The three are completely synonymous but *zeer* is rather formal or particularly emphatic and only *erg* can be used with negatives, eg. *Hij was niet erg groot. Heel* can also mean 'whole' and *erg* can mean 'terrfible', eg. *het was heel erg.* – It was quite awful.
Occasionally one gets a doubling up of *heel* and *erg* as adverbs, eg. *Het is heel erg moeilijk* – It is very, very difficult.
It is also common for the adverbs *erg* and particularly *heel* to inflect when preceding an inflected attributive adjective, but this should be avoided in writing, eg. *een hele mooie boom – een heel mooie boom.*

10.2.2
akelig	awful(ly)
ontzettend	
vreselijk	terrible (-y)
verschrikkelijk	frightful(ly)
ontzaglijk	awful(ly)
ontiegelijk	extremely
afschuwelijk	horrible (-y) – only followed by pejorative adjectives/adverbs

These adverbs, particularly the first three, are very commonly used in the spoken language (but may be written also) to intensify adjectives and other adverbs. They must never be inflected when occurring before attributive adjectives,

een ontzettend leuke jurk	an awfully nice dress
een verschrikkelijk lief kind	a terribly nice child
een afschuwelijk lelijk gezicht	a horribly ugly face

Ontiegelijk is rather a modern word and is increasing in popularity. Similarly the word *enorm* is very in at the moment. (see also *reuze*, p. 85)

een enorm duur gebouw	a tremendously expensive building
Ik heb enorm veel verkocht	I sold an enormous amount

10.2.3

especially	*bijzonder* (pronounced and sometimes written *biezonder/bizonder*)
exceptional(ly)	*buitengewoon*
too	*te*
much too	*veel te* (colloquially *veels te*)

One should take care with English 'especially': when it is used as an adjectival or adverbial intensifier in the above sense *bijzonder* is the appropriate word.

It was not especially (particularly) interesting.
Het was niet bijzonder interessant.

Not, however, in 'especially when it rains' or 'especially in summer' etc. when *vooral* is required, eg. *vooral wanneer het regent, vooral 's zomers.*

10.3   Adverbs of time

10.3.1   It is good style in Dutch to begin clauses with adverbs of time. It is particularly advisable to do this when there are also adverbs of manner and place in the same clause. Dutch insists on the order **Time, Manner, Place** whereas English usually has the reverse order.

He goes to school by bus every day.
              P   M   T

Hij gaat iedere dag met de bus naar school.
          T   M   P

By beginning clauses with time in Dutch, one then needs only concentrate on putting manner and place in the correct order.

Iedere dag gaat hij met de bus naar school.

Notice that if one begins the clause with time, inversion of subject and verb takes place.

Only statements can begin with time, never questions where the verb must be first.

Kom je morgen met de fiets of de tram?

The only exceptions to time always preceding manner and place are the short commonly occurring adverbs, *er, hier* and *daar*. *Er* (unemphatic 'there') always precedes time and *hier* and *daar* can stand at the beginning of the clause for emphasis and thus precede time; otherwise they follow time usually. (see 10.3.7)

> *Ik ben er al geweest.* (only possible order)
> *Daar ben ik al geweest./Ik ben al daar geweest.*
> *Hier heb ik vanochtend brood gekocht/Ik heb vanochtend hier brood gekocht./*
> *Vanochtend heb ik hier brood gekocht.*

10.3.2 When there are two expressions of time in a clause, the less definite always precedes the more definite.

> I get up at 10.00 a.m. every Sunday.
> *Ik sta iedere zondag om tien uur op /Iedere zondag sta ik om tien uur op.*

> He always reads till midnight.
> *Hij leest altijd tot middernacht/Altijd leest hij tot middernacht.* (unusual)

10.3.3 Note that in the above English sentence the adverb of time occurs between the subject and the finite verb. This is very common in English but must not be copied in Dutch.

> He seldom rings me up.
> *Hij belt me zelden op.*
> He never gave me the book.
> *Hij heeft me het boek nooit gegeven.*

10.3.4 When an expression of time occurs in a sentence with a nominal direct object, it precedes the object, not however, when the object is a pronoun.

> *Jullie moeten vanavond dit hoofdstuk lezen.*
> You must read this chapter tonight
> **but**
> *Jullie moeten het vanavond lezen.*

> *Ik heb hem gisteren het boek gegeven.*
> I gave him the book yesterday.

Note that this problem can be avoided by beginning with time.

> *Vanavond moeten jullie dit hoofdstuk lezen.*
> *Gisteren heb ik hem het boek gegeven.*

The same commonly occurs with an expression of place.

> *Hij zat in de tuin een boek te lezen.*
> *Zij zag overal vreemde dingen.*

10.3.5 Do not let the **word order in co-ordinate clauses** containing an adverb of time confuse you.

> *Gisteren is hij naar Amsterdam gevlogen maar morgen komt hij terug.*

Remember that the co-ordinating conjunctions *en, of, want* and *maar* do not effect the word order. Thus, in this example, *morgen* is taken as the first idea and consequently inversion of subject and verb takes place. A stylistic variant of the above is:

Hij is gisteren naar Amsterdam gevlogen maar (hij) komt morgen terug.

10.3.6   There can be a slight difference in the **word order in subordinate clauses** too.

*Zij ging vroeg naar bed, omdat ze **die dag** een lange wandeling had gemaakt.*

The only possible place for the adverb is after the subject. This is not the case in English.

She went to bed early because that day she had gone for a long walk **or** because she had gone for a long walk that day.

10.3.7   Note the presence or absence of 'for' in expressions of time.

a   *Voor hoe lang ga je? Ik ga er (voor) twee weken naar toe.*
How long are you going for? I'm going there for two weeks.

b   *Ik ben er twee weken geweest/Ik was er twee weken.*
I was there for two weeks.

c   *Ik woon hier al twee weken.*
I have been living here for two weeks.

a   *voor* (when in the future, but can also be omitted in such cases)
b   nothing (when in the past)
c   *al* (when in the past in English but lasting up till the present with the verb in the present in Dutch, see p. 114, 115)

Note the word order with *al twee weken* constructions:

Ik woon er/hier/daar al twee weken
but
Ik woon al twee weken in Amsterdam.
Ik wacht al twee uur op je.

Days of the week

on Sundays	*'s zondags*
	(**or** *op zondagen etc.*)
on Mondays	*'s maandags*
on Tuesdays	*dinsdags*
on Wednesdays	*'s woensdags*
on Thursdays	*donderdags*
on Fridays	*vrijdags*
on Saturdays	*zaterdags*
on Sunday etc. (past and coming)	*(op) zondag*
the Sunday after etc.	*de zondag daarna etc.*

Sunday morning, afternoon, evening/night	*zondagochtend, -morgen, -middag, -avond*
on Sunday evenings etc.	*op zondagavond etc.*
by Sunday	*vóór zondag*
next Sunday etc.	*aanstaande/volgende/komende zondag etc.*
last Sunday etc.	*verleden* (lit.)/*afgelopen zondag etc.*
from Sunday (on) etc.	*vanaf zondag etc.*
on working days	*op werkdagen*
on holidays	*op feestdagen*

Yesterday, today, tomorrow etc.

yesterday	*gister(en)*
yesterday morning, afternoon etc.	*gisterochtend, -morgen, -middag etc.*
yesterday evening or last night	Note: *gisteravond*
day before yesterday	*eergisteren*
morning of the day before yesterday etc.	*eergisterochtend, -middag etc.*
today	*vandaag*
today	*heden* (lit.)
from today on	*vanaf vandaag*
this morning, afternoon etc.	*vanochtend, -morgen, -middag, -avond etc.*
tonight (after midnight), last night (after midnight)	*vannacht*
tomorrow	*morgen*
tomorrow morning	*morgenochtend* (**not** *morgenmorgen*)
tomorrow afternoon, evening/night	*morgenmiddag, -avond*
day after tomorrow	*overmorgen*

Periods of the day

in the morning(s)	*'s morgens*
in the morning(s)	*'s ochtends*
in the afternoon(s)	*'s middags*
in the evening(s)	*'s avonds*
at night	*'s nachts*
during the day	*overdag*
late in the evening	*'s avonds laat*
early in the morning	*'s ochtends vroeg*
at lunch-time	*tussen de middag*
at one o'clock in the morning	*om een uur 's ochtends/in de ochtend*

Weekend

this/next weekend	*dit/volgend/komend weekend*
last weekend	*vorig/verleden/afgelopen weekend*
at the weekend	*in het weekend/weekeinde*

Seasons

next summer, winter, autumn, spring	*volgende/aanstaande/komende zomer, winter, herfst, lente*
last summer etc.	*vorige/verleden/afgelopen zomer etc.*
this summer etc. (i.e. both past and coming)	*van de zomer etc.*
in summer	*'s zomers, in de zomer*
in winter	*'s winters, in de winter*
in autumn	*in de herfst, in het najaar*
in spring	*in de lente, in het voorjaar*

Now

now	*thans* (lit.)
now	*nu* (colloquial *nou*)
from now on	*van nu af aan, vanaf nu, voortaan*
until now, up to now	*tot nu toe*, tot nog toe, tot dusver, tot op de dag van vandaag*
nowadays	*vandaag de dag, tegenwoordig*
now and then	*(zo) nu en dan, af en toe*
now and then, every so often	*om de zoveel tijd*

* Note that in this expression *nu* cannot be pronounced *nou*.

Hour

for hours	*urenlang*
hours ago	*uren geleden*
two hours ago	**but** *twee uur geleden*
in two hours' time	*over twee uur*

Note: *uur* always in sing, after numerals (see p. 216).

Day

one day, morning, evening etc.	*op een dag, morgen, avond etc.*
that day, morning, evening etc.	*die dag, morgen, avond etc.*
the day after	*de dag daarna*
the next day	*de dag daarop*
the day before	*de dag daarvoor/tevoren*
all day, evening, night etc	*de hele dag, avond, nacht etc.*
for days	*dagenlang*
days ago	*dagen geleden*
one of these days	*één dezer dagen*
(on) the same day	*(op) dezelfde dag*

once/twice a day	*één/twee keer per dag*
daily	*dagelijks*
the day after (that)	*de dag daarna/erna*
	daags nadien (lit.)
	daags daarna (lit.)

Week

this week	*deze week, van de week*
next week	*aanstaande/volgende/komende week*
last week	*vorige/verleden/afgelopen week*
in a week, in a week's time	*over een week*
in a fortnight, in a fortnight's time	*over twee weken, over veertien dagen*
within a week	*binnen een week*
a week ago	*een week geleden*
a fortnight ago	*twee weken geleden*
Friday week, a week from Friday	*vrijdag over een week*
during the week, on weekdays	*door de week, op werkdagen*
at the beginning/end of next/last week	*begin/eind volgende/vorige week*
the week after	*de week daarop*
all week (long)	*de hele week (door)*
from next week on	*vanaf volgende week*
once a week	*één keer in de week/per week*
twice a week etc.	*twee keer in de week/per week etc.*
every other/second week	*om de andere week*

Month

this month	*deze maand, van de maand*
next month	*volgende/aanstaande/komende maand*
last month	*vorige/verleden/afgelopen maand*
from next month (on)	*vanaf volgende maand*
in a month's time	*over een maand*
within a month	*binnen een maand*
a month ago	*een maand geleden*
for months	*maandenlang, maanden achtereen* (formal)
once a month	*één keer in de maand/per maand*
the month after	*de maand daarop*
at the beginning of January	*begin januari*
in the middle of January	*midden januari*
	half januari
	medio januari
at the end of January	*eind januari*
in June	*in juni*

Year

this year	*dit jaar*
from this year (on)	*vanaf dit jaar*
next year	*volgend/komend jaar*
last year	*vorig/verleden/afgelopen jaar*
in two years' time	*over twee jaar*
two years ago	*twee jaar geleden*
years ago	*jaren geleden*
	jaren her (lit.)
the last three years	*de afgelopen drie jaar*
all year long/through	*het hele jaar door*
the year after	*het jaar daarop*
once a year	*één keer per/in het jaar*

Note: *jaar* always in singular after numerals (see p. 216).

Holidays

on public holidays	*op feestdagen*
at Christmas time	*met (de) Kerst/Kerstmis*
at Easter	*met Pasen*
at Whitsuntide	*met Pinksteren*

GENERAL

always	*altijd*
	steeds
still	*nog*
	nog altijd
	nog steeds
not yet	*nog niet*
still not	*nog steeds niet*
for good	*voor altijd*
	voor goed
for ever (and ever)	*voor eeuwig (en altijd)*
seldom	*zelden*
ever	*ooit*
never	*nooit*
	nimmer
mostly	*meestal*
sometimes	*soms*
now and again	*af en toe*
meanwhile	*intussen*
	in de tussentijd
	ondertussen
	inmiddels

often	*vaak*
	dikwijls
more often	*vaker* (see p. 89)
usually	*gewoonlijk*
usually, generally	*doorgaans*
recently	*onlangs*
	kort geleden
lately	*laatst*
	de laatste tijd
at the latest	*op z'n laatst*
at the latest, not later than	*uiterlijk*
at the earliest	*op z'n vroegst*
late	*te laat*
these days	*tegenwoordig*
in the future	*in de toekomst*
	vervolgens
henceforth	*in het vervolg*
in the course of time	*op den duur*
	na verloop van tijd
	mettertijd
in due course	*te zijner tijd*
high time	*hoog tijd*
	de hoogste tijd
for the time being, provisionally	*voorlopig*
temporarily	*tijdelijk*
since, since then	*sindsdien*
	sedertdien (lit.)
of old	*vanouds (her)*
from way back	
from a child	*van kindsbeen af*
from childhood	

ADVERBS OF TIME WITH ALTERNATIVE TRANSLATIONS IN DUTCH

Afterwards

afterwards	*toen, daarna, naderhand*
afterwards, after that	*nadien* (lit.)
afterwards, later	*later*
shortly afterwards	*kort daarna*

Again

again	*weer*
(yet) again	*alweer*
(once) again	*opnieuw*
again and again	*steeds weer*
	telkens (weer)

Already

already   *al*
already   *(al)reeds* (lit.)

Before

before, earlier, formerly, previously   *vroeger*
(never) before   *(nooit) eerder*
before that   *voordien* (lit.)
as never before   *als nooit tevoren*

Finally

finally   *tenslotte* [1]
finally, at last, eventually   *eindelijk*
finally, at the end   *op 't laatst*
                                                 ten laatste (following *ten eerste,*
                                                 ten tweede etc.)

Firstly

firstly   *eerst*
for the first time   *voor 't eerst*
firstly (followed by secondly,   *ten eerste*
thirdly etc.)
first (as in 'show me the letter first',   *van tevoren*
i.e. before you send it)   *eerst*
at first   *in het begin*

Immediately

immediately   *onmiddellijk*
                                                 meteen

In a moment

as in 'I'll do it in a moment'   *zo meteen*
                                                 straks
                                                 dadelijk
                                                 zo
                                                 direct

Just

just   *net*
                                                 pas [2]
                                                 zojuist

1 *Tenslotte* also means 'after all'.
2 *Pas* also means 'only' and 'not until'; *juist* does not usually mean 'just', only *zojuist* does.

Soon

soon	*gauw*
soon, quickly	*spoedig*
soon afterwards	*kort daarna*
soon, shortly	*binnenkort, straks*
sooner	*vroeger*
sooner or later	*vroeger of later, vroeg of laat*
as soon as possible	*zo gauw mogelijk*[3]

Note: I'll do it **soon** (see 'in a moment').

Then

then	*dan*
then (past tense)	*toen*
then, at that time	*destijds*
	toentertijd
	indertijd

Note: *Dan* can occur in sentences in both the past and present tenses.

> *Ze waren van plan geweest om elkaar in de stad te ontmoeten. Ze wilden dan...*
> Here the verb is in the past but the action is not. It did not occur.

Compare:

> *Ze hebben elkaar in de stad ontmoet. Toen gingen ze...*

Toen means one occasion. The word *altijd* (repeated occasions) necessitates the use of *dan* in the following sentence, even if the verb is in the past.

> *Ik keek altijd eerst naar het nieuws en dan las ik de krant.*

Compare the use of *wanneer* when the verb is in the past. (see p. 184).

Time

at the same time	*tegelijk*
	tegelijkertijd
	tezelfdertijd
at the same time, as well as	*tevens*
some time ago	*een tijd(je) geleden*
a little while	*een tijdje, poosje*
	eventjes
all the time	*de hele tijd*
for a long time	*(al) lang*
(exactly) on time	*(stipt) op tijd*
	bijtijds

3　All expressions of this type, i.e. 'as (adj./adv.) as possible' take the form *zo* (adj./adv.) *mogelijk*, where the second 'as' is not translated.

at all times/any time	*te allen tijde*
once, one time	*een keer, eenmaal*
twice	*tweemaal*
a few times	*een paar keer*
	enige malen (formal)
last time	*de vorige keer*
next time	*de volgende keer*
this time	*deze/dit keer*
two times (twice) a day	*twee keer per dag/op een dag*

Note: the double gender of *keer* in the above expressions (see p. 32); *keer* is always used in the singular after numerals.

in the course of time	*in de loop der tijd*
	op den duur
	na verloop van tijd
	mettertijd

10.4 Adverbs of place and direction

It will be noticed that in many of the groups set out below there is a form with and without the preposition *naar*. In English there is usually one word to express both place and motion toward a place; in the latter case Dutch must express the motion with *naar* after verbs of motion.

Wanneer komt hij hiernaartoe?	When is he coming here?
Zij ging naar buiten.	She went outside.
Zij gingen naar boven.	The went upstairs.
hier	here
daar	there
er	there (*er* is an unemphatic form of *daar*. see p. 223)
hiervandaan, van hier	from here
daar-, ervandaan, van daar	from there
hiernaartoe	(to)here
daar-, ernaartoe	(to) there
hiernaast	next door
hierop	on this/these
hierin	in this/these
hierachter	behind this/these etc.

Similarly

daarop	on that/those
daarin	in that/those

daarachter	behind that/those etc.
erop	on it/them
erin	in it/them
erachter	behind it/them (see p. 222)
hier en daar, her en der	here and there
links	on the left
rechts	on the right
linksaf	(turn) left
rechtsaf	(turn) right
naar links	to the left
naar rechts	to the right
die/deze kant op/uit	that way, this way
in het midden	in the middle
rechtdoor	straight ahead
verderop	further on
naar voren (toe)	forward, ahead
naar achteren (toe)	back(wards)
voorin	in the front
voorop	up (on) the front
vooraan	at the head
achterin	in the back
achterop	on the back
achteraan	at the end
(see p. 207)	
boven	upstairs
beneden	downstairs
naar boven, de trap op	(to) upstairs
naar beneden, de trap af	(to) downstairs
bovenop, bovenaan	at the top (of)
onderaan	at the bottom (of)
binnen, binnenshuis	inside
buiten, buitenshuis	outside
naar binnen	(to) inside
naar buiten	(to) outside
naar huis	home
thuis	at home

Exception

thuiskomen	to come home

weg	away
ver weg	far away
onderweg	underway
bergop(waarts)	uphill
bergaf(waarts)	downhill
stroomop(waarts)	upstream
stroomaf(waarts)	downstream
alhier (lit.)	here, at this place
aldaar (lit.)	there, at the place mentioned
te Uwent (lit.)	at your place

10.4.1 INDEFINITE ADVERBS OF PLACE AND DIRECTION

overal	everywhere
ergens	somewhere (also an adverb of manner meaning 'somehow' – see p. 69)
nergens	nowhere (see p. 69)
ergens anders, elders	somewhere else
nergens anders	nowhere else
overal vandaan	from everywhere (see p. 69)
overal naartoe/heen	(to) everywhere
ergens vandaan	from somewhere
ergens naartoe/heen	(to) somewhere
nergens vandaan	from nowhere
nergens naartoe/heen	(to) nowhere

10.4.2 ADVERBS OF MANNER AND DEGREE

Adverbs of manner and degree are too numerous and diverse to list. The student is advised to consult a dictionary in such cases.

10.5 Interrogative adverbs *(vragende bijwoorden)*

Interrogative adverbs are those particles that introduce questions asking when, where, how and why etc. (see also Interrogative pronouns, p. 69). For interrogative adverbs in indirect questions see p. 190.

waarom	why
wanneer	when
sinds wanneer	since when
hoe	how
hoelang	how long

waar	where
waar...naartoe/heen	where...to
waar...vandaan	where...from

10.5.1 *Hoe* sometimes renders English 'what' , eg. What is your name? – *Hoe is je naam? Hoe heet je?* Also the question 'what is the date?' is *de hoeveelste is het vandaag? Hoe* is often followed by other adverbs in English.

hoe vaak – how often; *hoe veel* – how much/many

Note the interrogative clause *Hoe komt het dat je...?* 'How is it you...?'

10.5.2 Whenever *waar* occurs in a question with a verb of motion designating direction to or from a place, Dutch must use the compounds *waar...naartoe/heen* or *waar...vandaan.*

Waar woont u? **but** *Waar gaat u naartoe?*
Waar komt hij vandaan?

10.6 Adverbial conjunctions *(bijwoordelijke voegwoorden)*

See p. 187, 190

10.7 Formation of adverbs

-*s*   The addition of a final -*s* in various combinations is one of the main characteristics of adverbial formation:

heelhuids	unscathed, without a scratch
onverwachts	unexpectedly
(te)vergeefs	in vain

The *op z'n* noun +*s* constructions are still productive.

op z'n Hollands	as the Dutch do, à la hollandaise
op z'n Huismans	as Huisman does
op z'n janboerefluitjes	higgledy-piggledy

-*jes*   There is also a group of adverbial diminutives that are very commonly used in the spoken language. Some are permissible in the written language too (marked[+]). This ending is still productive. (see p. 46)

eventjes [+]	just a moment
frisjes [+]	coolish [4]
gezelligjes	cosy [4], cosily
kalmpjes (aan) [+]	calmly

---

4   It will be noticed that these words are occasionally used as predicative adjectives, eg. *Jij ziet er netjes uit.* – You look nice (i.e. nicely dressed).

knusjes [+]	cosy [4], snugly
losjes [+]	loosely
netjes [+]	nice [4], nicely, properly
slapjes [+]	weak [4], gutless
stiekempjes	secretly
stilletjes [+]	quietly
strakjes	in a moment, soon
zachtjes	quietly, gently

-gewijs   (rather) literary; basic meaning something like 'according to', 'by'

groepsgewijs	in groups
steekproefgewijs	by taking random samples
verhoudingsgewijs	relatively, proportionately

-halve   (basic meaning 'for the sake of')

gemakshalve	for convenience ('s sake)
volledigheidshalve	for the sake of completeness
veiligheidshalve	for safety's sake

-lijks   No longer productive. Actually an adverbial *-s* suffixed to the adjectival ending *-lijk*. Found only in the words *dagelijks* (daily), *maandelijks* (monthly), *jaarlijks* (yearly). All these words are also used as adjectives: eg. *ons dagelijks brood* – our daily bread.

-lings   No longer productive.

blindelings	blindly
beurtelings	in turns
ijlings	in haste
schrijlings	astride

-waarts   Comparable to English -'ward(s)' and still productive.

bergopwaarts	uphill
bergafwaarts	downhill
stroomopwaarts	upstream
stroomafwaarts	downstream
huiswaarts	home, homewards
stadwaarts	towards the city

-weg   This is quite a common ending for making adverbs of certain adjectives and is still productive to a degree, particularly in the spoken language

brutaalweg	coolly, barefacedly
domweg	(quite) simply
gewoonweg	(quite) simply
kortweg	in short
pakweg	about, approximately, say

11   Verbs *(werkwoorden)*

Dutch verbs can be weak, strong, mixed or irregular; modal auxiliary verbs and *zijn* and *hebben* belong to separate categories.

Weak verbs are simply regular verbs, the term 'weak' having been invented by Jacob Grimm and being peculiar to Germanic languages. Weak verbs are those that form their past tenses by the addition of a dental suffix, as is the case in English: compare worked – *werkte, gewerkt.*

Stong verbs. Colloquially strong verbs are often referred to as irregular verbs, but strictly speaking there is a difference between strong and irregular verbs. Strong verbs are those belonging to the seven original ablaut series common to all Germanic languages, i.e. they follow one of seven basic patterns (see p. 111). Irregular verbs, on the other hand, are those that show irregularities that are at odds with the seven ablaut series (see p. 128). Elsewhere the term 'mixed verb' is used to describe those verbs which have a strong past participle and a weak imperfect (see p. 127). Strong verbs form their present tense exactly as weak verbs. Only in the past tenses does it become obvious whether a verb is strong. All strong verbs have in common (a) a change in the vowel of the stem in the imperfect and/or the past participle and (c) all past participles end in *-en*.

Tense. The various tenses or 'times of action' of both weak and strong verbs will be looked at one by one in the following chapter. The complicated issue of tense is twofold: firstly it entails the **formation** of the various tenses and secondly the **use** of those tenses. The two are dealt with separately here.

11.1   Formation of tenses

11.1.1   PRESENT TENSE *(de onvoltooid tegenwoordige tijd – o.t.t.)*

With the exception of *komen, zijn, hebben* and the modals, all verbs are regular in the present tense and the irregularities of strong verbs will only emerge in the past tenses.

Example: *werken* – to work

Singular:	Plural:
1 *ik werk*	1 *wij werken*
2 *jij werkt*	2 *jullie werken, werkt* (lit.)
u werkt	*u werkt*
3 *hij, zij, het werkt*	3 *zij werken*

Note: Nowadays the form in *-en* is usual. In Belgium *gij* (you), both a singular and a plural, is in general use and it takes the plural *-t* einding. This form is also found in Holland in older texts and particularly in the Bible. (see p. 51)

The **interrogative** is formed simply by inverting the subject and the object, eg. *ik werk* – I work, I am working, I do work: *werk ik?* – am I working?, do I work? The *jij* form drops its *-t* when inversion occurs, eg. *jij werkt* **but** *werk jij?*

Note that the present progressive or continious tense (i.e. I am running etc.) is not rendered in Dutch. (for exceptions see p. 157)

Rules for the formation of the present tense of all verbs (i.e. weak and strong)

The plural is always identical to the infinitive; the singular is formed by isolating the stem of the verb and then adding *-t* to the second and third persons; the first person singular and the stem are always identical. The rules that apply for the spelling of the stem are the same as for the plural of nouns and the inflection of adjectives, but are in reverse, i.e. the *-en* ending of the infinitive is dropped and the phonetics of Dutch cause certain consonants to be written singularly instead of double, certain vowels to be written double instead of singularly, and v and z to be written f and s.
Examples:

liggen – to lie		*lopen* – to walk	
ik lig	*wij liggen*	*ik loop*	*wij lopen*
jij ligt	*jullie liggen*	*jij loopt*	*jullie lopen*
hij ligt	*zij liggen*	*hij loopt*	*zij lopen*

geloven – to believe		*reizen* – to travel	
ik geloof	*wij geloven*	*ik reis*	*wij reizen*
jij gelooft	*jullie geloven*	*jij reist*	*jullie reizen*
hij gelooft	*zij geloven*	*hij reist*	*zij reizen*

Sometimes, as with nouns and adjectives, a combination of these rules is applicable – see *geloven* above. If the stem already ends in *-t*, no further *t* is required, but if the stem ends in *-d* (pronounced *t*) then a *t* is added for the sake of form.

Examples:

bijten – to bite		*rijden* – to drive, ride	
ik bijt	*wij bijten*	*ik rijd*	*wij rijden*
jij bijt	*jullie bijten*	*jij rijdt*	*jullie rijden*
hij bijt	*zij bijten*	*hij rijdt*	*zij rijden*

The interrogative of *jij bijt* is *bijt jij?*, whereas that of *jij rijdt* is *rij(d) jij?*

Note: all verbs whose stem ends in *-d* and which have an *ij* or *ou* in the stem always drop the *d* in the first person singular and the interrogative of the second person singular; it may be written but is never pronounced, *ik rij(d), ik hou(d); rij(d) je, hou(d) je?*

There are five monosyllabic verbs that should be noted:

staan – to stand	*gaan* – to go	*slaan* – to hit
ik sta	*ik ga*	*ik sla*
jij staat	*jij gaat*	*jij slaat*
(sta je?)	*(ga je?)*	*(sla je?)*
hij slaat	*hij gaat*	*hij slaat*
pl. *staan*	pl. *gaan*	pl. *slaan*

zien – to see	*doen* – to do
ik zie	*ik doe*
jij ziet	*jij doet*
(zie je?)	*(doe je?)*
hij ziet	*hij doet*
pl. *zien*	pl. *doen*

The verb *komen* (to come) shows a slight irregularity in the present tense:

ik kom (not *koom*)	*wij komen*
jij komt	*jullie komen*
hij komt	*zij komen*

11.1.2   IMPERFECT TENSE *(de onvoltooid verleden tijd – o.v.t.)*

The imperfect or simple past in English is I worked (a weak verb), I sang (a strong verb). The progressive and emphatic forms I was working, I did work are not translatable into Dutch (for exceptions see p. 155).

Weak verbs

The imperfect is formed, as in English, by the addition of a dental ending to the stem of the verb. The rules for the isolation of the stem are given above. The only difficulty with the formation of the imperfect of weak verbs in Dutch is deciding whether to add *-te/-ten* or *-de/-den* to the stem. The two possible conjugations are as follows:

werken – to work

ik werkte	*wij werkten*
jij werkte	*jullie werkten*
u werkte	*u werkte*
hij, zij, het werkte	*zij werkten*

horen – to hear

ik hoorde	*wij hoorden*
jij hoorde	*jullie hoorden*
u hoorde	*u hoorde*
hij, zij, het hoorde	*zij hoorden*

gij forms end in *-tet* and *-det*

Those stems that end in the voiceless consonants *p, t, k, f, s, ch* add the voiceless ending *-te/-ten*. The word **'t kofschip** can serve as a mnemonic. Stems ending in any other sound, including those ending in a vowel, take *-de/-den*, eg. *bestellen* (to order) – *bestelde*, *bouwen* (to build) – *bouwde, gooien* (to throw) – *gooide* etc.

The endings *-te/-ten* and *-de/-den* are added to the stems of **all** weak verbs regardless of whether they already end in *t* or *d*, eg.:

praten (to talk) – *praatte, praatten*
branden (to burn) – *brandde, brandden*

Because of the tendency in ABN to drop final *n*'s in speech the following verbal forms are all pronounced identically: *praten, ik praatte, wij praatten.*

Sometimes the difference between present and past tense is not evident, eg. *zetten* (to put):
present tense: *ik zet, wij zetten*
past tense: *ik zette, wij zetten* (i.e. *-ten* added to the stem *zet-*)

Verbs with *v* of *z* in the infinitive:
The rule given above that states that the decision between *-te* and *-de* is based on the final sound of the stem is in fact a slight oversimplification, but it retains its validity if one remembers this one exception: verbs such as *reizen, verhuizen, geloven, leven* which contain a voiced consonant in the infinitive which becomes *s* and *f* in the stem i.e. *reis, verhuis, geloof, leef* add *-de/-den* to this stem, i.e. *reisde, verhuisde, geloofde, leefde.* The *s* and *f* in such cases are, however, pronounced voiced.

One should be careful of verbs ending in *-eren*. Those with the stress on the first *e* of this ending are of French origin and add *-de/-den* after doubling the *e* of the ending. eg. *reserveren* (to reserve) – *reserveerde(n)*. Those of Dutch origin with the stress on the stem vowel do not double the *e*, eg. *luisteren* (to listen) – *luisterde, herinneren* (to remind) – *herinnerde.*

Strong verbs

There is but one form for the singular and one for the plural, eg. *binden* (to tie):

ik bond	*wij bonden*
jij bond	*jullie bonden*
hij bond	*zij bonden*

One should learn both the singular **and** the plural (as well as the past participle) by heart because in some ablaut series the two differ. The following examples will illustrate this:

		Sing.	**Plur.**
1.	*schrijven* (to write)	*schreef*	*schreven*
2.	*schieten* (to shoot)	*schoot*	*schoten*
	buigen (to bend)	*boog*	*bogen*
	wegen (to weigh)	*woog*	*wogen*
3.	*drinken* (to drink)	*dronk*	*dronken*
4.	*nemen* (to take)	*nam*	*namen*
5.	*eten* (to eat)	*at*	*aten*
	zitten (to sit)	*zat*	*zaten*
6.	*dragen* (to wear)	*droeg*	*droegen*
7.	*hangen* (to hang)	*hing*	*hingen*
	slapen (to sleep)	*sliep*	*sliepen*

11.1.3 PERFECT TENSE *(de voltooid tegenwoordige tijd – v.t.t.)*

The perfect tense is a compound tense, i.e. it is formed from an auxiliary verb (either *hebben* of *zijn*, see p. 132) plus a derivative of the verb known as the past participle. In English the imperfect and the past participle of weak verbs are identical (eg. I worked, I have worked); in Dutch they are different and must not be confused.

As for the present and imperfect tenses, Dutch does not have an equivalent of the progressive or continuous form, i.e. I have been working (for exceptions see p. 155).

Weak verbs

1 Formation of the past participle: as for the imperfect of weak verbs the stem of the verb must be isolated; to this *ge-* is prefixed and *-t* or *-d* is suffixed: the rules for the choice of the latter are the same as for *-te* or *-de* in the imperfect (see p. 109), eg. *werken – gewerkt, horen – gehoord, reizen – gereisd, leven – geleefd*.

With the past participle, unlike the imperfect, if the stem already ends in *-t* or *-d*, no further *-t* or *-d* is added, eg. *zetten – gezet, branden – gebrand*. (It is in fact impossible in Dutch to have two of the same consonant at the end of a word.)

One should be careful with verbs ending in *-eren*. These are of two types:

a those where the suffix is of French origin with the stress on *-éren* and which thus double the *e* in the past participle to preserve the long vowels, eg. *reserveren – gereserveerd, waarderen – gewaardeerd*.

b those native Dutch words with the stress on the stem vowel which do not double the *e*, eg. *luisteren – geluisterd, herinneren – herinnerd*.

2   The past participle is invariable for all persons; only the auxiliary verb is conjugated, eg.

ik heb gewerkt   *wij hebben gewerkt*
jij hebt gewerkt   *jullie hebben gewerkt*
hij heeft gewerkt   *zij hebben gewerkt*

For the use of *zijn* as an auxiliary verb in the perfect tense see p. 132.

3   Those verbs beginning with any of the following unstressed prefixes do not add *ge-* (which would be yet another unstressed prefix):
be-, er-, ge-, her-, ont-, ver-.
Examples: *beloven* (to promise) – *beloofd*, *erkennen* (to recognise) – *erkend*, *geloven* (to believe) – *geloofd*, *herhalen* (to repeat) – *herhaald*, *ontmoeten* (to meet) – *ontmoet*, *vertalen* (to translate) – *vertaald*.

4   Past participles of weak verbs can be used as adjectives, as in English, and are inflected as normal adjectives, eg. *het vertaalde boek* – the translated book, *de gehate man* – the hated man (note spelling change).

Strong verbs

1   The past participle of strong verbs is formed by the prefixing of *ge-* to a root that may or may not have the same vowel as the stem or the imperfect (depending on the ablaut series), and the suffixing of *-en*. The past participles of those verbs given above, for example, are as follows:

1.	*schrijven*	*geschreven*
2.	*schieten*	*geschoten*
	buigen	*gebogen*
	wegen	*gewogen*
3.	*drinken*	*gedronken*
4.	*nemen*	*genomen*
5.	*eten*	*gegeten*
	zitten	*gezeten*
6.	*dragen*	*gedragen*
7.	*hangen*	*gehangen*
	slapen	*geslapen*

2   As for weak verbs the past participle of strong verbs in conjunction with an auxiliary verb (either *hebben* or *zijn*) is invariable.

3   As with weak verbs there are also strong verbs with the unstressed prefixes *be-, er-, ge-, her-, ont-* and *ver-*. Such verbs simply add no *ge-* but behave otherwise as strong verbs in the perfect, eg.:

verdrinken (to drown)   *verdronken*
bewegen (to move)   *bewogen*
ontvangen (to receive)   *ontvangen*

4 Past participles of strong verbs, like those of weak verbs, can be used as adjectives but there is one difference: as these all end by definition in -en, they are treated as adjectives like *open, eigen* and do not take an -e ending when used attributively, eg.:

> *de gesloten deur*   the closed door
> *de geschreven brief*   the written letter

When used substantively, however, they take both -e and -en, eg.:

> *de betrokkene(n)*   the one(s) concerned
> *de verbannene(n)*   the exiled one(s)

11.1.4 PLUPERFECT TENSE *(de voltooid verleden tijd – v.v.t)*

The pluperfect, a compound tense like the perfect, is formed from the imperfect of an auxiliary verb (either *hebben* of *zijn*, see p. 132) plus the past participle which remains invariable. The pluperfect can be described as a 'past in the past', eg.:

> He knew that I had worked – *Hij wist dat ik gewerkt had*
> We had drunk enough – *Wij hadden genoeg gedronken.*
> He had gone home – *Hij was naar huis gegaan.*

11.1.5 FUTURE TENSE *(de onvoltooid tegenwoordig toekomende tijd – o.t.t.t)*

1 The auxiliary used for the future tense which corresponds to English 'will' is the verb *zullen*: it is not the verb *willen* although there are occasions when an English non-temporal 'will' is translated by *willen* (see p. 144). *Zullen* is conjugated like a modal verb (singular – *zal*, plural – *zullen*) and can have modal as well as temporal qualities (see p. 117, 144). The future tense of all verbs is formed by the use of *zullen* plus the infinitive of the verb concerned; this infinitive is sent to the end of the clause, eg.:

> *Ik zal het brengen.*   I will bring it.
> *Wij zullen hem zien.*   We will see him.

2 The future can also be rendered by the verb *gaan* instead of *zullen*, as is the case in English, eg. I am going to buy a house tomorrow (I will...) *Ik ga morgen een huis kopen.* Is it going to rain? (i.e. will it rain?) *Gaat het regenen?* Never use *gaan* with *komen*, modal verbs or in contexts where it does not refer to an imminent action.

3 A third possible way of rendering the future, which also has a parallel in English, is by using the simple present tense, eg. He is buying a new car soon. (i.e. he will...) *Hij koopt binnenkort een nieuwe auto.* He is flying to Amsterdam tomorrow. (i.e. he will...) *Hij vliegt morgen naar Amsterdam.* This form of the future is possibly somewhat more common in Dutch than in English. These are occasions where we can use 'will' where the Dutchman would give preference to the present tense.

11.1.6 FUTURE PERFECT TENSE *(de voltooid tegenwoordig toekomende tijd – v.t.t.t.)*

The future perfect tense in Dutch corresponds exactly to that in English, eg. he will have done it – *hij zal het gedaan hebben* (or *hebben gedaan*), she will have gone home – *zij zal naar huis gegaan zijn* (or *zijn gegaan*), they will have shown it to me – *zij zullen het mij hebben laten zien.*

Note that the auxiliary 'have' is rendered by either *hebben* or *zijn* depending on which auxiliary the main verb normally takes in the perfect and pluperfect tenses, i.e. *hij heeft het gedaan, zij is naar huis gegaan.*

11.1.7 CONDITIONAL TENSE *(de onvoltooid verleden toekomende tijd – o.v.t.t.)*

1 The conditional can be described as the past in the future. It is the tense that employs 'would + infinitive' in English. Just as English uses the past tense of its future auxiliary 'will' to form the conditional, so Dutch employs the past tense of *zullen*, i.e. singular – *zou*, plural – *zouden.* (The *gij* form is *zoudt* but is often used with *u*, particularly in inverted constructions to facilitate pronounciation, eg. *zoudt u dat willen?*)

> (If...), she would believe him.
> *(Als...), zou zij hem geloven.*
> They would buy it, (if...)
> *Zij zouden het kopen (als...)*

2 *Zou(den)* is also used in Dutch to express 'was/were going to', eg. I was going to go to Germany last year but... – *Ik zou vorig jaar naar Duitsland gaan maar...*

3 There is one English 'would' which is not conditional in meaning and should not be translated with *zou(den)*, i.e. the one that means 'used to', eg. When I lived in Amsterdam I would often visit my aunt in Rotterdam – *Toen ik in Amsterdam woonde, heb ik* (or *bezocht ik) vaak mijn tante in Rotterdam bezocht.*

4 A 'should' which means 'would' is rendered by *zou(den)* but otherwise by a form of *moeten* (see p. 142), eg. I should do it if I were you – *Ik zou het doen als ik jou was.*

11.1.8 CONDITIONAL PERFECT TENSE *(de voltooid verleden toekomende tijd – v.v.t.t.)*

The conditional perfect is the past of the future perfect,

> He would have seen it.
> *Hij zou het gezien hebben* (or *hebben gezien).*
> She would have gone.
> *Zij zou gegaan zijn* (or *zijn gegaan).*
> They would have shown it to me.
> *Zij zouden het mij hebben laten zien.*

Contracted conditional perfects:

Because the conditional perfect employs two auxiliaries (*zou/zouden* + *hebben/ zijn*) in addition to one or two infinitives, there is a tendency to contract the auxiliaries into one form, i.e. as in German hätte and wäre. This is actually a remnant of the former imperfect subjunctive although the forms are identical to the imperfect of *hebben* and *zijn* nowadays,

> *hij* **zou** *het gezien* **hebben** – *hij* **had** *het gezien (als...)*
> *hij* **zou** *gegaan* **zijn** – *hij* **was** *gegaan (als...)*
> *hij* **zou** *het mij* **hebben** *laten zien – hij* **had** *het mij laten zien (als...)*

Confusion with the imperfect is usually avoided by context, i.e. there is always an 'if' clause preceding, following or implied.
Although it is not compulsory to contract, in cases like the third example where there are four verbs, it is preferable to reduce the number to three by such contraction. (For further verbal contractions see modal verbs.)

11.2   Use of tenses

11.2.1   PRESENT TENSE

The present tense is used as in English with the following exceptions:

1   Dutch has its own idiomatic way of expressing the present continuous (i.e. he is reading a book, see p. 155) and the emphatic present (i.e. he does like fish, see p. 156).

2   The present tense is used even more extensively in Dutch than in English to express the future; it is in fact the most usual way of expressing the future. (see p. 112)

3   An English perfect followed by 'for' plus an expression of time is rendered by the present tense in Dutch as the action of the verb is seen not to have been completed but still continuing into the present.

> I have been living here for ten years.
> *Ik woon hier al tien jaar.*

A similar construction is required in sentences introduced by 'how long',

> How long has he been learning Dutch?
> *Hoe lang leert hij al Nederlands?*
> (see p. 93)

11.2.2   IMPERFECT TENSE

1   Some confusion about when to use the imperfect arises because of the common practice in Dutch of using the perfect where English uses the imperfect (see Perfect tense). The real difficulty associated with the use of the imperfect in Dutch is in recognising the few occasions when it cannot be replaced by the perfect. It is also particularly difficult to give

rules for when it must be used. Generally speaking it tends to be used for narrating a series of events in the past. When mentioning isolated actions or listing a sequence of separate actions in the past, the perfect tense is normally preferred, however.

The verbs *zijn* and *hebben* are more commonly used in the imperfect than the perfect,

> *Wat had je in je hand?*
> What did you have in your hand?
> *Hoe was het weer die avond?*
> What was the weather like that night?

The perfect would, however, not be wrong in such cases.

In the following examples *hebben* and *zijn* indicate a permanent state rather than a momentary action like *zingen* and *doodgaan* and thus they must be in the imperfect:

> *Zij heeft langer gezongen dan ik en zij had een mooiere stem.*
> She sang longer than I and she had a nicer voice.
> *Onze hond is net doodgegaan. maar ja, hij was dan ook erg oud.*
> Our dog (has) just died but then he was very old.

A sentence such as 'Have you ever been to England?' containing the verb 'to be' which can be and usually is rendered literally by a perfect in Dutch, can also use an imperfect: *Ben je ooit in Engeland geweest?/Was je ooit in Engeland?*
The former sounds better, however.

The imperfect is always used after the conjunction *toen* (when).

> *Hij lag nog in bed toen ik bij hem kwam.*

Liggen must also be in the imperfect here as it describes a state, not an action, which was current when the action, i.e. arriving, occurred.

2   Dutch has its own idiomatic ways of expressing the imperfect continuous and emphatic, i.e. he was reading a book, he did like fish (see p. 155-156).

3   There is one imperfect in Dutch which replaces an English pluperfect.

> *Hij lag er al uren toen ik bij hem kwam.*
> He had been lying there for hours when I got to his place.

Here, as with the present tense (see Present tense point 3), the action of the first clause is seen as still continuing when the action of the second occurs and thus an imperfect must be used for the first action; a pluperfect (in Dutch) would imply that he was no longer lying there when I arrived, but that he had been lying there.

4   Two variant forms of the imperfect in English which often cause confusion are those indicating habit or custom which employ the auxiliaries 'used to' and 'would'.

> We used to live in Amsterdam.
> When we lived in Amsterdam we would often go to the National Museum.

In the first example the Dutch use either the imperfect or the perfect and express the habitual aspect with *vroeger* (earlier, formerly).

Wij woonden vroeger in A'dam; wij hebben vroeger in A'dam gewoond.

In the second example the conjunction *toen* determines the use of the imperfect in the first clause, and the 'would', which is equivalent in meaning to 'used to', is rendered as in the first example with an adverb, *dikwijls*.

Toen wij in A'dam woonden, gingen we dikwijls naar het Rijksmuseum.

Such sentences expressing habituality often employ the verb *plegen* (to be accustomed to) in very formal style,

Het karretje waarmee hij altijd naar de stad placht te rijden,...
The cart in which he would always (always used to) ride to town,...

5   One should also beware of what seem to be imperfects in Dutch but which are in fact contracted conditionals (see p. 117, 140). Imperfects in such 'if' clauses cannot be replaced by perfects.

11.2.3   PERFECT TENSE

1   It is in the use of the perfect that Dutch tenses differ most from those of English. The basic rule for the use of the perfect is as follows:

All perfects in English are rendered by perfects in Dutch (with one exception, see Present tense point 3), but most imperfects in English may be rendered by imperfects or perfects in Dutch, the perfect tense being more common, particularly in speech (for the few instances where English imperfects must be imperfects in Dutch, see Imperfect tense above).

For example, the sentence 'He bought a car yesterday.' can only use an imperfect in English as the time of the action is mentioned; 'He has bought a car', without any mention of the time, is possible however. In Dutch the latter would also always use a perfect but the former could employ either an imperfect or a perfect.

Hij heeft gisteren een auto gekocht; hij kocht gisteren een auto
but only
Hij heeft een auto gekocht.

11.2.4   PLUPERFECT TENSE

1   The pluperfect tense is used as in English (with one exception – see Imperfect tense point 3).

2   Dutch has its own idiomatic ways of expressing the pluperfect continuous, i.e. he had been reading a book for hours (see p. 155).

11.2.5 FUTURE TENSE

The use of the future tense is very similar in Dutch and English, including the tendency to use the verb 'to go' – *gaan* and the present tense for actions in the future (see p. 112). The main notable difference is that Dutch uses the present tense more than English to express the future (see p. 112, 114).
It should be noted that English 'will' often does not denote a future and in such instances Dutch uses *willen*, not *zullen* (see p. 144).

11.2.6 FUTURE PERFECT TENSE

There is no difference between English and Dutch in the use of this tense except the tendency for Dutch to use *zullen* in a modal sense with no connotation of the future.

> *Dat zal in andere landen ook wel gedaan zijn.*
> That's sure to have been done in other countries too.
> *Hij zal het zeker gedaan hebben.*
> He did it for sure.

It is possible to use a perfect where semantically a future perfect is implied: *Tegen die tijd heb ik het wel gedaan* – I will have done it by then.

11.2.7 CONDITIONAL TENSE

1   The conditional is used as in English except that the verb in the 'if' clause of a conditional sentence, which in English is often in the imperfect, can be either a conditional or an imperfect in Dutch.

> *Als je meer geld zou hebben (had), . . .*
> If you had more money, . . .
> *Als hij minder zou drinken (dronk), . . .*
> If he drank less, . . .

By using the conditional in such instances the Dutch are trying to compensate for an historical simplification that has affected both English and Dutch, i.e. the falling together of the imperfect subjunctive with the imperfect.
Compare: If I were rich... – *Als ik rijk was (zou zijn)...*
(see p. 114)

2   *Zou(den)* is often used to render English 'was/were going to' or 'intended to'.

> *Vader zou mij voor Sinterklaas een brommer geven maar ik kreeg een fiets.*
> Father was going to give me a moped for St. Nicholas but I got a bike.

11.2.8 CONDITIONAL PERFECT TENSE

There are no differences between English and Dutch in the use of this tense but beware of contractions (see p. 114).

11.3 Alphabetical list of strong and irregular verbs

Roman numerals refer to the class to which the verb belongs (see p. 121). The abbreviation m.v. stands for mixed verbs, i.v. for irregular verbs and mo. for modal verbs.

bakken	m.v.	*duiken*	II
barsten	m.v.	*dunken*	i.v.
bedelven	III, m.v.	*durven*	mo.
bederven	III	*dwingen*	III
bedriegen	II	*eten*	V
beginnen	III	*fluiten*	II
begrijpen	I	*gaan*	i.v.
belijden	I	*gelden*	III
(op)bergen	III	*genezen*	V
bevelen	IV	*genieten*	II
bewegen	II	*geven*	V
bezwijken	I	*gieten*	II
bidden	V	*glijden*	I
bieden	II	*glimmen*	III
bijten	I	*graven*	VI
binden	III	*grijpen*	I
blazen	VII	*hangen*	VII
blijken	I	*hebben*	i.v.
blijven	I	*heffen*	VII
blinken	III	*helpen*	III
braden	m.v.	*heten*	m.v.
breken	IV	*hijsen*	I
brengen	i.v.	*houden*	VII
brouwen	m.v.	*houwen*	VII
buigen	II	*jagen*	VI, m.v.
delven	III, m.v.	*kiezen*	II
denken	i.v.	*kijken*	I
dingen	III	*kijven*	I
doen	i.v.	*klimmen*	III
dragen	VI	*klinken*	III
drijven	I	*kluiven*	II
dringen	III	*knijpen*	I
drinken	III	*komen*	IV
druipen	II	*kopen*	i.v.

krijgen	I		*slaan*	VI, i.v.
krimpen	III		*slapen*	VII
kruipen	II		*slijpen*	I
kunnen	mo.		*slijten*	I
kwijten	I		*slinken*	III
lachen	m.v.		*sluipen*	II
laden	m.v.		*sluiten*	II
laten	VII		*smelten*	III
lezen	IV		*smijten*	I
liegen	II		*snijden*	I
liggen	V		*snuiten*	II
lijden	I		*snuiven*	II
lijken	I		*spannen*	m.v.
lopen	VII		*spijten*	I
malen	m.v.		*spinnen*	III
melken	III		*splijten*	I
meten	IV		*spreken*	IV
mijden	I		*springen*	III
moeten	mo.		*spruiten*	II
mogen	mo.		*spugen*	II
nemen	IV		*spuiten*	II
nijgen	I		*staan*	I
nijpen	I		*steken*	IV
ontginnen	III		*stelen*	IV
overlijden	I		*sterven*	III
plegen	i.v.		*stijgen*	I
pluizen	II		*stijven*	I
prijzen	I		*stinken*	III
raden	VII, m.v.		*stoten*	VII, m.v.
rijden	I		*strijden*	I
rijgen	I		*strijken*	I
rijten	I		*stuiven*	II
rijzen	I		*treden*	V
roepen	VII		*treffen*	III
ruiken	II		*trekken*	III
scheiden	m.v.		*vallen*	VII
schelden	III		*vangen*	VII
schenden	III		*varen*	VI
schenken	III		*vechten*	III
scheppen	VII		*verbieden*	II
scheren	II		*verdelgen*	III
schieten	II		*verdrieten*	II
schijnen	I		*verdwijnen*	I
schrijden	I		*vergelijken*	I
schrijven	I		*vergeten*	V
schrikken	III		*verliezen*	II
schuiven	II		*vermijden*	I

verraden	VII	*willen*	mo.
verschuilen	II, m.v.	*winden*	III
verslijten	I	*winnen*	III
verslinden	III	*worden*	i.v.
verwijten	I	*wreken*	m.v.
verwijzen	I	*wrijven*	I
verzinnen	III	*wringen*	III
verzwelgen	III	*zeggen*	i.v.
vinden	III	*zenden*	III
vlechten	III	*zien*	IV, i.v.
vlieden	II	*zijn*	i.v.
vliegen	II	*zingen*	III
vragen	VI, m.v.	*zinken*	III
vrouwen	m.v.	*zinnen*	III
vreten	IV	*zitten*	V
vriezen	II	*zoeken*	i.v.
waaien	VI, m.v.	*zouten*	m.v.
wassen	VII, m.v.	*zuigen*	II
wegen	II	*zuipen*	II
werpen	III	*zullen*	mo.
werven	III	*zwelgen*	III
weten	i.v.	*zwellen*	III
weven	m.v.	*zwemmen*	III
wijken	I	*zweren*	II, m.v.
wijten	I	*zwerven*	III
wijzen	I	*zwijgen*	I

11.3.1 STRONG AND IRREGULAR VERBS

The numbers refer to the ablaut series to which these verbs belong historically (see p. 106, 111).
* = verbs conjugated only with *zijn*
+ = verbs conjugated with *hebben* or *zijn*

I All verbs with *ij* in the stem belong in this group except for a few formed from non-verbal parts of speech, eg. *benijden* (to envy), *bevrijden* (to liberate), *kastijden* (to chastise), *verblijden* (to gladden), *verslijken* (to silt up), *wijden* (to consecrate, to devote) etc.; these are weak.

begrijpen	*begreep*	*begrepen*	*begrepen*	to understand
belijden	*beleed*	*beleden*	*beleden*	to confess
bezwijken*	*bezweek*	*bezweken*	*bezweken*	to succumb
bijten	*beet*	*beten*	*gebeten*	to bite
blijken*	*bleek*	*bleken*	*gebleken*	to appear
blijven*	*bleef*	*bleven*	*gebleven*	to remain, stay
drijven+	*dreef*	*dreven*	*gedreven*	to float, drive
glijden+	*gleed*	*gleden*	*gegleden*	to glide, slide
grijpen	*greep*	*grepen*	*gegrepen*	to seize, grab
hijsen	*hees*	*hesen*	*gehesen*	to hoist, lift
kijken	*keek*	*keken*	*gekeken*	to look
kijven	*keef*	*keven*	*gekeven*	to quarrel
(k)nijpen	*(k)neep*	*(k)nepen*	*ge(k)nepen*	to pinch
krijgen	*kreeg*	*kregen*	*gekregen*	to get, receive
zich kwijten van	*kweet*	*kweten*	*gekweten*	to acquit oneself of
lijden	*leed*	*leden*	*geleden*	to suffer
lijken	*leek*	*leken*	*geleken*	to seem, resemble
nijgen	*neeg*	*negen*	*genegen*	to bow
overlijden*	*overleed*	*overleden*	*overleden*	to pass away
prijzen	*prees*	*prezen*	*geprezen*	to praise
rijden+	*reed*	*reden*	*gereden*	to ride, drive
rijgen	*reeg*	*regen*	*geregen*	to string (beads), tack
rijten	*reet*	*reten*	*gereten*	to tear
rijzen*	*rees*	*rezen*	*gerezen*	to rise
schijnen	*scheen*	*schenen*	*geschenen*	to seem, shine
schrijden+	*schreed*	*schreden*	*geschreden*	to stride
schrijven	*schreef*	*schreven*	*geschreven*	to write
slijpen	*sleep*	*slepen*	*geslepen*	to sharpen
smijten	*smeet*	*smeten*	*gesmeten*	to throw
snijden	*sneed*	*sneden*	*gesneden*	to cut
spijten	*speet*	*speten*	*gespeten*	to be sorry
splijten	*spleet*	*spleten*	*gespleten*	to split
stijgen*	*steeg*	*stegen*	*gestegen*	to rise, climb
stijven	*steef*	*steven*	*gesteven*	to stiffen

strijden	*streed*	*streden*	*gestreden*	to fight
strijken	*streek*	*streken*	*gestreken*	to iron, lower (flag)
*verdwijnen**	*verdween*	*verdwenen*	*verdwenen*	to disappear
vergelijken	*vergeleek*	*vergeleken*	*vergeleken*	to compare
(ver)mijden	*(ver)meed*	*(ver)meden*	*(ver)meden*	to avoid
(ver)slijten+	*(ver)sleet*	*(ver)sleten*	*(ver)sleten*	to wear (out)
(ver)wijten	*(ver)weet*	*(ver)weten*	*(ver)weten*	to reproach
(ver)wijzen	*(ver)wees*	*(ver)wezen*	*(ver)wezen)*	to (refer), show
wijken+	*week*	*weken*	*geweken*	to yield, retreat
wrijven	*wreef*	*wreven*	*gewreven*	to rub
zwijgen	*zweeg*	*zwegen*	*gezwegen*	to be silent

II Not all verbs with *ui* and *ie* are irregular,

> *huilen* (to cry), *huilde, gehuild*
> *spieden* (to spy), *spiedde, gespied*

also

> *bruisen* (to fizz), *gebruiken* (to use), *getuigen* (to testify), *kruisen* (to cross), *verhuizen* (to shift), *wuiven* (to wave), *geschieden* (to happen), *wieden*, (to weed) etc.

buigen	*boog*	*bogen*	*gebogen*	to bend, bow
druipen	*droop*	*dropen*	*gedropen*	to drip
duiken+	*dook*	*doken*	*gedoken*	to dive
fluiten	*floot*	*floten*	*gefloten*	to whistle
kluiven	*kloof*	*kloven*	*gekloven*	to pick a bone
kruipen+	*kroop*	*kropen*	*gekropen*	to crawl, creep
pluizen	*ploos*	*plozen*	*geplozen*	to give off fluff
ruiken	*rook*	*roken*	*geroken*	to smell
schuiven+	*schoof*	*schoven*	*geschoven*	to push, shove
sluipen	*sloop*	*slopen*	*geslopen*	to steal, sneak
sluiten	*sloot*	*sloten*	*gesloten*	to close
snuiten	*snoot*	*snoten*	*gesnoten*	to blow one's nose
snuiven	*snoof*	*snoven*	*gesnoven*	to sniff
*spruiten**	*sproot*	*sproten*	*gespoten*	to sprout
spuiten	*spoot*	*spoten*	*gespoten*	to spout, squirt, spray
stuiven	*stoof*	*stoven*	*gestoven*	to be dusty, rush
verschuilen	*verschool* *verschuilde*	*verscholen* *verschuilden*	*verscholen* *verscholen*	to hide
*zuigen*¹	*zoog*	*zogen*	*gezogen*	to suck
zuipen	*zoop*	*zopen*	*gezopen*	to booze
spugen	*spoog*	*spogen*	*gespogen*	to spit

1 *Stofzuigen* is regular, i.e. *stofzuigde, gestofzuigd.*

bedriegen	*bedroog*	*bedrogen*	*bedrogen*	to deceive
bieden	*bood*	*boden*	*geboden*	to offer
genieten	*genoot*	*genoten*	*genoten*	to enjoy
gieten	*goot*	*goten*	*gegoten*	to pour
kiezen	*koos*	*kozen*	*gekozen*	to choose
liegen	*loog*	*logen*	*gelogen*	to lie, tell lies
schieten	*schoot*	*schoten*	*geschoten*	to shoot
verbieden	*verbood*	*verboden*	*verboden*	to forbid
verdrieten	*verdroot*	*verdroten*	*verdroten*	to vex; sadden
verliezen[2]	*verloor*	*verloren*	*verloren*	to lose
vlieden+ (lit.)	*vlood*	*vloden*	*gevloden*	to flee
vliegen+	*vloog*	*vlogen*	*gevlogen*	to fly
vriezen	*vroor*	*vroren*	*gevroren*	to freeze
wegen	*woog*	*wogen*	*gewogen*	to weigh
bewegen	*bewoog*	*bewogen*	*bewogen*	to move
scheren	*schoor*	*schoren*	*geschoren*	to shear, shave (see p. 128)
zweren[3]	*zweerde*	*zweerden*	*gezworen*	to fester
archaic:	*zwoor*	*zworen*		

III

*beginnen**	*begon*	*begonnen*	*begonnen*	to begin
(op)bergen	*borg (op)*	*borgen (op)*	*(op)geborgen*	to store
binden	*bond*	*bonden*	*gebonden*	to bind
blinken	*blonk*	*blonken*	*geblonken*	to shine
(be)delven	*delfde*	*delfden*	*gedolven*	to (bury), dig
archaic:	*dolf*	*dolven*		
dingen	*dong*	*dongen*	*gedongen*	to haggle
dringen+	*drong*	*drongen*	*gedrongen*	to push, crowd
drinken	*dronk*	*dronken*	*gedronken*	to drink
dwingen	*dwong*	*dwongen*	*gedwongen*	to force
gelden	*gold*	*golden*	*gegolden*	to be valid
glimmen	*glom*	*glommen*	*geglommen*	to glimmer, shine
klimmen+	*klom*	*klommen*	*geklommen*	to climb
klinken	*klonk*	*klonken*	*geklonken*	to sound
krimpen+	*kromp*	*krompen*	*gekrompen*	to shrink
melken	*molk*	*molken*	*gemolken*	to milk
ontginnen	*ontgon*	*ontgonnen*	*ontgonnen*	to open up, reclaim (land)
schelden	*schold*	*scholden*	*gescholden*	to abuse
schenden	*schond*	*schonden*	*geschonden*	to violate
schenken	*schonk*	*schonken*	*geschonken*	to pour, give

2 One will hear both *Ik ben mijn pen verloren* and *Ik heb mijn pen verloren* with no difference in meaning. See also *vergeten*.
3 See group VI for *zweren* – to swear.

schrikken*[4]	schrok	schrokken	geschrokken	to be frightened
slinken*	slonk	slonken	geslonken	to shrink
smelten+	smolt	smolten	gesmolten	to melt
spinnen	spon	sponnen	gesponnen	to spin
springen+	sprong	sprongen	gesprongen	to jump
stinken	stonk	stonken	gestonken	to stink, smell
treffen	trof	troffen	getroffen	to hit
trekken+5	trok	trokken	getrokken	to pull
vechten	vocht	vochten	gevochten	to fight
verslinden	verslond	verslonden	verslonden	to devour
verzwelgen	verzwolg	verzwolgen	verzwolgen	to swallow up
vinden	vond	vonden	gevonden	to find
vlechten	vlocht	vlochten	gevlochten	to plait
winden	wond	wonden	gewonden	to wind
winnen	won	wonnen	gewonnen	to win
wringen	wrong	wrongen	gewrongen	to wring
zenden	zond	zonden	gezonden	to send
zingen	zong	zongen	gezongen	to sing
zinken*	zonk	zonken	gezonken	to sink
(ver)zinnen	zon	zonnen	gezonnen	to ponder, muse
zwelgen	zwolg	zwolgen	gezwolgen	to guzzle
zwellen*	zwol	zwollen	gezwollen	to swell
zwemmen+	zwom	zwommen	gezwommen	to swim
bederven	bedierf	bedierven	bedorven	to spoil
helpen	hielp	hielpen	geholpen	to help
sterven*	stierf	stierven	gestorven	to die
werpen	wierp	wierpen	geworpen	to throw
werven	wierf	wierven	geworven	to recruit
zwerven	zwierf	zwierven	gezworven	to wander, roam

IV

bevelen	beval	bevalen	bevolen	to order, command
breken	brak	braken	gebroken	to break
komen*	kwam	kwamen	gekomen	to come
nemen	nam	namen	genomen	to take
spreken	sprak	spraken	gesproken	to speak
steken	stak	staken	gestoken	to stab
stelen	stal	stalen	gestolen	to steal

V

bidden	bad	baden	gebeden	to pray
eten	at	aten	gegeten	to eat

4 The related verbs *verschrikken* and *opschrikken* are regular.
5 *Trekken* takes *zijn* in various compounds, eg. *vertrekken* (to depart), *wegtrekken* (to go away).

genezen[+]	*genas*	*genazen*	*genezen*	to heal
geven	*gaf*	*gaven*	*gegeven*	to give
lezen	*las*	*lazen*	*gelezen*	to read
liggen	*lag*	*lagen*	*gelegen*	to lie
meten	*mat*	*maten*	*gemeten*	to measure
treden[*]	*trad*	*traden*	*getreden*	to tread, step
vergeten[+6]	*vergat*	*vergaten*	*vergeten*	to forget
vreten	*vrat*	*vraten*	*gevreten*	to gorge, eat (of animals)
zien	*zag*	*zagen*	*gezien*	to see
zitten	*zat*	*zaten*	*gezeten*	to sit

VI

dragen	*droeg*	*droegen*	*gedragen*	to carry
graven	*groef*	*groeven*	*gegraven*	to dig
jagen	*joeg*	*joegen*	*gejaagd*	to chase
	jaagde	*jaagden*	*gejaagd*	to hunt
slaan[7]	*sloeg*	*sloegen*	*geslagen*	to hit
varen[+]	*voer*	*voeren*	*gevaren*	to sail, go (by ship)
vragen	*vroeg*	*vroegen*	*gevraagd*	to ask
waaien	*woei*	*woeien*	*gewaaid*	to blow (wind)
	waaide	*waaiden*	*gewaaid*	
zweren	*zwoer*	*zwoeren*	*gezworen*	to swear (an oath)

VII

blazen	*blies*	*bliezen*	*geblazen*	to blow
hangen	*hing*	*hingen*	*gehangen*	to hang
heffen	*hief*	*hieven*	*geheven*	to lift
houden	*hield*	*hielden*	*gehouden*	to hold
houwen[8]	*hieuw*	*hieuwen*	*gehouwen*	to hew
laten	*liet*	*lieten*	*gelaten*	to let, leave
lopen[+]	*liep*	*liepen*	*gelopen*	to walk
raden[9]	*raadde*	*raadden*	*geraden*	to guess, advise
archaic:	*ried*	*rieden*		

6   The criteria for the use of *zijn* or *hebben* with *vergeten* are different from other verbs marked[+]: when the meaning is 'to have left something behind' *hebben* may be used but when a fact etc. has been forgotten only *zijn* can be employed; in practice *zijn* is more commonly used in both cases. (see p. 136).

  Ik ben (heb) mijn regenjas vergeten.
  Ik ben het woord nu vergeten.

7   *Slaan* should not be confused with the regular verb *slagen* (to succeed; pass an exam). Note the past participle is *geslagen*, not *geslaan*.

8   The compound *beeldhouwen* (to sculpt) is weak: *beeldhouwde, gebeeldhouwd*.

9   Nowadays *raden* is only used in the meaning of to guess. To advise is rendered by *aanraden* which is weak.

roepen	*riep*	*riepen*	*geroepen*	to call
scheppen[10]	*schiep*	*schiepen*	*geschapen*	to create
slapen	*sliep*	*sliepen*	*geslapen*	to sleep
stoten	*stootte*	*stootten*	*gestoten*	to push, shove
archaic:	*stiet*	*stieten*		
vallen*	*viel*	*vielen*	*gevallen*	to fall
vangen	*ving*	*vingen*	*gevangen*	to catch
verraden	*verried*	*verrieden*	*verraden*	to betray
wassen* [11]	*wies*	*wiesen*	*gewassen*	to grow, wax
wassen	*waste*	*wasten*	*gewassen*	to wash
archaic:	*wies*	*wiesen*		

11.3.2 MIXED VERBS

bakken	*bakte*	*bakten*	*gebakken*	to bake
barsten*	*barstte*	*barstten*	*gebarsten*	to burst
braden	*braadde*	*braadden*	*gebraden*	to roast
brouwen	*brouwde*	*brouwden*	*gebrouwen*	to brew
heten	*heette*	*heetten*	*geheten*	to be called
lachen[12]	*lachte*	*lachten*	*gelachen*	to laugh
laden	*laadde*	*laadden*	*geladen*	to load
malen	*maalde*	*maalden*	*gemalen*	to grind
scheiden	*scheidde*	*scheidden*	*gescheiden*	to separate
spannen	*spande*	*spanden*	*gespannen*	to stretch
vouwen	*vouwde*	*vouwden*	*gevouwen*	to fold
weven	*weefde*	*weefden*	*geweven*	to weave
wreken	*wreekte*	*wreekten*	*gewroken*	to avenge, revenge
zouten	*zoutte*	*zoutten*	*gezouten*	to salt

Verbs in this sub-group also have an archaic strong imperfect. See list of strong verbs.

(be)delven	*delfde*	*delfden*	*gedolven*	to (bury), dig
raden	*raadde*	*raadden*	*geraden*	to advise, guess
stoten	*stootte*	*stootten*	*gestoten*	to push, shove
wassen	*waste*	*wasten*	*gewassen*	to wash
zweren	*zweerde*	*zweerden*	*gezworen*	to fester

Jagen and *waaien* also have a weak imperfect; in the case of *jagen* the weak imperfect has a different meaning, i.e. to hunt.

jagen	*joeg*	*joegen*	*gejaagd*	to chase
waaien	*woei*	*woeien*	*gewaaid*	to blow (wind)
vragen	*vroeg*	*vroegen*	*gevraagd*	to ask

10 There is also a regular verb *scheppen* (to scoop, ladle).
11 *Wassen* (to grow) is archaic and is usually replaced by *groeien*, except in standard expressions, eg. *de wassende maan* – the waxing moon.
12 Note that *glimlachen* (to smile) is weak, i.e. *glimlachte, geglimlacht.*

11.3.3 IRREGULAR VERBS

brengen	*bracht*	*brachten*	*gebracht*	to bring
denken	*dacht*	*dachten*	*gedacht*	to think
dunken[13]	*docht*			to think, seem (see p. 168)
kopen	*kocht*	*kochten*	*gekocht*	to buy
plegen[13]	*placht*	*plachten*		to be used to
zoeken	*zocht*	*zochten*	*gezocht*	to look for, seek
doen	*deed*	*deden*	*gedaan*	to do
gaan*	*ging*	*gingen*	*gegaan*	to go
slaan	*sloeg*	*sloegen*	*geslagen*	to hit
staan	*stond*	*stonden*	*gestaan*	to stand
zien	*zag*	*zagen*	*gezien*	to see
hebben	*had*	*hadden*	*gehad*	to have
weten	*wist*	*wisten*	*geweten*	to know
worden*	*werd*	*werden*	*geworden*	to become
zeggen	*zei*	*zeiden*	*gezegd*	to say
zijn*	*was*	*waren*	*geweest*	to be

11.3.4 MODAL VERBS

durven	*durfde*	*durfden*	*gedurfd*	to dare
archaic:	*dorst*	*dorsten*		
kunnen	*kon*	*konden*	*gekund*	to be able
moeten	*moest*	*moesten*	*gemoeten*	to have to
mogen	*mocht*	*mochten*	*gemogen*[14]	to be allowed to
willen	*wilde*	*wilden*	*gewild*	to want to
	wou			
zullen	*zou*	*zouden*		will

11.4 Mixed verbs

1 Mixed is the name given to those verbs which for historical reasons have a weak imperfect and a stong past participle (or occasionally vise versa)

    bakken (to bake) *bakte, bakten, gebakken*

For a complete list of such verbs see p. 126.

---

13 See p. 128.
14 See p. 139.

2 There are five verbs,
delven (to dig), *raden* (to guess, advise), *stoten* (to push), *wassen* (to wash) and *zweren* (to fester), which have a strong imperfect which is now archaic (see p. 126).

dolf	*dolven*
ried	*rieden*
stiet	*stieten*
wies	*wiesen*
zwoor	*zworen*

Also *verschuilen* (to hide) but its strong imperfect is not archaic (see p. 122).

3 *Jagen* (to hunt, chase) and *waaien* (to blow, as of the wind) and *vragen* (to ask) are exceptional mixed verbs and they all have a strong imperfect and a weak past participle. *Jagen* and *waaien* also have a weak imperfect.

jagen	*joeg/joegen, jaagde/jaagden*	*gejaagd*
waaien	*woei/woeien, waaide/waaiden*	*gewaaid*
vragen	*vroeg/vroegen*	*gevraagd*

It should be noted, however, that there is a difference in meaning between the weak and strong imperfects of *jagen*:
joeg/jagen = chased (away); *jaagde/jaagden* = hunted
Scheren (to shave, shear-a sheep) is usually regarded as a strong verb (see p. 123) but as the imperfect of 'to shave' one commonly hears *scheerde*.
Ervaren (to experience, discover) should follow *varen* (see p. 125) but *ervaarde* is frequently heard in the imperfect.

11.5 Irregular verbs

Colloquially the term 'irregular' is used as a synonym for 'strong' with reference to verbs. Strictly speaking, however, irregular verbs are those that show irregularities that do not follow any of the seven basic patterns of strong verbs.

There are three groups of irregular verbs:

1 those that are historically weak verbs that all show a change of vowel in the past tenses, which they have in common with strong verbs, and also a dental ending, which they have in common with weak verbs. There are only six such verbs, two of which are not used in the spoken language, i.e. *dunken* and *plegen* (see p. 127).
All derivatives of these verbs have the same irregularities, eg. *verkopen* (to sell), *verzoeken* (to request).
There is also a verb *plegen* which means 'to commit' but it is a regular verb, i.e. *pleegde, gepleegd*.

2 there are five monosyllabic verbs that belong historically to one of the seven groups of strong verbs (except *doen*), but which show certain peculiarities other strong verbs don't. (see p. 108, 127)

3 there are a few isolated verbs that follow no particular pattern at all. (see p. 127)
Zeggen has a singular form *zeide* which is occasionally found in literature. Compounds of *zeggen* are regular, however.

ontzeggen (to deny)   *ontzegde*
opzeggen (to recite; cancel) *zegde...op*

11.6 *Hebben* – to have

11.6.1 FORMS OF *HEBBEN*

The verb *hebben* shows several irregularities that the other irregular and strong verbs don't.

Present tense: *ik heb*   *wij hebben*
                        jij hebt   *jullie hebben, hebt*
                        u hebt, heeft   *u hebt, heeft*
                        hij heeft   *zij hebben*

The *gij* form is *hebt*.
As with *zijn*, *u* can take a second or third person verb; both are equally common.
Jullie hebben is more common than *jullie hebt*. In 'plat' Dutch the form *hij heb* is often heard.

Imperfect tense: singular: *had*   plural: *hadden*
Perfect tense: *ik heb gehad* etc.   – I have had
Pluperfect tense: *ik had gehad*   – I had had
Future tense: *ik zal hebben*   – I will have
Future perfect tense: *ik zal gehad hebben* – I will have had
Conditional tense: *ik zou hebben*   – I would have
                          (or contracted to *ik had*, see p. 117)
Conditional perfect tense: *ik zou gehad hebben* – I would have had
                          (or contracted to *ik had gehad*, see p. 114)

Imperative: *heb!*
                          The imperative forms *hebt u* and *hebben jullie* exist but are not common, as indeed in the imperative of *hebben* as a whole.
Subjunctive: the third person of the present subjunctive occurs in certain standard expressions, eg. *God hebbe zijn ziel* – (May) God rest his soul.
                          Occasionally in literature the past subjunctive is also met – *hadde*.

11.6.2 USES OF *HEBBEN*

1 For *hebben* as an auxiliary verb in perfect tenses see p. 110, 135

2 The following expressions employ the verb 'to be' in English but *hebben* in Dutch.

dienst hebben	to be on duty	
dorst hebben	to be thirsty	
(on)gelijk hebben	to be (wrong) right	
geluk hebben	to be in luck	
haast hebben	to be in a hurry	(see p. 228)
honger hebben	to be hungry	
pech hebben	to be unlucky	
slaap hebben	to be sleepy	
vakantie hebben	to be on holidays	
vrij hebben	to be off (from work)	

Note: to be very hungry etc.   *– erge honger hebben*
to be not hungry etc.   *– geen honger hebben*

The following *hebben* constructions which employ 'to be' in English contain an idiomatic *het* which is usually written *'t*. They are only used with personal subjects.

Note: *ik heb het druk* **but** *het is erg druk*.

't benauwd hebben	to feel off
't druk hebben	to be busy
't koud hebben	to be cold
't moeilijk hebben	to be in trouble
't warm hebben	to be hot
't hebben over	to be talking about

11.7 *Zijn* – to be

11.7.1 FORMS OF THE VERB *ZIJN*

The verb 'to be', as in all European languages, is extremely irregular.

Present tense:		
	1 *ik ben* – I am	*wij zijn*
	2 *jij bent* – you are etc.	*jullie zijn, bent*
	u bent, is	*u bent*
	3 *hij is*	*zij zijn*

The *gij* form, which is common in Belgium, is *gij zijt*.
U can take a second or third person verb but *bent* is more common.
Jullie zijn is more common than *jullie bent*.

Imperfect tense:		
	1 *ik was* – I was	*wij waren*
	2 *jij was* – you were etc.	*jullie waren*
	u was	*u was*
	3 *hij was*	*zij waren*

The *gij* form is *waart*.

Perfect tense: the past participle is *geweest* and is formed from another infinitive *wezen* (see below). The perfect tense of *zijn* takes *zijn*.
ik ben geweest – I have been
jij bent geweest – you have been etc.

There is an adjective formed from the past participle but it is strong in form:
eg. *de gewezen burgemeester* – the former mayor

Pluperfect tense: 1 *ik was geweest* – I had been
2 *jij was geweest* – you had been etc.

Future tense: 1 *ik zal zijn* – I will be
2 *jij zult zijn* – you will be etc.

Future perfect tense: 1 *ik zal geweest zijn* – I will have been
2 *jij zult geweest zijn* – you will have been etc.

Conditional tense: 1 *Ik zou zijn* (or contracted to *ik was*, see p. 117) –
I would be
2 *jij zou zijn* (or contracted to *jij was*) – you would be etc.

hij zou rijk zijn als hij gewerkt had   he would be rich if
hij was rijk als hij gewerkt had   he had worked

Conditional perfect tense: 1 *ik zou geweest zijn* (or contracted to *ik was geweest*)
– I would have been
2 *jij zou geweest zijn* (or contracted to *jij was geweest*)
– you would have been etc.

Note: One often hears *dat had leuk geweest* but in such cases the conditional perfect of *kunnen* is actually implied, i.e. *dat had leuk kunnen zijn.*

Imperative: in the imperative a derivative of the second infinitive *wezen* is used as for the past participle and the imperfect.
wees! – for all persons
the forms *weest u, wezen jullie* are also commonly found.

Subjunctive: subjunctive forms of 'to be' are still found in some standard expressions:
God zij dank! – Thank God!
Volledigheidshalve zij hier vermeld dat – For the sake of completeness it be said that
als het ware – as it were

Notes on *wezen*

Wezen, which was originally a synonym of *zijn*, is used nowadays (other than in the imperative as described above) in two ways:

to replace *zijn* when the latter stands in the infinitive (rather colloquial).

> *het zou erg leuk kunnen wezen* – it could be really nice
> *weg wezen* – be off with you

to replace *zijn* in double infinitive constructions (i.e. functions in fact as a past participle). (see p. 147)

> *ik ben wezen kijken* – I have been to look
> *hij is wezen vissen* – he has been fishing

11.7.2   USES OF THE VERB *ZIJN*

***Zijn* as an auxiliary verb in compound tenses.**

Many verbs in Dutch, unlike in English, employ the verb 'to be' as the auxiliary in compound tenses:

> I **have** bought a car.   *Ik **heb** een auto gekocht.*
>
> but
> He **has** gone home.   *Hij **is** naar huis gegaan.*
> They **had** fallen over.   *Ze **waren** omgevallen.*

Verbs that denote a **change from one position or state to another** belong to this category.

> *komen* (to come), *vallen* (to fall), *stijgen* (to rise)

denote a motion from one point to another.

> *worden* (to become), *sterven* (to die), *groeien* (to grow)

denote a change from one state to another.
It is not always immediately evident, however, that the verbs concerned imply a change of position or state.

The verbs in this group are all **intransitive** (for exceptions see p. 133, 135-136).

Both weak and strong verbs can be conjugated with *zijn*. This raises another problem: most Dutch-English dictionaries and grammars will indicate in the list of strong verbs (see p. 121) whether those verbs take *zijn* in their compound tenses, but as weak verbs are never listed, those weak verbs that take *zijn* are more difficult to isolate and learn. For this reason the list given below is incomplete.

11.8.1 The following verbs **always take** *zijn* in the perfect, pluperfect, future perfect and conditional perfect tenses:

vallen (to fall)
perfect	: I have fallen	– *ik ben gevallen*
pluperfect	: I had fallen	– *ik was gevallen*
future perfect	: I will have fallen	– *ik zal gevallen zijn*
conditional perfect	: I would have fallen	– *ik zou gevallen zijn/ik was gevallen*

It is impossible to give a complete list but the following will suffice to give an indication of the sort of verb that takes *zijn*:

af-, toenemen	to increase/decrease	*dalen*	to descend
barsten	to burst	*doorschieten*	to go to seed
bedaren	to calm/die down	*emigreren*	to emigrate
beginnen [15]	to start	*gaan* [16]	to go
belanden	to land, end up	*gebeuren*	to happen
bevallen	to like (impers.)	*geschieden*	to happen
bevriezen	to freeze	*groeien*	to grow
blijken	to appear	*immigreren*	to immigrate
blijven	to remain, stay		

15 There are just a few transitive verbs that use *zijn: beginnen* (to begin), *naderen* (to approach), *nagaan* (to follow up), *oversteken* (to cross – a road etc.), *tegenkomen* (to bump into s.o.).

beginnen (see p. 146) often turns the direct object into an indirect object by the use of a preposition.
Hij is een zaak in de stad begonnen.
He's started a business in town.
Zij is al aan (met) haar huiswerk begonnen.
She's already started her homework.
Ik ben er al aan (mee) begonnen.
I've already started it.

The verbs *aankomen* and *afvallen* (to gain and to lose weight) take *zijn* although they seem to be used transitively in expressions such as *ze is twee kilo afgevallen* – 'she has lost 2 kilos'. (see p. 218) For other transitive verbs using *zijn* see p. 135-136).

16 Many derivatives of these and other verbs also take *zijn*, eg. *ondergaan* (to set of the sun), *vergaan* (to pass), *binnenkomen* (to come in), *opvallen* (to strike) but not all derivatives do: sometimes the prefixes make transitive verbs of these otherwise intransitive verbs and then *hebben* is used, eg. *ondergáan* (to undergo), *nagaan* (to check, trace), *voorkómen* (to prevent), *betreden* (to tread on), *bestijgen* (to ascend the throne). *Schoolgaan* (to go to school) also takes *hebben*.
On the other hand there are sometimes derivatives that thake *zijn* when the root verb in its literal sense does not,

opstaan (to get up) – *ik ben opgestaan* but *staan* (to stand) – *ik heb twee uur gestaan*
afbranden (to burn down) – *het huis is afgebrand* but *branden* (to burn, intransitive) – *het huis heeft urenlang gebrand*
dichtvriezen (to freeze up) – *de rivier is dichtgevroren* but *vriezen* (to freeze) – *het heeft gevroren.*

komen[16]	to come	*stijgen*[16]	to rise
krimpen	to shrink	*stoppen*	to stop
landen	to land (plane)	*tegenvallen*	to be disappointing
meevallen	to exceed expectations	*treden*[16]	to tread
(mis)lukken	to succeed (fail)	*uitslapen*[17]	to sleep in
ontsnappen	to escape	*vallen*	to fall
ontstaan	to originate	*verbleken*[18]	to turn pale
opgroeien	to grow up	*verdorren*[18]	to wither
ophouden	to stop	*verdwijnen*[18]	to disappear
opschieten	to make progress	*verkleuren*[18]	to change colour
opstaan	to get up, stand up	*verouderen*[18]	to get old
opstijgen	to take off (plane), to mount (horse)	*verschieten*[18]	to fade, run (colours)
		verschijnen[18]	to appear
overlijden	to pass away	*vertrekken*[18]	to leave, depart
rijzen	to rise	*verwelken*[18]	to wither
slagen	to pass (exams), succeed	*vluchten*	to flee
		(uit)wijken	to give way to
spruiten	to sprout	*worden*	to become
stappen (in-,	to step (get in,	*zakken*	to fail (exams)
uit-, over-)	out etc.)	*zijn*	to be
sterven	to die	*zinken*	to sink
stikken	to suffocate	*zwellen*	to swell

17 Many Dutch verbs can take the prefix *uit-* giving the meaning 'to be finished doing'. These compound verbs all take *zijn* even if the verbs from which they are formed do not:
uitslapen – to sleep in, have one's fill of sleep
uitpraten – to finish saying what one has to say
uitkijken – to finish looking

> *Ik was nog niet uitgepraat of hij begon al te zingen.*
> I had hardly finished talking when he began to sing.
> *Ben je uitgekeken?* – Have you seen enough/finished looking?

18 The prefix *ver-* basically means 'change' (see p. 172) and thus many *ver-* verbs are found in this group; not all *ver-* verbs belong here, however, as many are transitive, eg. *verstaan* (to understand), *vertalen* (to translate, i.e. to change from one language to antoher).

11.8.2 There is also a group of verbs that can take **either** *hebben* **or** *zijn* as the auxiliary in the perfect tenses. There are four categories of such verbs.

1 The following verbs are conjugated with *zijn* if a motion to or from a particular place is mentioned (in which case they do not differ from the verbs in group I); if, however, there is no motion but merely an action, they are conjugated with *hebben*.

fietsen	– to cycle	*rijden**	– to drive, ride
glijden	– to slide	*roeien**	– to row
klimmen	– to climb	*springen*	– to jump
kruipen	– to crawl	*trappen*	– to pedal, tread
lopen	– to walk	*varen**	– to go (by sea)
rennen	– to run	*vliegen**	– to fly
hollen	– to run	*wandelen*	– to walk, stroll
overstreken	– to cross	*zeilen*	– to sail
reizen	– to travel	*zwemmen*	– to swim

lopen (to run)	*hij is naar huis gelopen*
	hij heeft de hele dag gelopen
rijden (to drive)	*ik ben in drie kwartier naar Rotterdam gereden*
	ik heb vandaag erg veel gereden
zwemmen (to swim)	*gisteren is er een Engelsman van Calais naar Dover gezwommen*
	heb je ooit in de Oostzee gezwommen?

2 Some of the verbs mentioned above can also be used transitively, in which case they take *hebben*, as do all transitive verbs. They are marked*.

rijden: Ik heb de auto voor mijn moeder naar Amsterdam gereden.
roeien: Ik heb hem naar de overkant van de rivier geroeid.

3 There is in addition a small group of verbs that take *zijn* when used intransitively, but *hebben* when used transitively. They have nothing to do with motion like those in (2), however.

bederven (to spoil)	*ontdooien* (to defrost)
breken (to break)	*smelten* (to melt)
genezen (to heal, cure)	*veranderen* (to change)

Het is bedorven	It has spoiled
Jij hebt het bedorven.	You've spoilt it.
De stoel is gebroken.	The chair has broken.
Jij hebt hem gebroken.	You broke it.
De wond is genezen.	The wound has healed.
De dokter heeft me genezen.	The doctor (has) cured me.
De kip is ontdooid.	The chicken has defrosted.
Ik heb de kip ontdooid.	I have defrosted the chicken.

De boter is gesmolten.	The butter has melted.
Jij hebt hem in de pan gesmolten.	You melted it in the pot.
Het weer is veranderd.	The weather has changed.
Ik heb het veranderd.	I altered it.

It should be noted that when such verbs are used intransitively in Dutch they are conjugated with *zijn*. The past participles are indistinguishable from predicative adjectives.

4   The verbs dealt with here can be conjugated with *zijn* or *hebben* but the criteria for their use are separate in each case:

vergeten (to forget): with *hebben* the meaning is 'did not think of s.t.', 'neglected to do s.t.' or 'left s.t. behind'.

> *Ik heb vergeten te schrijven.*
> *Ik heb mijn paraplu vergeten.*

With *zijn* the meaning is 'has gone from one's memory'.

> *Ik ben glad vergeten waar ik het gelaten heb.*
> *Ik ben je naam vergeten.*

In practice most Dutch people use *zijn* in all cases.

verleren (to forget s.t. learnt): this verb can be conjugated with *hebben* of *zijn* with no difference in meaning:

> *Ik heb/ben het Frans geheel verleerd.*

verliezen (to lose): should always be conjugated with *hebben* but is commonly heard with *zijn* either by analogy with *vergeten* or with *kwijt zijn*.

> *Ik ben mijn sleutels kwijt.*
> *Ik heb mijn sleutels verloren.*

volgen (to follow) when this verb means 'to pursue' it is conjugated with *zijn*.

> *De buurman is zijn hond gevolgd.*

Otherwise *hebben* is used.

> *Ik heb colleges bij hem gevolgd.*
> *Zij heeft de politieke ontwikkelingen in Zuid-Afrika gevolgd.*

The verb *opvolgen* (to succeed, follow) is found with both.

> *Juliana heeft/is haar moeder in 1948 opgevolgd.*

Note: Because only one auxiliary (i.e. have) is used in the perfect and pluperfect tenses in English one can often have several past participles following, all dependent on the one 'have'. In Dutch this is only possible if all past participles require *hebben*; the auxiliary must be repeated if one requires *hebben* and the other *zijn*,

> He has hired a plane and flown to Russia.
> *Hij heeft een vliegtuig gehuurd en is naar Rusland gevlogen.*

Alternative translations of 'to be':

Very often the English verb 'to be', when indicating the position of something, is rendered in Dutch by the verbs *hangen* (to hang), *liggen* (to lie), *lopen* (to run), *staan* (to stand) and *zitten* (to sit). They are usually found in repletive *er* constructions (see p. 221).

There are many trees here.	*Er staan hier veel bomen.*
Behind our house is a canal.	*Achter ons huis loopt een gracht.*
There is a picture on the wall.	*Er hangt een schilderij aan de muur.*
What is in that glass?	*Wat zit er in dat glas?*

11.9 Modal auxiliary verbs *(modale hulpwerkwoorden)*

Modal verbs form a special class of their own because they show a variety of irregular forms and, due to their auxiliary nature in expressing mood, also a variety of meanings. There are four true modals (*kunnen, moeten, mogen, willen*) plus the verbs *durven, hoeven,* and *zullen* which share one or more modal characteristics.

One feature common to both Dutch and English modals is the lack of a *te* before the infinitive for which it is acting as an auxiliary,
eg. he can do it – *hij kan het doen.*

11.9.1 FORMS

1 **kunnen** (to be able to, can)

present:

1. *ik kan* = I am able, can	*wij kunnen*
2. *jij kunt, kan*	*jullie kunnen, kunt*
u kunt	*u kunt*
3. *hij kan*	*zij kunnen*

Jij can take either *kunt* or *kan* and both are equally common; when inverted, *jij kunt* becomes *kun jij.*
Jullie kunnen is more common than *jullie kunt.*
In 'plat' Dutch *kennen* (to know) and *kunnen* are often confused.

imperfect:

ik, jij, u, hij kon = I was able, could
wij, jullie, zij konden

past participle:

gekund (see Perfect tenses of modal verbs, p. 139)

2 **moeten** (to have to, must)
For the negative of *moeten* using *hoeven* see p. 142.

present:
1. *ik moet* = I have to, must   *wij moeten*
2. *jij, u moet*   *jullie moeten, moet*
3. *hij moet*   *zij moeten*

Jullie moet is not common.

imperfect:

ik, jij, u, hij moest = I had to
wij, jullie, zij moesten

past participle:

gemoeten (see Perfect tenses of modal verbs, p. 139).

3 **mogen** (to be allowed to, may)

present:

1. *ik mag* = I am allowed, may   *wij mogen*
2. *jij, u mag*   *jullie mogen, mag*
3. *hij mag*   *zij mogen*

Jullie mag is not common. The *gij* form is *moogt*.

imperfect:

ik, jij, u, hij mocht = I was allowed to
wij, jullie, zij mochten

past participle:

One finds *gemogen, gemocht* and *gemoogd*, but in practice most people say *gemogen*. (see Perfect tenses of modal verbs. below).

4 **willen** (to want to)

present:

1. *ik wil*   *wij willen*
2. *jij wilt, wil*   *jullie willen, wilt*
    u wilt   *u wilt*
3. *hij wil*   *zij willen*

Jij can take either *wilt* or *wil* and both are equally common; when inverted *jij wilt* becomes *wil jij. Jullie wilt* is not common.

imperfect:

ik, jij, u, hij wilde, wou = I wanted to
wij, jullie, zij wilden

One often hears a plural form *wouwen* but this is never written and should be avoided in more careful speech; the singular form *wou* is permissible in both writing and speech, however. (see also Contracted modals in conditional tenses. p. 140).

past participle: *gewild* (see Perfect tenses of modal verbs below).

11.9.2 PERFECT TENSES OF MODAL VERBS

The past participle of modal verbs is not often used. Because of the auxiliary functions of modals a perfect tense (including pluperfects, future perfects and conditional perfects) is usually followed by another infinitive and in this case the so-called 'double infinitive rule' applies, i.e. if one has an English sentence where the past participle of a modal verb is followed by an infinitive, Dutch does not use the past participle but the infinitive of the modal concerned. (see also p. 146-147).

I have not **been able to** visit him.	*Ik heb hem niet **kunnen** bezoeken.*
They had **been allowed to** go.	*Ze hadden **mogen** gaan.*
She will have **had to** spend it.	*Zij zal het hebben **moeten** uitgeven.*

Only when the infinitive for which the modal is acting as auxiliary is not mentioned (but simply implied), is the past participle used.

Ik heb het niet gekund.	I have not been able to (see him).
Zij hadden het gemogen.	They had been allowed to (go)
Zij zal het hebben gemoeten.	She will have had to (spend it).

Note the use of *het* in such cases.

The following is commonly done by Dutch people with the perfect tense of modals: modals all take *hebben* as their auxiliary verb in the perfect tense but the speaker is often misled by the infinitive that follows the perfect of the modal,

Hij is niet kunnen komen.

Here he anticipates the verb of motion which follows the modal and which requires *zijn* in its perfect tense, but in actual fact it is the perfect of *kunnen* which is required here and *kunnen* requires *hebben*, eg. *hij heeft niet kunnen komen*. Similarly *hij is weggemoeten,* which is an abbreviated form of *hij heeft moeten weggaan* where *gaan* is not mentioned but simply implied. (see also 11.9.4).

11.9.3 CONTRACTED MODALS IN CONDITIONAL TENSES

1   Conditional tense:
The modal auxiliary verbs have in common with the auxiliaries *hebben* and *zijn* the fact that they have contracted forms in the conditional. In the case of the conditional the concept is not unknown in English either: for example 'I could do it' can mean either 'I was able to do it' (an imperfect) or 'I would be able to do it' (a conditional).

Kunnen

Similarly the Dutch sentence *ik kon het doen* is ambiguous without a context and in the latter meaning it replaces *ik zou het kunnen doen,* where *kon* is the contracted form of *zou kunnen*. Either form is permissible but the latter avoids any ambiguity.

Moeten

In the same way, *moest, moesten* can mean 'should, ought to' as well as 'had to', eg. *je moest meer eten* – you should eat more. *Jij zou meer moeten eten* is equally correct and preferable if ambiguity is likely.

Willen

It has a contracted form too which means 'would like to, want to' and which is also identical to the past tense.

>   *Ik wou graag twee kilo appels (hebben)* =
>   *Ik zou graag twee kilo appels willen (hebben).*

The adverb *graag* is commonly used in such 'would like' constructions but not in questions eg. Would you like a cup of coffee – *Wil je een kopje koffie?*

Note the following use of *wou: ik wou dat ik rijk was* – I wish I were rich.

Wilde(n) can never be used in this conditional sense.

Mogen

There is a contraction of *mogen* in the conditional which is rather formal style and which is translated by 'should' in English.

>   *Mocht het regenen, dan komen we niet.*
>   Should it rain, we won't be coming.

2   Conditional perfect of *kunnen* and *moeten* (see also p. 154).

Kunnen

The English phrase 'could have done' is a contraction of 'would have been able to do' and as such can be rendered in Dutch by *hij zou het hebben kunnen doen* but the following contracted form is more commonly used: *hij had het kunnen doen* (for contraction of *zou... hebben* to *had/hadden*, see p. 114).

It is best to learn *had/hadden kunnen doen* parrot-fashion and to apply it as follows: she could have sung the song better – *zij had het liedje beter kunnen zingen*.

Moeten

The construction 'should have done' is similar to the above but is difficult to rephrase sensibly in 'would' terms in English. In this case it is advisable to learn *had/hadden moeten doen* parrot-fashion and to apply it as follows: The gentlemen should have read the newspaper – *De heren hadden de krant moeten lezen*.

Note that the contracted conditional perfect forms *had kunnen doen* and *had moeten doen* are identical to the pluperfect (as a result of the double infinitive rule, see p. 139), but context always makes the meaning clear.

> *Als ik het had moeten doen, zou ik geweigerd hebben.*
> If I had had to do it, I would have refused. (pluperfect)
> *Ik had het moeten doen maar ik had er geen zin in.*
> I should have done it but I didn't feel like it. (conditional perfect).
> See uses of *zullen* on p. 144.

11.9.4   USE OF INDEPENDENT MODALS

There is one use of modals which differs considerably from English: *kunnen, moeten, mogen* and *willen* often stand alone and the verb that follows in English is simply implied in Dutch; this is particularly the case when the implied verbs are *doen, gaan, komen, hebben* and *worden*.

Ik kan het niet.	I can't do it.
Dat moet.	That must be done.
Je mag naar binnen.	You may go inside.
Hij zou het niet willen.	He wouldn't want to do (or to have) it.
Kan dat?	Is that possible?
Mag dat?	Is that allowed?

11.9.5   SEMANTIC DIFFICULTIES WITH MODALS

1   Kunnen

a   As in English, *kunnen* (can) and *mogen* (may) are often confused, eg. 'Can I borrow your bicycle?' should actually read 'May I borrow your bicycle?' but in practice the semantic distinction between the two is ignored; in Dutch too *Kan ik je fiets even lenen?* will often be heard for *Mag ik je fiets even lenen?*
In addition English 'may' is often rendered by *kunnen* in Dutch:

That may be true.	*Dat kan wel waar zijn.*
The king may come at any moment.	*De koning kan elk ogenblik komen.*

b *Kunnen* is commonly used in polite requests:

Kunt u het raam even dichtdoen?/Zou u het raam even dicht kunnen doen?

c *Kunnen* + *beter* renders English 'had better':

You had better not buy a car.   *Je kan beter geen auto kopen.*

d A conditional of *kunnen* is often used to render 'might' (see p. 143).

Note that *kunnen* is not used with verbs of perception, unlike English:

I can see/hear nothing.   *Ik zie/hoor niets.*
I can't understand you.   *Ik versta je niet.*

2 Moeten

a *Moeten* has two meanings:
1. to be obliged to, have to
2. to be advised to

Je moet je vader helpen.
You must (are obliged to) help your father.
You must (i.e. I advise you to) help your father.

English has the same ambiguity. When the above English examples are negated, the following occurs:

meaning 1: You don't have to help your father.
meaning 2: You mustn't help your father.

Similarly in Dutch a different verb is used to negate the former:

meaning 1: *Je hoeft je vader niet te helpen.*
meaning 2: *Je moet je vader niet helpen.*

Hoeven is a semi-modal verb; it replaces *moeten* in the above sense; it can be used independently like *moeten*, eg. *dat hoeft niet* – that's not necessary; but there are cases when it must be followed by *te* (an unmodal trait) and others where one has the option, i.e. *te* is always used in the present and imperfect tenses but may be omitted in compound tenses where double infinitive constructions occur.

Dat zul je nooit hoeven (te) doen.
Dat heeft hij nooit hoeven (te) doen.

Note the following use with the negative conjunction *zonder: Zonder iets voor me te hoeven doen, heeft hij zijn diensten aangeboden* – Without having to do anything for me, he offered his services.

b 'Should, ought to' are expressed by *moeten* in Dutch. (see also *mogen*, p. 140).

Note: not, however, 'should' which means 'would', i.e. I should do it, if I were you – *ik zou het doen als ik jou was.*

Although the contracted conditional form *moest(en)* (see 11.9.3) is often used in this sense, the present tense is also very common and is certainly simpler.

You should write more often.   *Je moet (moest) vaker schrijven.*
That should be forbidden.   *Dat moet (moest) verboden worden.*

c   In formal style the verbs **dienen** and **(be)horen** often replace *moeten* in the sense of 'to be obliged to'. They are always followed by *te*,

Alle passagiers dienen zich vóór acht uur bij loket vier te melden.
Bestellingen (be)horen vóór 31 januari te worden geplaatst.

3   Mogen

a   In addition to the basic meaning of 'to be allowed to', *mogen* also renders the verb 'to like' (of people), eg. *Ik mag hem graag* – I like him a lot, as distinct from *ik hou van hem* – I love him; otherwise one must say *ik vind hem aardig* to express 'to like'.

b   There is a *mogen* commonly used with the adverb *wel eens* which means 'could, would be better if',

Je mag je kamer wel eens opruimen.
You could tidy up your room (to begin with).
Hij mag zich wel eens verkleden.
He could change his clothes (for once).

c   There is an obsolete first person present tense form of *mogen* that is sometimes used in formal letters (see also p. 150):

Naar aanleiding van uw schrijven van 21 december jl. moge ik u mededelen dat...
With reference to your letter of the 21st December last I **would like** to inform you that...

d   English 'might', a form derived from 'may', is usually expressed in Dutch simply by the addition of *misschien* (perhaps) to the sentence, but the conditional of *kunnen* is also possible.

He might come tomorrow.
Hij komt misschien morgen/Hij zou morgen kunnen komen.
That might be difficult.
Dat zal misschien moeilijk zijn/Dat zou moeilijk kunnen zijn.

'Might' in the following example is semantically different, however, and *misschien* cannot be used: He might have asked me if I wanted it – i.e. he could have asked, thus *hij had mij kunnen vragen of ik het hebben wilde*.

e   Note the following idiomatic use of *mocht(en)* which expresses a lack of ability: *Ik heb alles geprobeerd om af te vallen maar niets mocht lukken* – I tried everything to lose weight but nothing worked.

4 Willen

a In addition to the meaning 'want', the Dutch verb *willen* also often renders English 'will'; in such cases no futurity is expressed but a polite imperative (also English 'would you mind...').

Will you please shut the window.
Wilt u het raam even dichtdoen.

b English 'would like' is expressed by the conditional of *willen* (see p. 140).

I would like a cup of tea.
Ik zou graag een kopje thee willen hebben/Ik wou graag een kopje thee.
I would like to meet you – *Ik zou u graag willen ontmoeten.* (note the word order)

c *Ik wil dat jij...*etc. renders 'I want you to...etc.', eg. *Moeder wil dat ik mijn broertje meeneem* – Mother wants me to take my brother along.

5 Zullen

In addition to being the auxiliary used to form the future tense, *zullen* can also have other connotations.

Zullen we gaan? – Shall we go?
i.e. *Laten we gaan* – Let's go.

It also renders biblical 'shall' (i.e. must).

Gij zult niet stelen – Thou shalt not steal.

The idiom *dat zal wel* (that's probably so) is very common. (see p. 117)
Gezuld is quite rare but *zullen* occurs in double infinitive constructions (see p. 139). In such cases it is very close in meaning to *moeten* (see p. 141) although here the emphasis is on the intention rather than the obligation.

Ze had het zullen doen maar ze deed het niet.
She intended/was going to do it but she didn't (do it).

Note the following idiomatic use of *zullen* in the infinitive: *Ze hebben beloofd om bombardementen niet te zullen hervatten* – They promised not to resume bombing.

11.10   The infinitive *(de onbepaalde wijs)*

11.10.1   CHARACTERISTICS OF THE INFINITIVE

The infinitive or basic undeclined form of the verb always ends in *-en* in Dutch,

lopen (to run), *jagen* (to hunt) etc.

There are six monosyllabic verbs ending in *-n* in the infinitive.

doen, gaan, slaan, staan, zien, zijn

English always puts 'to' before the infinitive in isolation. One should learn each new verb as follows: *lopen* = to run. In context, however, there are occasions when this 'to' may or may not be used. Similarly in Dutch, although the infinitive in isolation is never preceded by *te*, in context there are rules for when it is and is not used.

11.10.2   RULES FOR THE USE OF *TE*

As a general rule one can say that an infinitive at the end of a clause is always preceded by *te* in the following cases:

1   When the infinitive is used as a general impersonal imperative (see p. 150).

niet roken, geen lawaai maken, niet zo langzaam lopen.

2   It is never used after modal verbs, i.e. when a modal is the finite verb in the clause. Dutch shares this feature with English.

Hij kan het niet doen.
He can't do it/He isn't able to do it.
Wij hebben tien boeken moeten lezen.
We had to read ten books.

Note the English modal 'to want to', where a 'to' is used (compare 'to be able to' and 'to have to' above), unlike Dutch.

He wants to go – *Hij wil gaan.*

3   The auxiliary *hoeven* which is used to form the negative of *moeten*, is commonly followed by *te*, unlike the modals. (see p. 142-143).

4   The verbs *durven* (to dare), *staan* (to stand), *liggen* (to lie) and *zitten* (to sit) behave in a similar way to *hoeven*:

Durf je dat te doen?
Do you dare (to) do that?
Dat heb ik nooit durven (te) zeggen.
I never dared (to) say that.
Hij zit een boek te lezen.
He's sitting reading a book.

Hij heeft de hele dag een boek zitten lezen.
He has been (sitting) reading a book all day.
Zij stond naar een koe te kijken.
She stood looking at a cow.
Ze kan urenlang naar koeien staan kijken.
She can stand looking at cows for hours.
(see 11.14.2).

The verbs *proberen* and *trachten* (to try) know a double infinitive construction like that of the above verbs but it is always followed by *te*:

Hij probeerde mij te helpen.
He tried to help me.
Hij heeft mij proberen te helpen/Hij heeft geprobeerd mij te helpen.
He (has) tried to help me.

The verb *beginnen*, when used in the perfect tense and followed by another infinitive, usually follows the regular pattern of past participle + *te* + infinitive but it can also follow the same pattern as *proberen*, using the infinitive instead of the past participle:

Toen is het kind begonnen te schreeuwen/
Toen is het kind beginnen te schreeuwen.
Then the child started to scream/screaming
Hij is begonnen een brief te schrijven/
Hij is een brief beginnen te schrijven.
He began to write/writing a letter.

Similarly the verb *weten* which literally means 'to know' but renders English 'to manage to' in such constructions:

He wist te ontsnappen.	He managed to escape.
Hij heeft het weten te vinden.	He (has) managed to find it.

5 a When the following verbs are used as finite verbs and are followed by an infinitive, the infinitive is not preceded by *te*:

komen	*zien*	*doen*
gaan	*leren*	*blijven*
horen	*helpen*	*wezen* (see p. 132)
vinden	*laten*	*hebben*
voelen		

Zij hoorde mij komen – She heard me coming.
Ik vond hem bij het raam staan – I found him standing by the window.

b All these verbs (except *hebben*, see top p. 160) employ a double infinitive construction in the perfect tense, i.e. they use an infinitive, not a past participle when followed by another infinitive (see also Perfect tenses of modal verbs, p. 139). Such constructions are very common because of the tendency in Dutch to use the perfect tense instead of the imperfect – see the translations of the following examples:

Ik heb hem horen komen – I heard him coming.
Hij is gaan kijken – He has gone (went) to look.

Note: Use of *zijn* – perfect tense of *gaan*, a verb of motion.

Hij heeft zijn hart voelen kloppen.
He felt his heart beating.
Ik heb mijn zoontje leren zwemmen.
I taught my son to swim.
De aardappels hebben koud staan worden.
The potatoes have been getting cold.
Hij heeft zijn handen leren gebruiken.
He has learnt to use his hands.
He is blijven doorpraten.
He went on talking.

Note: *zijn* has a special alternative infinitive used only in such double infinitive constructions:

Ze zijn wezen kijken.
They have been to have a look. (see p. 132)

In *Hij heeft lezen en schrijven geleerd* reading and writing are acting as nouns.

c *Laten* in such constructions is often rendered by a passive in English:

Hij heeft een huis laten bouwen.
He has had a house built.
Ik heb mijn haar laten knippen.
I (have) had my hair cut.

Doen often replaces *laten* in more formal style:

De regering heeft het parlementsgebouw doen ontruimen.
The government (has) had parliament house evacuated.

Note: *Doen* can be used as a sort of auxiliary in combination with another infinitive provided the sentence begins with that infinitive:

Lezen doet ze wel – She does read.

d There are some pairs of infinitives incorporating the above verbs which render a new concept in English:

blijven zitten – to fail, stay down (at school)
gaan zitten – to sit down
blijven staan – to stop still
doen denken – to remind (someone of something)

e   Note the following idiomatic use of *hebben* which requires no *te* before the infinitive that follows it:

> *Ik heb een tante in Friesland zitten.*
> I have an aunt living in Friesland.
> *Zij heeft een prachtige lamp in de hoek staan.*
> She has a beautiful lamp standing in the corner.

11.10.3   USE OF *OM... TE* BEFORE INFINITIVES

This is a complicated issue in Dutch and seems to be in the process of changing. There are a few instances where only *te* can be used (see 11.10.2) and a few cases where only *om...te* can be used:

1   When in English 'to' means 'in order to' (compare the poetic form 'for to cross the road'),

> *Ik ga naar de stad om een hoed te kopen.*
> I am going to town to buy a hat.
> *Het is niet nodig (om) de weg over te steken om bij de winkels te komen.*
> It is not necessary to cross the road to reach the shops.

2   When a sentence begins with an infinitive clause:

> *Om te besluiten zou ik...* – To finish, I woud...

3   When an infinitive construction follows a noun that it is describing; in such cases *om* is always followed by a preposition:
> *Een pad om op te fietsen.*
> A path to ride on.
> *Een surfboot is een boot om mee door de branding te gaan.*
> A surfboat is a boat to go through the surf with.
> *Nieuwe huizen zijn niet prettig om in te wonen.*
> New houses are not nice to live in.
> *Ik heb al mijn kinderen om voor te zorgen.*
> I have all my children to look after.

Note: There is one specific use of *om...te* which renders English 'only to...', eg. *Het vliegtuig steeg op om een half uur later neer te storten.* – The plane took off only to crash half an hour later.

In all other cases the use of *om...te* is optional but nowadays there is a tendency to include *om* wherever possible.

> *Ze weigerde (om) mee te gaan.* [19]
> She refused to go along.

19   *te* used with a separable verb goes between the prefix and the verb and the three words are written separately.

Het is daar niet (om) uit te houden.
It is impossible to bear there.
Het is stom (om) een oude auto te kopen.
It is stupid to buy an old car.
Ik ben vergeten (om) te vragen.
I forgot to ask.
Zij was van plan (om) een uitstapje naar Marken te maken.
She intended making a trip to Marken.
Dat is niet (om) te doen.
That can't be done.

11.10.4 THE INFINITIVE AS A NOUN

The infinitive is also used as a neuter noun:

blaffen – to bark, thus *het blaffen* – the barking
behangen – to wallpaper, thus *het behangen* – the wallpapering

Ik ben tegen het roken.
I am against smoking.
Het uit je hoofd leren van werkwoorden valt tegen.
Learning verbs by heart isn't easy.
Vermijd het te veel drinken van wodka als je in Rusland bent.
Avoid drinking too much vodka when you're in Russia

11.11 The imperative mood *(de gebiedende wijs)*

11.11.1   As the imperative is an order form addressed to a second person there is a *jij, jullie*
and *u* form.

werk
werken jullie   work!
werkt u

The form derived from the simple stem can actually be used for all persons whether singular
of plural, familiar or polite.

The *u* form is used only when being particularly polite,

Komt u binnen en gaat u zitten.

The simple stem can sound a little harsh and it is often softened by the use of the adverbs
eens of *even.*

Geef me eens (pronounced *'s) je boek.*
Doe het raam eens even dicht.
Lees dat eens even voor.

Sometimes *jij, u* or *jullie* is added for the same reason,

Ga jij nou daar zitten.

Note the following common idiomatic imperatives employing the word *ze: werk ze* – work hard, *slaap ze* - sleep well, *eet ze* – bon appétit.

11.11.2   In formal written style (and often in advertisements too) one meets an imperative formed from the stem + t, actually a plural form.

Leest de Bijbel.

11.11.3   The infinitive is also commonly used as a general hyper-impersonal imperative; this is particularly common on signs and is also used in recipes (the simple stem is common in recipes too).

signs: *niet roken* – don't smoke
           voorrang verlenen – give way (i.e. in traffic)

recipes: *het vlees met kruiden inwrijven en dan twee dagen op een koele plaats laten staan.*

11.11.4   Occasionally the past participle is used as a general impersonal imperative, particularly with the verbs *opletten* and *oppassen*.

opgelet, opgepast – watch out, take care!

11.11.5   The imperative form 'let' as in 'Let's go home' etc. can be expressed in two ways in Dutch:

a   either by the simple imperative formed from the stem plus the object pronoun as in English:

Laat ons naar huis gaan; laat me het zo zeggen.

b   or by using the subject pronoun and the appropriate form of the verb,

Laten we naar huis gaan; laat ik het zo zeggen.

11.12   The subjunctive mood *(de aanvoegende wijs)*

The subjunctive mood, which was formerly quite common in Dutch and may still be met in older literature, is not actively used any more. It has suffered the same fate in Dutch as in English; it is only preserved in certain standard expressions. As in English, it is used to express actions that are wished for, feared, doubted or are conditional on other occasions. (see p. 131)

The **present subjunctive** differs from the present indicative in that the first and third persons singular end in -*e*, eg. *ik werke, hij worde*. (*Jij*, being a familiar form, is never found with a subjunctive form.) Note that sometimes in formal letter style an archaic first person present tense form ending in -*e* is used; this should not be confused with the subjunctive (see p. 143):

Naar aanleiding van uw brief van 21 december moge ik u mededelen...
Verblijve met de meeste hoogachting

The **imperfect subjunctive** of weak verbs is the same as the indicative, but that of strong verbs ends in -e in the first person singular and is otherwise the same as the imperfect indicative, eg. *ik hadde, hij kwame*.

The monosyllabic verbs *doen, gaan, slaan, staan* and *zien* add no -e but employ the stem only. *Zijn* has the irregular forms *zij* (first and third persons present subjunctive) and *ware* (first and third persons imperfect subjunctive).

Examples of some commonly used subjunctives:

leve de koningin	long live the Queen
het koste wat het wil	cost what it may
het ga u goed	may all go well for you
God zij dank	thanks be to God
wat hij ook moge doen	whatever he may do
als het ware	as it were

Note the final example has a parallel in English; the English imperfect subjunctive preserved in 'if I/he were rich...' no longer exists in Dutch, however, i.e. *als ik/hij rijk was...*

There is one present subjunctive that is still productive: in formal writing a third person singular subjunctive with the subject pronoun *men* renders an imperative, eg. *men lette hierop, men herleze mijn openingswoord ter gelegenheid van het derde colloquium*. This form is sometimes used in recipes.

11.13 The passive *(de lijdende vorm)*

11.13.1 THE TENSES OF THE PASSIVE

Present : *De auto wordt (door hem) gewassen.*
The car is (being) washed (by him).

Imperfect : *De auto werd (door hem) gewassen.*
The was (being) washed (by him).

Perfect : *De auto is (door hem) gewassen [geworden].*[20]
The car has been washed (by him).

Pluperfect : *De auto was (door hem) gewassen [geworden].*
The car had been washed (by him).

---

20 Because of the Dutch tendency to use the perfect tense where English uses the imperfect, this can also be translated with 'was washed'.
As *zijn* is also used to form the active perfect tense of some intransitive verbs, there is no formal difference between the active perfect of those verbs and the passive perfects of all other verbs.

Hij is in Amsterdam aangekomen – He (has) arrived in Amsterdam.
Hij is in Amsterdam gezien – He has been/was seen in Amsterdam.

Future : *De auto zal (door hem) gewassen worden.*
The car will be washed (by him).

Conditional : *De auto zou (door hem) gewassen worden.*
The car would be washed (by him).

Future perfect : *De auto zal (door hem) gewassen [geworden] zijn.*
The car will have been washed (by him).

Conditional perfect : *De auto zou (door hem) gewassen [geworden] zijn.*
The car would have been washed (by him).

11.13.2   WHAT IS THE PASSIVE?

The passive is a voice, not a tense, because all tenses of the active extend to the passive too. A passive construction is one where the logical object of the action becomes the subject of the finite verb, i.e.

active : he washes the car – *hij wast de auto.*
passive: the car is washed (by him) – *de auto wordt (door hem) gewassen.*

In the passive the agent of the action may be left unmentioned if so desired, but it is always implied.

11.13.3   HOW TO CONSTRUCT THE PASSIVE

The passive is constructed in English by a form of the verb 'to be' plus a past participle plus an optional agent introduced by the preposition 'by'.

i.e. subject	+	to be	+	past participle	(+ by + noun/pronoun)
e.g. the car		is being		washed	by him

The Dutch passive differs in that the verb *worden* is used, not *zijn*, to translate the verb 'to be' and 'by' is translated by *door*.

i.e. subject	+	*worden*	(+ *door* + noun/pronoun)	+	past participle
e.g. *de auto*		*wordt*	*door* *hem*		*gewassen*

11.13.4   DIFFICULTIES WITH THE PASSIVE

1   Perfect and pluperfect passive

A complication arises where the auxiliary *worden* is required in the perfect tense,

i.e. the car has been washed.

Here one would expect: *de auto is gewassen geworden*
has washed   been

This double participle is not liked, however, and the Dutchman simply drops the *geworden*, claiming that if 'a car has been washed' then it 'is washed', i.e. *is gewassen*.
Similarly in the pluperfect 'the car had been washed' should be: *de auto was gewassen geworden,* but the *geworden* is dropped because if 'the car had been washed' then it 'was washed', i.e. *was gewassen.*

These two forms *is/was gewassen* lead the English speaker, however, to think that a sentence like 'the car is/was washed by him' is *de auto is/was door hem gewassen.* Be careful here. In this case the present or past of *worden* is required.

Note: The perfect tense is more common in Dutch than in English because of the tendency to render English imperfects with perfects in Dutch.

> The car was washed by him yesterday.
> *De auto werd gisteren door hem gewassen/De auto is gisteren door hem gewassen.*

2   Action versus state with the past participle

A further difficulty arises with a sentence like 'the door is closed'. If one is describing an action, i.e. if the sentence is 'the door is (being) closed (by him)', then the present tense of *worden* must be used: *de deur wordt (door hem) gesloten.*

Similarly, in the past 'the door was shut'; if it means 'the door was (being) shut (by him)', it will be in Dutch *de deur werd (door hem) gesloten.*

But perhaps only a state, not an action, is implied, i.e. the door is/was closed. Here the past participle can be regarded as an adjective as in 'the door is/was red' and no agent is implied. If this is the case then the sentence is translated: *de deur is/was gesloten.*
We thus see that 'the door has (had) been closed' and 'the door is (was) closed' are both *de deur is (was) gesloten* and the context tells us what is intended.

3   Passives with indirect objects

A special difficulty arises in passive sentences such as the following: I was given a book (by them). If one looks firstly at the active of this sentence 'They gave a book to me' one sees that the English 'I' is an indirect object in meaning: I was not given, a book was given **to me**. Such indirect objects in passive sentences can be rendered in three ways in Dutch:

> *(Aan) mij werd een boek gegeven.* (less common)
> *Een boek werd aan mij gegeven.* (less common)
> *Er werd een boek aan mij gegeven/Er werd mij een boek gegeven.*

The last alternative, which utilizes a repletive *er*, is very common in the passive in Dutch, especially when the agent is not mentioned. (see p. 221)

> *Er werden gisteren veel auto's gewassen* – Many cars were washed yesterday.

> *Er moet wat gedaan worden* – Something must be done.

> *Er werden felicitaties aan hen gestuurd* – They were sent congratulations.

4 Use of modals with the passive

Modal verbs often act as auxiliaries in the passive too as in English and should simply be translated literally.

> It must be done – *Het moet gedaan worden.*
> It couldn't be cleaned – *Het kon niet schoongemaakt worden.*

The following modal constructions differ considerably from English (see p. 141):

> That could have been done. – *Dat had gedaan kunnen worden.*
> That should have been done. – *Dat had gedaan moeten worden.*

> A decision could/should have been taken by now.
> *Een beslissing had nu al genomen kunnen/moeten zijn.*

5 Word order with modals

In main clauses the order of the constituent parts of the passive with a modal verb can be either:

> *Dat kan gedaan worden/Dat kan worden gedaan.*
> *Dat zou gedaan moeten worden/Dat zou moeten worden gedaan.*

In subordinate clauses the following alternatives exist (the finite verb is never placed after the verbal cluster).

> *Ik weet dat het gedaan kan worden/Ik weet dat het kan worden gedaan.*
> *Hij zei dat het gedaan zou moeten worden/Hij zei dat het zou moeten worden gedaan.*

6 Contracted conditionals in the passive

Contracted forms of *zijn* are common in the passive. (see p. 114)

> The city would have been destroyed if...
> *De stad was vernietigd als.../De stad zou vernietigd zijn als...*
> The book would have been read sooner if...
> *Het boek was eerder gelezen als.../Het boek zou eerder gelezen zijn als...*

7 Passives rendered by adjectival adjuncts (see p. 65)

It is common in journalese and other written style to replace clauses containing a passive with adjectival adjuncts placed before the relevant noun.

> *Het huis dat gisteren door hem werd geverfd.*
> *Het gisteren door hem geverfde huis.*

> *Het bedrag dat nog door hem betaald moet worden.*
> *Het nog door hem te betalen bedrag.*

Such constructions must be translated into English with relative clauses.

8   There are some impersonal English passives which are rendered in Dutch by an infinitive construction, thus avoiding the passive.

There was nobody to be seen.   *Er was niemand te zien.*
That was to be expected.   *Dat was te verwachten.*
That is to be hoped.   *Dat is te hopen.*
Where can that book be got?   *Waar is dat boek te krijgen?*

9   Use of *men/je/ze* instead of the passive

It should be noted that the passive in all its forms is more common in English than in Dutch. Very often the Dutchman uses an active form of the verb with *men* (one) or *je* (you) as its subject.

Dutch is spoken here.   *Men spreekt hier Nederlands.*
Cows can be milked by hand.   *Men/je kan koeien met de hand melken.*

Men is as formal in Dutch as 'one' is in English. In everyday speech *je* (never *jij*) is used, just as in English.

English can also use a non-personal 'they' instead of the passive; Dutch has this too and uses *ze* (never *zij*).

They say it's going to rain. (= it is said that)
Ze zeggen dat het gaat regenen.

11.14   Progressive or continuous tenses

When first learning Dutch verbs one is told that a form such as 'I am working' is *ik werk*, 'I was working' is *ik werkte* and 'I have been working' is *ik heb gewerkt*. This is indeed usually the case but there are instances where the continuous aspect needs to be expressed and there are three ways of doing so in Dutch:

11.14.1   *zijn aan 't* + infinitive:

Ik ben druk aan 't koken.
I am busy cooking.
Ik was de hele middag aan 't timmeren.
I was hammering away all afternoon.
Ik ben urenlang aan 't koken geweest.
I have been cooking for hours (and have finished, see 11.2.1).

This is the most common way.

11.14.2   *zitten, staan, liggen* or *lopen* + *te* + infinitive:

Ze zit een boek te lezen.
She is reading a book.
Hij stond buiten met de buurman te praten.
He was (standing) talking to the neighbour outside.

Jantje ligt te slapen.
Jantje is sleeping.

Note: *Zij zit al een hele tijd dat boek te lezen.*
She has been reading that book for ages. (see p. 145)

Hij heeft urenlang liggen slapen.
He was asleep for hours.
Ik heb ernaar lopen zoeken.
I have been looking for it.

This is also a very common construction.

11.14.3   *zijn bezig te* + infinitive:

Ik ben bezig een boek te schrijven.
I am (busy) writing a book.
Zij waren bezig het hele appartement te verven.
They were painting the whole flat.

This is not as common as 11.14.1 and 11.14.2.

11.15   Emphatic present and imperfect tenses formed with 'to do'

One usually learns that a form such as *ik werk* renders three English forms, i.e. I work, I am working, I do work and the imperfect *ik werkte* renders I worked, I was working, I did work. This is so, but just as the am/was working forms can be expressed in a different way in Dutch (see 11.14), so can the emphatic forms using 'do' have an equivalent in Dutch. In this case, however, the adverb *wel* can follow the verb to give it the required emphasis.

Let er wel goed op.   Do take note of it.
Ik heb het wel gedaan.   I did do it.
(the opposite of:
Ik heb het niet gedaan)

11.16   The present participle *(het tegenwoordig deelwoord)*

The present participle in Dutch is formed by adding *-d(e)* to the infinitive, eg. *zijnde* – being, *lopend(e)* – walking, *kijkend(e)* – looking. Sentence or word rhythm determines whether the *-e* is added: for example, all monosyllabic verbs add *-de*.
The present participle is not commonly used in Dutch as most English -ing constructions are expressed in other ways (see p. 160). It is used in the following instances:

11.16.1 Many adjectives are formed from the infinitive + -d:

een lachende vrouw	a laughing woman
een roerend verhaal	a moving story
dit is uitstekend	this is excellent
volgende week	next week
volgend jaar	next year
de wassende maan	the waxing moon

11.16.2 It is commonly used as an adverb of manner, in which case it has a direct parallel in English:

Het kind kwam huilend binnen.	The child came in crying.
Ik ging er lopend naartoe.	I went there on foot.

11.16.3 It renders some English -ing forms in certain standard expressions:

(als) vrouw zijnde,...[21]	being a woman,...
jou kennende,...	knowing you,...
zodoende,...	by so doing,...

In addition, the form *al -de* meaning 'while -ing' is quite common in good style:

al reizende leert men veel	one learns a lot while travelling
al lezende ontdekte hij dat...	while reading he discovered that...

11.16.4 In the written language it is often used in much the same way as -ing in English (see 11.17 for alternative constructions commonly used in the spoken language).

Aankomende op de Grote Markt in Brussel verbaasde hij zich dat...
Arriving at the Grand' Place in Brussels he was amazed that...
Uitgaande van wat hier geschreven staat...
Going on what is written here...
Daar stond een ruïne, bestaande uit een toren en een gedeelte van de stadsmuur.
There was a ruin there consisting of a tower and a section of the city wall.
Dit zeggend verliet hij de kamer.
Saying this he left the room.

11.16.5 It can also be used to form nouns, in which case it always ends in -de and takes a plural in -n.

de overlevende(n)	the survivor(s)
de inzittende(n)	the passenger(s) (in a car)

11.16.6 A few present participles have assumed the function of prepositions:

gedurende	during
betreffende } *aangaande* }	concerning, with regard to

---

21 Although a common expression, some people would disapprove of the use of *als* in this case.

11.17 How to render English '-ing' forms in Dutch

The use of -ing constructions in the formation of the progressive continuous form of the present and imperfect tenses (i.e. I am/was buying a book) is described on p. 107 and p. 108 and is thus not discussed here.

Although there is the possibility of expressing the English present participle literally in Dutch on occasions, this is rarely done in colloquial speech and such forms are reserved for literary or more formal style (see p. 156-157).

The present participle is usually avoided in Dutch. It is generally necessary to paraphrase an English sentence containing an -ing construction in order to translate it into natural Dutch. The following are the most common ways of doing so. (When seeking the appropriate translation, look at the phrase in bold type for the construction which most resembles the one you have to put into Dutch).

11.17.1   With the infinitive plus *te*:

It is lovely **being here.**
Het is heerlijk hier te zijn.
I succeeded in seeing the queen.
Het lukte mij de koningin te zien.
I like staying at home.
Ik hou ervan thuis te blijven. (also: *Ik blijf graag thuis.* see 11.17.11)
He left **without saying** a word.
Hij vertrok zonder een woord the zeggen. (see 11.17.3)
He remained seated **instead of standing** up.
Hij bleef zitten in plaats van op te staan. (see 11.17.3, also p. 202)

11.17.2   English -ing clauses introduced by 'by' or 'from' are rendered in Dutch by infinitive clauses introduced by *door* or *van* (see 12.5):

I'm trying to lose weight **by eating** nothing.
Ik probeer af te vallen door niets te eten.
By doing that you'll achieve nothing.
Door dat te doen zul je niets bereiken.
You get tired **from reading** so much.
Je wordt erg moe van zo veel te lezen.

11.17.3   Some -ing clauses are avoided by using *dat* constructions in Dutch:

They had already arrived there **without our knowing** it.
Ze waren er al aangekomen zonder dat wij het wisten.
(Compare: *We waren er al aangekomen zonder het te weten*
where the subject of both parts is the same, see 11.17.1)
Instead of him doing it I had to do it. (compare 11.17.1)
In plaats van dat hij het deed, moest ik het doen. (see p. 190)

11.17.4 Some -ing clauses can be paraphrased by 'since/because' clauses which are rendered in Dutch by the conjunctions *daar/omdat*, the former being rather formal:

Being sick he could not come.
Daar hij ziek was, kon hij niet komen. (i.e. Since he was sick...)
Being students we didn't need to pay anything.
Omdat wij studenten waren, hoefden we niets te betalen.

11.17.5 When there is a temporal sense expressed in the English -ing construction, subordinating conjunctions of time are used in Dutch.

Finding the house uninhabited, he didn't want to...
Toen hij merkte dat het huis onbewoond was, wilde hij niet...
Having recovered he went home.
Toen hij hersteld was, ging hij naar huis.
Before going to bed we drank a cup of tea.
Voordat we naar bed gingen, dronken we een kopje thee.
(After) having written a letter to his mother he went and sat in front of the T.V.
Na een brief aan zijn moeder te hebben geschreven, ging hij voor de televisie zitten.
This could also be translated as follows:
Nadat hij een brief aan zijn moeder geschreven had, ging hij...
When writing a letter you must be neat.
Wanneer je een brief schrijft, moet je netjes zijn.

11.17.6 Some -ing clauses can be paraphrased with 'while' and these are rendered in Dutch by a subordinate clause introduced by *terwijl*.

Saying that he smiled.
Terwijl hij dat zei, glimlachte hij.

11.17.7 If the English construction is 'to stand, sit or lie doing something', Dutch translates the present participle with an infinitive.

He **stood waving** at the window.
Hij stond aan het raam te wuiven.
They **were sitting (sat) watching** the film.
Zij zaten naar de film te kijken.

When such constructions are put in the (plu-)perfect tense one is dealing with double infinitives.

We **were standing (stood) talking** the whole time.
Wij hebben de hele tijd staan praten.

Similarly of course the other verbs that occur in double infinitive constructions translate -ing in this way (see p. 146-147).

I **saw him coming.**
Ik zag hem komen/Ik heb hem zien komen.
He **heard me singing.**
Hij hoorde mij zingen/Hij heeft mij horen zingen.

Note: **I have** an aunt **living** in Friesland.
Ik heb een tante in Friesland wonen.
He **has** a painting by R. **hanging** on the wall.
Hij heeft een schilderij van R. aan de muur hangen.

11.17.8   Some English -ing constructions are disguised relative clauses and must be translated as such into Dutch.

The tree standing in the park is very old.
De boom die in het park staat, is erg oud.
The man in the corner **reading** the paper is my uncle.
De man in de hoek die de krant zit te lezen, is mijn oom.

11.17.9   An infinitive noun construction also exists but can usually be avoided by other means:

You must be careful **when getting in.**
Je moet oppassen bij het instappen.

This could of course be translated as follows:

Je moet oppassen wanneer/als je instapt.

11.17.10   The so-called gerund in English, i.e. the present participle used as a noun, is rendered in Dutch by the infinitive – such nouns are always neuter (see 11.17.9).

The cooking of vegetables is a great art.
Het koken van groente is een grote kunst.
Writing novels doesn't interest me.
Het schrijven van romans interesseert me niet.
Going out is very expensive.
Uitgaan is erg duur.

Note: No smoking.
Niet roken. (an imperative in Dutch)

11.17.11   'To like/prefer doing something' is rendered by the very commonly used construction *iets graag/liever doen.*

I **like watching** him.
Ik kijk graag naar hem.
They **prefer sitting** inside.
Zij zitten liever binnen.
also: He **likes getting** up early.
Hij houdt ervan vroeg op te staan.

11.17.12   Constructions such as 'to think of doing something' are rendered by a clause containing a prepositional object followed by an infinitieve clause (see *er*, p. 222-223).

He is **thinking of buying** a boat.
Hij denkt erover een boot te kopen.

I **suspected** my family **of having sold** the house.
Ik verdacht er mijn familie van het huis te hebben verkocht.
Does anyone **feel like going** to the cinema?
Heeft er iemand zin in naar de bioscoop te gaan?

11.17.13   Occasionally an -ing construction introduces a new clause and can be avoided in Dutch by inserting a conjunction and making a normal co-ordinate clause of it.

As he was very ill he stayed in bed all day, **not getting up** till the evening.
Daar hij erg ziek was, bleef hij de hele dag in bed liggen en stond pas 's avonds op.

11.18   Reflexive verbs *(wederkerende werkwoorden)*

Reflexive verbs are verbs which have as their object[22] a reflexive pronoun, i.e. the action reflects back on the subject of the verb. The concept is known to English but is not nearly as common. For example, the verb 'to shave' can be used in two ways: I shave every day; the barber shaved me. In Dutch the verb *scheren* must have an object; that is to say, if you are not shaving someone else (eg. *de kapper schoor me*) then you must be shaving yourself and must thus say so, i.e. *ik schoor me iedere dag.* To omit this reflexive pronoun would be incorrect and is an error commonly committed by English speakers.

There are two basic sorts of reflexive verbs:

a   those that are always reflexive;
b   those that may be used reflexively but which can also be used as transitive verbs with direct objects (such as *scheren* above).

It is impossible to list all the verbs in both groups but the list under 11.18.1 will serve to illustrate the concept.

---

22   Some reflexive verbs can also take a direct object and thus behave as transitive verbs at the same time, eg. *ik herinnerde me hem erg goed, zij kon het zich niet veroorloven.*
Note: if a reflexive verb governs a direct object *het* (although most reflexive verbs are intransitive) the *het* precedes the reflexive pronoun:

Hij herinnerde het zich niet meer.
Ik kan het me niet veroorloven.

Compare:

Hij herinnerde zich mijn moeder niet meer.
Ik kan me geen auto veroorloven.

The reflexive pronouns are as follows:

	singular		plural	
1st person	*me* (lit. *mij*)	– myself	*ons*	– ourselves
2nd person	*je*	– yourself	*je*	– yourselves
	u }	– yourself	*u* }	– yourselves
	zich		*zich*	
3rd person	*zich*	– himself	*zich*	– themselves
		– herself		
		– itself		
		– oneself		

Example:

> *ik heb me gewassen*   *wij hebben ons gewassen*
> (I washed [myself] etc.)
> *jij hebt je gewassen*   *jullie hebben je gewassen*
> *u hebt u gewassen*   *u hebt u gewassen*
> *u heeft zich gewassen*   *u heeft zich gewassen*
> *hij heeft zich gewassen*   *zij hebben zich gewassen*
> *zij heeft zich gewassen*
> *het heeft zich gewassen*

The reflexive *u* should be used with *hebt* and *zich* with *heeft*, i.e. a second person reflexive pronoun with a second person verb and a third person reflexive pronoun with a third person verb, although this is often ignored in practice. When the subject pronoun and the reflexive are not separated by other words, there is a definite preference for *zich*: *Heeft u zich vergist?* – Were you mistaken? *Denkt u dat u zich vergist heeft?* – Do you think you were mistaken?
Notice also *Heeft u dat boek bij zich?* Have you got that book on you?

Note: All reflexive verbs are conjugated with *hebben*, unlike Romance languages. Exception: *zich rot/kapot schrikken* (to get a terrible shock/fright), eg. *Ik ben me rot geschrokken.*

11.18.1 VERBS THAT ARE ALWAYS REFLEXIVE (exemplary list only)

zich aanstellen	to show off, carry on
zich afvragen	to wonder
zich begeven	to proceed, make one's way
zich bemoeien met	to meddle with
zich bevinden	to find oneself
zich bewust zijn van	to be aware of
zich gedragen, misdragen	to behave, misbehave
zich generen	to feel embarrassed
zich haasten	to hurry
zich herinneren	to remember

zich herstellen	to recover
zich indenken	to imagine, visualize
zich inspannen	to exert oneself
zich in acht nemen voor	to be on one's guard against
zich onthouden van	to refrain from
zich realiseren	to realize
zich schamen voor	to be ashamed of
zich uitsloven	to go to trouble (for someone)
zich verbeelden	to imagine
zich verdiepen in	to go (deeply) into (a problem)
zich vergissen in	to be mistaken
zich verhangen	to hang oneself
zich verheugen op	to look forward to
zich verkijken	to make a mistake (in looking at s.t.)
zich verschrijven	to make a mistake (in writing)
zich verslapen	to sleep in (by mistake), oversleep
zich verslikken in	to choke on, swallow (wrong way)
zich voordoen	to happen, occur
zich voorstellen	to imagine

Note that some such verbs can also be used as transitive verbs (like those in 11.18.2) but then their meaning is quite different from that given here:

> *herstellen* – to repair, *herinneren* – to remind, *verdiepen* – to deepen, *voorstellen* – to introduce.

Verbs in this group are never used with *-zelf.* (see 11.8.3).

11.18.2   TRANSITIVE VERBS THAT CAN BE USED REFLEXIVELY

All the verbs in this group also occur as normal transitive verbs, eg. *hij verdedigde zich* – he defended himself, but also *het leger verdedigde de stad* – the army defended the town.
The verbs in this category are actually too numerous to list in their entirety. For instance, one would not normally call the verb *verkopen* (to sell) a reflexive verb, but there can be occasions when one wants to express 'to sell oneself' and this must be rendered by *zich verkopen.*
The following list, although very limited, will serve to illustrate:

*	*zich aankleden*	to dress (oneself), get dressed
	zich amuseren	to amuse, enjoy oneself
*	*zich bewegen*	to move
	zich bezighouden met	to busy oneself with
*	*zich ergeren*	to get irritated
*	*zich inschrijven*	to enrol
*	*zich melden*	to report (for duty, sick)
	zich noemen	to call oneself
*	*zich omdraaien*	to turn around
	zich opgeven	to give oneself up

zich opofferen voor	to sacrifice oneself for
* *zich opstapelen*	to pile up, accumulate
zich opwinden	to get excited
zich overeten	to overeat
* *zich overgeven*	to surrender
* *zich scheren*	to shave
zich snijden[23]	to cut oneself
* *zich terugtrekken*	to retreat, pull back
* *zich uitkleden*	to undress oneself, get undressed
* *zich verbazen*	to be amazed
* *zich verbergen* ⎫	
* *zich verschuilen* ⎬	to hide (oneself)
* *zich verstoppen* ⎭	
zich verdedigen	to defend oneself
* *zich verkleden*	to change one's clothes
* *zich veroorloven*	to afford[24]
* *zich vervelen*	to be bored
* *zich voelen*	to feel
zich voorbereiden op	to prepare oneself for
zich voorstellen	to introduce oneself
* *zich wassen*	to wash (oneself)
zich wegen	to weigh oneself
zich wijden aan	to devote oneself to

*   The verbs marked with an asterisk illustrate the problem involved with Dutch reflexives: in English these verbs would seldom be reflexive.

he dressed	*hij kleedde zich aan*
he turned around	*hij draaide zich om*
he remembered me	*hij herinnerde zich mij*
he hid	*hij verstopte zich*

---

23   Note the following peculiarity of *zich snijden*: if the part of the body one has cut is mentioned, it is preceded by *in* and the definite article is commonly used (see 8.2.4).

   Ik heb me in mijn/de vinger gesneden.

24   There are three ways of expressing 'to afford' (actually always expressed in English and Dutch as 'to be able to afford').

   Ik kan het me niet veroorloven.
   Ik kan het me niet permitteren.
   Ik kan het niet bekostigen. (i.e. not reflexive)

11.18.3 USE OF *ZICHZELF*

1 All verbs in group 11.18.2 (i.e. those that can also occur as transitive verbs) can on occasion use *zichzelf* instead of a simple *zich*, but only when one needs to emphasize that one washed or dressed **oneself** and not somebody else.

> *Ik kleedde Jantje aan en toen kleedde ik mezelf aan.* (stress on *zelf*)
> *Ik woog de koffers en toen mezelf.* (stress on *zelf*)
> *Zij hebben haar niet verdedigd maar alleen zichzelf.* (stress on *zelf*)

2 There is also a group of verbs that one would not normally regard as reflexive verbs but which can be used reflexively, but then always with *zichzelf*. Such verbs cause complications for the English-speaking student who is often inclined to use *zichzelf* with the other more numerous verbs that require only *zich*. All verbs requiring *zichzelf* imply an emphasis on the self.

zichzelf iets aandoen	to do something (harmful) to oneself
bij zichzelf denken	to think to oneself
zichzelf haten	to hate oneself
alleen met zichzelf rekening houden	to take only onself into account
zichzelf kennen	to know oneself
in zichzelf lachen	to laugh to oneself
over zichzelf praten	to talk about oneself
bij zichzelf zeggen	to say to oneself
zichzelf zien als	to see onseself as
zichzelf zijn	to be oneself
voor zichzelf zorgen	to care for, look after oneself

11.18.4 USE OF INDEPENDENT *ZELF*

English often uses myself, yourself etc. with verbs that would not normally be classified as reflexive verbs. In such cases the reflexive pronoun is used to emphasize who the doer of the action concerned is. In Dutch these pronouns are expressed simply by *zelf*.

> I did it myself.
> *Ik heb het zelf gedaan.*
> They painted the house themselves.
> *Zij hebben het huis zelf geverfd.*

11.18.5 USE OF INDEPENDENT *ZICH*

In sentences where the prepositional object and the subject pronouns are one and the same person, the simple reflexive pronoun is used in Dutch.

> I have no money on me.
> *Ik heb geen geld bij me.*
> He looked behind him.
> *Hij keek achter zich.*

The commanders had a lot of soldiers under them.
De commandanten hadden veel soldaten onder zich.

The expression *op zich(zelf)*, which grammatically speaking belongs in this category, is usually best translated by 'actually' or 'in fact'.

Op zich is dat niet zo erg.
Actually that's not so bad.
Het is op zich een vreemde uitdrukking.
It's a strange expression in fact.

11.18.6   USE OF *Z'N EIGEN* AS A REFLEXIVE PRONOUN

In substandard speech one often hears *m'n eigen, je eigen, z'n eigen* etc. instead of the reflexive *me, je, zich* etc. This practice, although common, is not to be copied.

Ik ben m'n eigen kapot geschrokken.
I got a terrible shock.
Jij kent je eigen niet.
You don't know yourself.

Note: Dutch, like English, uses the reciprocal pronoun *elkaar* in sentences such as the following, not the reflexive as is the case in French and German.

We hebben elkaar in de stad ontmoet.
We met each other in town.

11.19   Transitive and intransitive verbs (*overgankelijke en onovergankelijke werkwoorden*)

11.19.1   Very often difficulties arise with verbs because the distinction between transitive and intransitive is not fully understood: transitive verbs are those that can take a direct object and intransitive verbs are those that can't. Verbs that are transitive in English may not necessarily be so in Dutch. For example, if one wants to translate 'I answer the question' one will find in the dictionary under 'to answer' the words *antwoorden* and *beantwoorden*. A good dictionary will indicate that the former is intransitive and the latter transitive. The above example will thus be translated by either *ik beantwoord de vraag* or *ik antwoord op de vraag* (intransitive verbs often take prepositional objects).

It is not possible to give rules for such difficulties but the following common examples will serve to illustrate what one has to be wary of:

to burn	= *branden* (intr.)	– *het hout brandde*
	verbranden (trans.)	– *hij verbrandde het hout*
to leave	= *vertrekken* (intr.)	– *de trein vertrok om tien uur*
	verlaten (trans.)	– *de trein verliet Amsterdam om tien uur*
to taste	= *smaken* (intr.)	– *de appel smaakt goed*
	proeven (trans.)	– *proef deze appel*

11.19.2 Sometimes a verb which is both transitive and intransitive in English, but only intransitive in Dutch, is made transitive by the use of *laten* as an auxiliary (in more formal style *doen*). This is done when no separate transitive verb exists in Dutch.

to sink	= *zinken* (intr.)		– *het stuk metaal zonk*
(trans. & intr.)			the piece of metal sank
	laten zinken (intr.)		– *ik heb het laten zinken*
			I sank it
to shrink	= *krimpen* (intr.)		– *de trui is gekrompen*
(trans. & intr.)			the jumper has shrunk
	laten krimpen (trans.)		– *ik heb hem laten krimpen*
			I shrank it.
to run	= *lopen* (intr.)		– *het paard liep langs het strand*
(trans. & intr.)			the horse ran along the beach
	laten lopen (trans.)		– *ik heb het langs het strand laten lopen*
			I ran it along the beach

Such *laten* constructions are very common in Dutch (see p. 147).

11.19.3 Transitive verbs are usually conjugated with *hebben* in the perfect tenses (see p. 133 for the very few exceptions). Intransitive verbs, on the other hand, use either *hebben* or *zijn*,
eg. *hij is gestorven; het huis heeft urenlang gebrand*.

11.19.4 Intransitive verbs cannot be used in the passive as the passive is by definition a construction where the object of the active sentence becomes the subject. (see note 20, p. 51)

11.20 Impersonal verbs

Impersonal verbs are those which only occur in the third person (usually only in the singular, but some can occur in the plural too). In the third person singular the subject is always *het*. English has impersonal verbs too but Dutch has more.

11.20.1 VERBS THAT ARE IMPERSONAL IN ENGLISH AND DUTCH

1 Verbs denoting weather conditions which are used only in the third person singular:

het bliksemt	there's lightning
het dondert	it's thundering
het dooit	it's thawing
het hagelt	it's hailing
het mist	there's a fog
het onweert	there's a thunderstorm
het regent	it's raining
het schemert	it's dawning, it's twilight

het sneeuwt	it's snowing
het stormt	there's a storm
het trekt/tocht	there's a draught

2   Several other verbs that can only be used in the third person singular:

gebeuren, geschieden (lit.):
het gebeurde 's nachts   it happened at night
betreffen:
wat mij betreft,...   as far as I'm concerned,...
overkomen:
het overkwam me   it happened to me
dunken:
mij dunkt   it seems to me

11.20.2   VERBS THAT ARE IMPERSONAL IN DUTCH BUT NOT IN ENGLISH

These verbs often denote a feeling or reaction.

bevallen:
het bevalt[25] *me*   I like it
spijten:
het spijt me   I'm sorry
lukken:
het lukte me (niet)   I succeeded (didn't succeed)
zwaar vallen:
het valt me zwaar   I find it difficult
mee-, tegenvallen:
het valt[25] *me mee (tegen)*   I (don't) like it
verbazen:
het verbaast[25] *me*   I'm amazed
verheugen:
het verheugt[25] *me*   I'm pleased
verwonderen:
het verwondert[25] me   I'm surprised

These verbs are often followed by *dat* clauses.

---

25   These verbs can be used with other persons, eg. *ik beviel hem niet, jij valt me tegen etc.*, but are commonly found in the third person and in such contexts are rendered by personal constructions in English as is shown in the above examples. In addition, *bevallen*, as well as *mee-* and *tegenvallen*, takes *zijn* in the perfect.

11.21 Verbal prefixes *(werkwoordelijke voorvoegsels)*

In Dutch both separable and inseparable verbal prefixes are used to form new words. This is a very economical means of vocabulary building. In many instances there are parallel examples in English, eg. to go = *gaan*, to undergó = *ondergáan*; to look = *kijken*, to look úp = *ópkijken*. (The accents are not normally written but merely serve to indicate the stress.) Often, however, the addition of a prefix in Dutch renders a totally new word, eg. *spreken* = to speak, *tegenspreken* = to contradict; *huren* = to hire/rent, *verhuren* = to rent out; *geven* = to give, *toegeven* = to admit.

Separable verbs are recognised by the fact that the prefix bears the stress; this is not the case with inseparable verbs, eg. *vóórstellen* = to introduce, *voorspéllen* = to predict.
A verb that normally takes *hebben* in the perfect tense may, by the addition of a prefix, take on a new meaning which requires *zijn* in the same tense; the reverse is also true, eg. *staan* (to stand) takes *hebben* but *opstaan* (to get/stand up) takes *zijn*; *komen* (to come) takes *zijn* but *voorkómen* (to prevent) takes *hebben*.

11.21.1 SEPARABLE VERBS *(scheidbare werkwoorden)*

There are three sorts of separable prefixes:

1 Prepositional prefixes, many of which can also be inseparable, eg. *aan, bij, door, mee*[*26] (from *mede* = *met*), *om, onder, op*[*], *over, tegen*[*], *toe*[*26] (from *tot*), *uit*[*], *voor*.
(* those that can only be separable)

2 Nominal prefixes formed from what is actually the object of the verb but which has been used so frequently with certain verbs that the object has come to be regarded as a verbal prefix and behaves as a separable prefix, i.e. is joined to the verb in the infinitive and the past participle. It is not wrong, however, to write these prefixes separately, eg. *koffiedrinken* (to drink coffee), *haarknippen* (to cut hair), *boekbinden* (to bind books), *lesgeven* (to teach), *gelukwensen* (to congratulate), *televisiekijken* (to watch television), *schaatsenrijden* (to skate).

3 There are also many verbs whose prefix is adverbial rather than nominal, eg. *goedkeuren* (to approve), *misrekenen* (to calculate incorrectly), *samengaan* (to go along), *tegemoetkomen* (to meet, fall in with), *teleurstellen* (to disappoint), *terechtzetten* (to set straight), *thuiskomen* (to come home), *weergeven* (to return, reproduce).

Tenses of separable verbs

When a separable verb is conjugated in the **present** and **imperfect** tenses and in the **imperative** the prefix goes to the end of the clause:

meegaan (to go along) – *hij gaat/ging vanmiddag mee*
opstaan (to get up) – *sta onmiddellijk op!*

26 See p. 178

These prefixes can, however, precede prepositional adjuncts in which case they do not have to stand at the very end of the clause:

Wij gingen samen weg na afloop van het programma.

In formal writing the prefix may go to the end of the clause in such cases, but the above is more common.

In the **future** tense or after modals the infinitive stays together at the end of the clause:

Ik zal je later opbellen.
Hij moest me aan haar voorstellen.

When other verbs also stand at the end of the clause, there is a tendency (very common in speech) to split the separable verb and place the prefix before the other verbs:

Ik zou hem op kunnen bellen.
Ik begrijp niet waarom je niet vroeger op had kunnen staan.

This is often avoided in more formal written style.

The **past participle** of separable verbs is formed by inserting *ge-* between the prefix and the verbal stem, eg. *voorstellen – voorgesteld, opgraven – opgegraven*. Such compound past participles are often split (particularly in speech) just like the infinitives above:

Ik weet dat hij je op heeft gebeld.
Ik begrijp niet waarom hij niet mee is gegaan.

When the **infinitive** of a separable verb is accompanied by *te*, the *te* is placed between the prefix and the verb and the three parts are written separately, unlike German:

Hij hoopt zijn vakantie in Spanje door te brengen.
(also *door te kunnen brengen*)
Probeer vóór middernacht terug te komen.

Note: Often confusion arises between separable verbs with prepositional prefixes and verbs followed by prepositional objects,

opkijken – to look up; *kijken op* – to look at (a watch)
overschrijven – to copy; *schrijven over* – to write about
doorlopen – to continue walking; *lopen door* – to walk through

A verb like *lopen door* further complicates the issue because of the tendency for some prepositions to follow the object to which they refer in order to indicate a motion (p. 105-206): such cases as *doorlopen* and *lopen door* look and sound the same but remain semantically different:

doorlopen   ik liep gewoon door
ik ben gewoon doorgelopen

lopen door   ik liep door het bos
ik liep het bos door
ik ben door het bos gelopen
ik ben het bos door gelopen/doorgelopen

(see also p. 224)

11.21.2 INSEPARABLE VERBS (onscheidbare werkoorden)

There are three sorts of inseparable prefixes:

1 Prefixes that can only be inseparable, eg. be-, er-, ge-, her-, ont-, ver-.

2 Prepositional prefixes which can also act as separable prefixes (see p. 169), eg. aan, door, mis (actually an adverb), om, onder, over, vol (actually an adverb), voor, weer (actually an adverb).

3 There are just a few compound verbs which do not separate but which, unlike the verbs in groups 1 & 2, bear the stress:

> beeldhouwen (to sculpt), glimlachen (to smile), huisvesten (to house), knipogen (to wink), raadplegen (to consult), rangschikken (to arrange in order), stofzuigen (to vacuum clean), stroomlijnen (to streamline), voetballen (to play football), waarschuwen (to warn).

All the verbs in groups 1 & 2 are conjugated like normal verbs in all tenses, never divide, and because they already contain an unstressed prefix, no ge- (a further unstressed prefix) is added to form the past participle:

> hij herstèlde de televisie   – hij heeft de televisie herstèld
> hij voorspèlde slecht weer   – hij had slecht weer voorspèld

(The above accents should not be copied in writing; they are only to illustrate the stress.)

Verbs in group 3 do take ge-, but this does not go between the prefix and the verb as with separable verbs:

> Wij hebben de hele dag gevoetbald.

It is not always possible to isolate the meaning of these prefixes but there are a few patterns which can be described:

Meaning of the prefixes in group 1 (those in groups 2 and 3 are usually self-evident)

be- is an extremely common prefix and has a variety of functions:

a   it can be used to make the intransitive verbs that take a prepositional object transitive, sometimes with a slight change in meaning,

> antwoorden op – beantwoorden (to answer), kijken naar – bekijken (to look at), luisteren naar (to listen to) – beluisteren (to listen to), oordelen over – beoordelen (to judge, assess), spreken over (to talk about) – bespreken (to discuss).
> Also: eindigen (intr.) – beëindigen (trans.) (to finish, end).

b   sometimes the verb assumes a slightly different meaning, as is often the case in group a, but there is no question of a preposition being replaced,

> kritiseren (to criticise) – bekritiseren (= kritiek hebben op), denken (to think) – bedenken (to think of, devise, concoct), dienen (to serve God etc.) – bedienen (to

serve, attend to guests, wait upon customers), *groeten* (to greet) – *begroeten* (to receive, welcome), *rekenen* (to do sums, count) – *berekenen* (to calculate, figure out), *studeren* (to learn, study a subject) – *bestuderen* (to analyse, study a book).

c   in a few isolated cases the *be-* has no force at all and is merely a more formal form of the verb concerned

> *hoeven – behoeven* (to need + neg.),
> *horen – behoren* (to be fitting, proper).

Note: the verbs *danken/bedanken* (to thank) do not differ in meaning but do differ in usage.

> *Ik dank u, meneer.* (direct speech)
> *Zij heeft haar tante bedankt.*

er-   is of German origin and is found in only three words and it is not possible to define a meaning:

> *zich erbarmen over* (to have pity on), *erkennen* (to acknowledge, recognize), *ervaren* (to experience).
> *West-Duitsland heeft de DDR erkend.*
> West Germany has recognised the German Democratic Republic.

ge-   is not a common prefix and its meaning avoids definition:

> *geloven* (to believe), *gelijken* (to resemble), *zich gedragen* (to behave), *gebeuren* (to happen).
> *Ik heb hem niet geloofd.*
> I didn't believe him.
> *Hij heeft zich slecht gedragen.*
> He behaved disgracefully.

In the case of *gelukken* (to succeed) and *geraken* (to get, attain) the prefix is superfluous, and is usually not used. As with *behoeven* and *behoren* (see above) the forms with *ge-* sound rather formal.

her-   is very common and still productive; it is similar in meaning and function to English re- (i.e. again):

> *heradverteren* (to readvertise), *herbenoemen* (to reappoint), *herkennen* (to recog- nise), *herschrijven* (to rewrite).
> *Ik heb mijn eigen moeder niet herkend.*
> I didn't recognise my own mother. (see *er-* above)

ont-   basically means 'away' but this meaning is sometimes hard to isolate. It is a common prefix:

> *ontsnappen* (to escape), *ontkomen* (to get away), *ontstaan* (to originate), *ontploffen* (to explode), *ontmoeten* (to meet)

ver-   is the most common of all inseparable prefixes and has a variety of meanings and functions:

it commonly means 'change':

veranderen (to change), *vertalen* (to translate), *verwisselen* (to confuse), *verneder-landsen* (to 'dutchify'), *verkopen* (to sell), *verhuren* (to rent out), *verhuizen* (to move)

it also commonly means 'wrong' (in which case the verbs are usually reflexive):

zich vergissen (to make a mistake), *zich verkijken* (to look wrongly), *zich verspreken* (to make an error in speech), *zich verschrijven* (to make a mistake in writing)

it is productively prefixed to existing verbs to indicate that the object of the resulting transitive verb is wasted (always a negative connotation):

de tijd verpraten (to talk away the time), *benzine verrijden* (to use up petrol by superfluous driving), *zich verslapen* (to sleep in, oversleep)

it is used to make *branden* (to burn, intr.) a transitive verb *verbranden* (to burn, trans.):

ik heb de kist verbrand; hij brandde niet makkelijk.

Examples of verbs in group 2 with prepositional prefixes:

It is impossible to give a complete list but the following will illustrate the concept. When the same compound exists as both a separable and an inseparable verb, the meaning of the former is usually more literal than that of the latter, eg. *óndergaan* – to go down, set (of the sun), *ondergáan* – to undergo:

aanváarden	to accept	*onderbréken*	to interrupt
aanbídden	to worship	*ondernémen*	to undertake
doordénken	to consider	*overléven*	to survive
doorzóeken	to search	*overtuígen*	to convince
misbruiken	to misuse, abuse	*volbréngen*	to fulfil
zich misdrágen	to misbehave	*voldóen*	to satisfy
omhélzen	to embrace	*voorkómen*	to prevent
omschríjven	to describe	*voorspéllen*	to predict
omsíngelen	to surround	*weerspíegelen*	to reflect
omvátten	to comprise	*weerstáan*	to resist

11.22   Verbs followed by prepositional objects

Some of the verbs below will be found under more than one preposition with a difference in meaning. Many verbs are followed by the same preposition in English and are thus not always included here. Others require no preposition in English but do in Dutch, eg. *trouwen met* – to marry, *genieten van* – to enjoy, *houden van* – to love. The verbs are grouped under the Dutch prepositions they are followed by in order to give the student a feeling for the use of the prepositions in Dutch. This approach then fulfils a function the dictionary does not.

aan

(zich) aanpassen	to adapt to, assimilate	*meedoen*	to take part in
beantwoorden	to correspond with	*onderwerpen*	to subject to
behoren	to belong to	*ontkomen*	to evade (a tax etc.)
besteden	to spend on	*ontlenen*	to borrow (words from Latin etc.)
bijdragen	to contribute to	*ontsnappen*	to escape from s.o.
binden	to tie to	*(zich) onttrekken*	to withdraw from
deelnemen	to take part in	*overdragen*	to transfer to
denken	to think of	*overhandigen*	to hand over to
doen	to take part in, go in for (sport)	*overlijden*	to die from
		schrijven	to write to
doen denken	to remind s.o. of s.t.	*sterven*	to die from
zich ergeren	to be irritated by	*sturen*	to send to
geloven	to believe in (God)	*toeschrijven*	to attribute to
geven	to give to	*toevertrouwen*	to entrust to
grenzen	to border to	*toevoegen*	to add to
behoefte hebben	to be in need of	*twijfelen*	to doubt s.t.
gebrek hebben	to be short of	*vertellen*	to tell to s.o.
hechten	to believe in	*voldoen*	to satisfy (demands)
herinneren	to remind s.o. of s.t.	*voorafgaan*	to precede s.t.
zich houden	to stick to (an agreement)	*voorstellen*	to introduce to
laten zien	to show to	*wennen*	to get used to
lenen	to lend to	*zich wijden*	to devote o.s. to
leveren	to deliver to	*wijten*	to blame s.o. for s.t.
lijden	to suffer from (a disease)	*zenden*	to send to s.o.

bij

aankomen	to arrive at s.o.'s place	*passen*	to match
(be)horen	to belong together	*vergelijken*	to compare with
		wonen	to live with (i.e. at s.o.'s place)

boven

verkiezen	to prefer to

door

vervangen	to replace by

in

aankomen	to arrive at	*veranderen*	to change into
belangstellen	to be interested in	*zich verdiepen*	to go deeply into, lose o.s. (in one's work)
bijten	to bite (a part of s.o.'s body, see p. 58)	*geïnteresseerd zijn*	to be interested in
geloven	to believe in s.o.		
trek/zin hebben	to feel like	*verdelen*	to divide into
slagen	to succeed at, in	*voorzien (in een behoefte)*	to satisfy a need
zich specialiseren	to specialise in		

met (see note p. 178)

zich bemoeien	to mind (one's own business), interfere in	*overeenstemmen*	to be in keeping with
condoleren	to condole with s.o. on s.t.	*praten*	to talk to
feliciteren	to congratulate	*spotten*	to scoff at
akkoord gaan	to agree with	*spreken*	to speak to
gebeuren	to happen to	*trouwen*	to marry
gelukwensen	to congratulate on	*vergelijken*	to compare with
overeenkomen	to correspond with, agree with s.t.	*wonen*	to live with
		het eens zijn	to agree with s.o.

naar

geuren	to smell of	*stinken*	to stink of
gluren	to peep, peer at	*streven*[28]	to strive for
gooien	to throw at	*sturen*[27]	to send to
graven	to dig for	*uitkijken*	to look out for, look forward to
grijpen	to grab at		
hunkeren	to pine for	*er uitzien*	to look (like)
kijken	to look at	*uitzien*	to look forward to
luisteren	to listen to	*verlangen*	to long for
oordelen	to judge from	*vertrekken*	to leave, depart for
pikken	to pick at	*verwijzen*	to refer to
rieken	to smell of	*vissen*	to fish for
ruiken	to smell of	*vragen*	to ask for s.o.
schrijven[27]	to write to	*werpen*	to throw at
smaken	to taste of	*wijzen*	to point at
snakken	to yearn, pine for	*zenden*[27]	to send for
solliciteren	to apply for	*zoeken*	to look for (*naar* often optional)
staren	to stare at		

om

bédelen	to beg for	*smeken*	to plead for
benijden	to envy s.o. s.t.	*soebatten*	to implore, beseech for
denken	to think of, remember	*treuren*	to grieve, weep for
geven	to care about	*verzoeken*	to ask for s.t., request
huilen	to cry for, about s.t.	*vragen*	to ask for s.t.
(glim)lachen[29]	to (smile) laugh at	*wenen*	to cry, weep for

onder

lijden	to suffer under, by (eg. a regime)

27 *schrijven, sturen, zenden aan* someone, but *naar* a country. One will also hear *naar* someone.
28 compare *nastreven* (to pursue, aspire to, strive after)
29 to laugh at s.o. = *iemand uitlachen*.

op

aandringen	to insist on	*richten*	to direct at
zich abonneren	to subscribe to	*schatten*	to value at
antwoorden	to answer to (a question)	*schieten*	to shoot at
zich beroepen	to appeal to	*staan*	to insist on
berusten	to be founded, based on	*stemmen*	to vote for
drinken	to drink to	*storten*	to deposit in (an account)
duiden	to point to	*terugkomen*	to return to (a point, issue)
gokken	to bet on	*zich toeleggen*	to apply o.s. to
kritiek hebben	to be critical of	*toepassen*	to apply to
betrekking hebben	to refer to	*trakteren*	to treat to
recht hebben	to be entitled to	*zich verheugen*	to look forward to,
hopen	to hope for		rejoice at
ingaan	to go further into (a matter)	*zich verlaten*	to rely, depend on
jagen	to hunt (after)	*veroveren*	to conquer, capture from
kijken	to look at (a watch, clock)	*vertrouwen*	to rely, depend on
komen	to hit upon, think of	*vestigen*	to fix upon
	(a name etc.)	*vissen*	to fish for
lijken	to look like	*volgen*	to follow after, on
letten	to pay attention to	*zich voorbereiden*	to prepare for
loeren	to lie in wait for	*vuren*	to fire at
attent maken	to draw one's attention to	*vliegen*	to fly to (a country) [30]
mikken	to aim at	*wachten*	to wait for
neerkomen	to boil down to	*wedden*	to bet on
passen	to look after	*wijzen*	to point to, out
reageren	to react to	*ja zeggen*	to say yes to
rekenen	to rely on	*zinspelen*	to allude to, hint at

over

beschikken	to have at one's disposal	*oordelen*	to judge
beslissen	to decide on	*prakkezeren*	to think of
zich ergeren	to get irritated at	(coll.)	
huilen	to cry about	*roddelen*	to gossip about
klagen	to complain about	*zich schamen*	to be ashamed of
peinzen	to think about, ponder on	*schrijven*	to write about
praten	to talk about	*spreken*	to speak, talk about
zich druk maken	to get excited, make a	*zich verheugen*	to rejoice at
	fuss about	*vertellen*	to tell about
mopperen	to grumble about	*wenen*	to cry about
nadenken	to think about		

tegen

blaffen	to bark at	*spreken*	to speak to
glimlachen	to smile at	*zich verzetten*	to risist
knikken	to nod at	*vloeken*	to swear at
opzien	to look up to s.o., dread s.t.	*zeggen*	to say to
ruilen	to exchange for		

30 *De KLM vliegt op Australië* – KLM flies to (= serves) Australia.

tot (see note p. 178)

aansporen	to incite, urge to	*aanleiding geven*	to give cause for
aanzetten	to incite, urge to	*kiezen*	to choose for, as
behoren	to belong to, be part of	*leiden*	to lead to
bekeren	to convert to	*zich richten*	to apply to
zich beperken	to limit o.s. to	*toelaten*	to admit to (university)
besluiten	to decide on	*veroordelen*	to condemn to
bidden	to pray	*zich verplichten*	to commit o.s. to
bijdragen	to contribute to	*zich wenden*	to turn to s.o.

uit

afleiden	to infer from	*opmaken*	to gather, conclude from
bestaan	to consist		
concluderen	to conclude, infer from	*verbannen*	to banish from
dateren	to date from	*vertalen*	to translate from
drinken	to drink from (a glass)	*voortvloeien*	to result from
komen	to come from (a country, town)		
ontstaan	to arise, spring from		

van

afhangen	to depend on	*ontsnappen*	to escape form
afstammen	to be descended from	*overtuigen*	to convince of
balen	to be fed up with	*schrikken*	to be shocked by
barsten	to burst with	*stikken*	to suffocate from, swarm with
beroven	to deprive of		
beven	to tremble with	*veranderen*	to change (one's opinion, intention)
bevrijden	to liberate, free from		
blozen	to blush with	*verdenken*	to suspect of
genieten	to enjoy	*verliezen*	to lose to s.o.
houden	to like	*verschillen*	to differ from
huilen	to cry with	*voorzien*	to supply with
krioelen	to swarm, teem with	*wemelen*	to swarm, teem with
leven	live on	*weten*	to know of

voor

behoeden	to guard, protect from	*zich in acht nemen*	to be on one's guard against
bezwijken	to succumb, yield to (the enemy)	*oppassen*	to look out for
danken	thank for	*slagen*	to pass (an exam)
doorgaan	to pass for	*zich uitgeven*	to pass off for, as
gelden	to count for, be valid for	*verslijten*	to take s.o. for
belangstelling hebben	to be interested in	*vrezen*	to be afraid of
		waarschuwen	to warn against
zich hoeden	to beware of, guard against	*wijken*	to give way/yield to
zich interesseren	to be interested in	*zakken*	to fail (an exam)
in aanmerking komen	to be considered for	*bang zijn*	to be afraid of
		zorgen	to take care of, look after

Note on *met/mee, tot/toe:*

When verbs followed by *met* or *tot* govern a noun or pronominal object there is no complication

Ik heb jouw moeder met de mijne vergeleken.
De vakbond heeft de mannen tot staken aangezet.

When the noun or pronoun is replaced by a pronominal *er, hier* or *daar* (see p. 54, 222) or the relative *waar* (see p. 61) the alternative forms *mee* and *toe* must be used.

Ik heb ze daarmee vergeleken.
Zij hebben ze ertoe aangespoord.
De pen waar ik de brief mee schreef, is leeg.

Note on verbs with prepositional objects which are transitive in English. A few Dutch verbs are followed by a preposition where English requires none, eg.

bijten in – De hond heeft hem in zijn been gebeten (see p. 58)/The dog bit his leg.
klappen in – Ze klapten in hun handen/They clapped their hands.
lezen in – Hij zit (in) een boek te lezen (optional)/He's reading a book.
rijden in – Heb je ooit in een Mercedes gereden?/Have you ever driven a Mercedes?
snijden in – Ik heb me in mijn vinger gesneden (see p. 58)/I've cut my finger.
trouwen met – De filmster trouwde met de prins/The filmstar married the prince.

12 Conjunctions *(voegwoorden)*

The distinction between conjunctions and certain sorts of adverbs is sometimes difficult to make. This section deals thus with those words, whether they be classed as conjunctions or adverbs, that join two or more clauses in a sentence.

12.1 Co-ordinating conjunctions *(nevenschikkende voegwoorden)*

The main distinguishing feature of a co-ordinating conjunction in Dutch is that it does not have any effect on the word order of the following clause.

en[1]	– and
want[2]	– for, because
of[3]	– or
maar	– but
doch (lit.)[5]	– but, nevertheless
dus[4]	– thus, therefore
alleen (lit.)[5]	– only, but

Ik ben zeer arm **maar** *ik heb toch een auto.*
Kom je vandaag **of** *kom je morgen?*
Hij heeft het beloofd **doch** *hij heeft het niet gedaan.*

Notes

1 Note that the following English conjunctional constructions with 'and' are avoided in Dutch.

We went and sat down.
We gingen zitten.
They then went and sang a song together.
Ze gingen toen samen een liedje zingen.
He is sitting outside (and) reading a book.
Hij zit buiten een boek te lezen.

2 The conjunction 'for' is rather formal in English and is usually replaced by 'because'; in Dutch the reverse is the case, however. A sentence such as 'he dropped the cup because it was hot' would usually be rendered as *hij liet het kopje vallen want het was heet,* although *omdat* plus subordinate word order would be quite correct too. Note that just as not all English 'becauses' can be 'for', so in Dutch not all *omdat's* can be *want,* i.e. when a compound sentence begins with the subordinate clause, then 'because'/*omdat* must be used.

Because I felt ill I left the room.
Omdat ik me misselijk voelde, verliet ik de kamer.

3 In more emphatic speech or writing *of* is often replaced by *ofwel* particularly with the meaning 'or...either'.
eg. *Hij gaat morgen terug, ofwel overmorgen.*
The co-ordinating conjunction *of* is commonly found after negative clauses in which case it can be translated in various ways into English.

> *Het scheelde niet veel of hij was overreden.*
> He was very nearly run over.
> *Nauwelijks was ik thuis of ik moest weer weg.*
> I was hardly home when I had to leave again.
> *Het duurde niet lang of ze stopten vóór een groot ijzeren hek.*
> It wasn't long before they stopped in front of a large iron gate.

In addition, *of* is used idiomatically in the following expressions to render 'approximately':
een stuk of tien	about ten (pieces, books, apples, etc.)
een man of acht	about eight people
om een uur of acht	at about eight o'clock

Note the expression *nou en of:*
Kun je lekker koffie zetten? Nou en of!
I certainly can/And how!
Het heeft veel geregend, niet waar? Nou en of!
It certainly has/And how!

Of can also be a subordinating conjunction with a further set of complex meanings (see p. 182).

4 *Dus* can act as an ordinary co-ordinating conjunction not affecting word order, but can also cause inversion, in which case it acts as an adverbial conjunction.
Ruud bleef thuis dus Karel ging ook niet uit. (co-ordinating)
Ruud bleef thuis dus ging Karel ook niet uit. (adverbial)

Note, however, when *dus* is preceded by *en*, only the adverbial construction is possible.
eg. *Ruud bleef thuis en dus ging Karel ook niet uit.*

5 The co-ordinating conjunctions *doch* and *alleen* are usually replaced by the adverbial conjunctions *toch* and *alleen* in the spoken language (see p. 187).

12.2 Subordinating conjunctions *(onderschikkende voegwoorden)*

There is a large number of such conjunctions, most of which are listed below. The distinguishing feature of these is that the verb of the dependent clause is sent to the end of that clause.
The following pitfalls with subordinating conjunctions should be noted.

Beware of the word order when a subordinating conjunction governs two subordinate clauses which are joined by a co-ordinating conjunction.

I stayed home because I was sick and (because I) didn't want to go to the fair.
Ik bleef thuis, omdat ik ziek was en (omdat ik) niet naar de kermis wilde gaan.
How glad she was when she heard his voice and (when she) saw his face.
Wat was ze blij, toen ze zijn stem hoorde en (toen ze) zijn gezicht zag.
Our friends had told us (that) it was a very interesting place and (that) we could easily spend a few days there.
Onze kennissen hadden ons verteld, dat het een zeer interessante plaats was en (dat) we er makkelijk een paar dagen zouden kunnen doorbrengen.

When a co-ordinating conjunction is followed by a subordinating conjunction, the subordinating one governs the word order of the following clause, but not that of the co-ordinate clause; the subject and verb of the following co-ordinate clause invert because the subordinate clause takes on the role of first idea.

Ik blijf thuis en omdat ik me misselijk voel, ga ik naar bed.

Sometimes a subordinate clause can be inserted into another, in which case one must remember to put the verb of the interrupted clause to the end when one returns to it.

Ik vind ook dat als je een andere taal leert, je gewoonlijk je eigen taal beter kunt begrijpen.

dat[1]	that
voordat, voor[2]	before (see also p. 189)
eerdat, eer (lit.)	before
nadat, na[2]	after (see also p. 189)
totdat, tot	until
omdat[3]	because, as, since*
zodat[4]	so that (result)
opdat[4]	so that (purpose)
doordat	by, because (see also p. 189)
mede doordat	also because
in plaats van dat	instead of (see also p. 189)
zonder dat	without (see also p. 189)
behalve dat	except that
zodanig dat	such that
vandaar dat	for that reason, thus
alsmede dat	as well as (the fact that)
inzover(re) dat	to the extent that
zoals[8]	(just) as
alsof[9]	as if

* Where 'as' or 'since' (see *daar*) mean 'because' they should be translated by *omdat*, eg. As he feels sick, he's staying at home.

als [2, 5, 6, 8, 9]	when, if
wanneer [2, 6]	when, whenever
toen [6]	when
indien (lit.) [5]	if
daar (lit.)	since, because
aangezien	since, because, seeing
terwijl [7]	while, whereas
ofschoon (lit.)	although
schoon (lit.)	
(al)hoewel	
sinds	since (temporal)
sedert	
nu	now that
zodra (coll. also *zo gauw*)	as soon as
zolang	as long as
(voor)zover	as far as
gelijk (lit.)	just as (= *net zoals*)
evenals	
evenmin als	just as little as, no more than
tenzij	unless
mits	provided that
vermits (lit.)	whereas, since
of [9]	whether
of dat [9]	or whether
onverschillig of	regardless of whether
naar [10]	as
naarmate	as
naar gelang	as
niettegenstaande	notwithstanding that
ingeval	in case, in the event (that)

The following is a list of commonly used phrases/clauses that introduce subordinate clauses:

daar staat tegenover dat	on the other hand
stel/veronderstel/gesteld (lit.) *dat*	let's say/assume (that)
tegen de tijd dat	by the time (that)
dat neemt niet weg dat	that does not alter the fact that
dat wil (niet) zeggen dat	that means (doesn't mean) that
dat maakt dat	that means that, has as a result that
gezien het feit dat	as, in the light of the fact that
ondanks het feit dat	in spite of the fact that
voor het geval dat	in case
daar komt (nog) bij dat	in addition
laat staan dat/als/wanneer	let alone that/if/when
't toeval wilde dat	chance would have it that
met dien verstande dat	on the understanding that
het ziet ernaar uit dat/alsof	it looks as if

Notes

1 *dat*

Note that **'that'** is often omitted in English but never in Dutch.

> He said he would come – *Hij zei dat hij komen zou.*
> The first time she said it – *De eerste keer dat ze het zei.*

In uncultivated speech a superfluous *dat* is sometimes used after other subordinate conjunctions and interrogative adverbs in indirect questions

> *Ik weet niet waar dat ze wonen* – I don't know where they live.
> *Nu dat ik rijk ben,...* – Now (that) I am rich,...

It is, for example, very common after *naarmate, naar gelang* and *niettegenstaande.*

A rather idiomatic usage of *dat* is the following:

> *Een stank dat er was!* – There was a terrible smell!
> *En eten dat hij kan!* – How he can eat!

Note also the use of *dat* in the following instances where it could be confused with the relative pronoun:

> *De tweede keer dat hij kwam.*
> The second time he came.
> *Dit is een pot uit de tijd dat er hier nog geen blanken leefden.*
> This is a pot from the time that/before there weren't any whites living here.

2 The conjunctions *voordat* and *nadat* are commonly preceded by *kort* (shortly before/after), *daags* (the day before/after) and *lang* (long before/after).

Wanneer and *als* (meaning 'when') are commonly preceded by *pas* (only when, not untill, see p. 228), *zelfs* (even when) and *vooral* (especially when).

3 For substitution of *omdat* with *want* see p. 179.

4 In colloquial Dutch the subtle distinction between *zodat* and *opdat* is often ignored and *zodat* is used in both senses.

> *Het heeft de hele dag geregend zodat we niet uit konden gaan.* (with the result that)
> *De regering heeft het bedrag van de steun verhoogd opdat de armsten geen honger zullen lijden.* (with the purpose that)

5 As in English, *als/indien* (if) in conditional sentences can be omitted in higher style and the clause can begin with the verb; the main clause is then always introduced by *dan*.

> Had he come, we could have done it/If he had come, we could have done it.
> *Was hij gekomen, dan hadden wij het kunnen doen/Als hij gekomen was, hadden wij het kunnen doen.*

Should war come, then we'll leave Germany/If war comes, we'll leave Germany.
Komt er oorlog, dan zullen we Duitsland verlaten/Als er oorlog komt, zullen we Duitsland verlaten. (see *mogen* on p. 140).

Note: The following syntactical device can occur in higher style where the conjunctionless 'if' clause comes second:

Holidays have to be exceptional if they want to appear in that brochure.
Vakanties moeten uitzonderlijk zijn, willen ze in die brochure staan.

6   The translation of English 'when' into Dutch is a complex issue. There are three words: *wanneer, als, toen.*

Wanneer is always used in interrogative clauses both direct and indirect.

Wanneer komt hij thuis? Ik weet niet wanneer hij thuiskomt.

It is also used to translate 'when' in subordinate clauses when the verb is in the present, future or perfect tense. In this case it can be replaced by *als.*

Wanneer (als) het regent, wil ik thuis blijven.

It can only be used in a clause with the verb in the imperfect or pluperfect when it means 'whenever', otherwise *toen* is used (see below). This *wanneer* can also be replaced by *als.*

Wanneer (als) hij thuiskwam was ik altijd boos op hem.

Als, apart from replacing *wanneer* in instances such as the above, also renders 'if' (not the 'if' which means 'whether', see *of*), in which case an ambiguity can arise.

Als het regent, wil ik thuis blijven.
When/if it rains,...

See 9 below for *als* as an abbreviation of *alsof*. See Prepositions for *als* as a preposition (p. 193).

Toen replaces *wanneer/als* when the verb is in the imperfect or the pluperfect, i.e. when the meaning is 'when on one occasion'. *Wanneer/als* are, however, used when the verb is in the imperfect and the meaning is 'whenever', i.e. 'when on repeated occasions'.

Toen hij thuiskwam, was ik al weg.

Compare: *Wanneer (als) hij thuiskwam, was ik altijd al weg.*
Ik heb de brief meteen gepost toen ik hem geschreven had.

Note: There is also an adverb *toen* (then) which should not be confused with the conjunction *toen* (when). (see p. 100)

Toen ging hij weg.   He then left.
Toen hij wegging,...   When he left,...

7   *Terwijl* often helps one out of certain difficult English verbal -ing constructions. (see p. 159)

Walking around in town I bumped into him.
Terwijl ik in de stad rondliep, ben ik hem tegengekomen.

8 *Als* as a subordinating conjunction has a variety of meanings:

'when, whenever' (see note 6 above)

'if', in which case it can be omitted (see notes 5 and 6 above)

'as long as', in which case it replaces *zolang*.

> *Het kan me niet schelen hoe, als je het maar doet.*
> I don't care how, so long as you do it.

'as', in which case it can be confused with *zoals* – not a common usage.

> *Als volgt* – As follows.

'than', used after comparatives (often followed by simple nouns and pronouns rather than clauses). In this sense it is considered rather colloquial and should be replaced by *dan*.

> *Hij is groter als (dan) ik.*
> *Hij deed het beter als (dan) ik het had kunnen doen.*

Als also can be used as an adverbial conjunction replacing the subordinating conjunction *alsof*.

> *Hij deed als hoorde hij me niet.*
> He pretended he didn't hear me.
> (*doen alsof* renders 'to pretend')
> *Ze renden als vreesden zij voor hun leven.*
> They were running as if they were afraid for their lives.

alsof – als – as if.

de vrees – fear.

vrezen – to fear.

Also:

> *Toen lachte hij als om zich te verontschuldigen.*
> Then he laughed as if to apologise.

Als can also be a preposition meaning 'as':

> *Als kind werkte ik in een goudmijn.*
> As a child I worked in a gold mine.
> *Ik gebruikte het als asbak.*
> I used it as an ashtray.
> *Zich gedragen als een heer.*
> To behave as (like) a gentleman.
> *Iemand erkennen als koning.*
> To recognize someone as king.

Zoals can only be used as a subordinating conjunction whereas *als* has both adverbial and prepositional functions in addition to that of a conjunction.

(such) as, in such a way as

> *Hij zong zoals hij nog nooit gezongen heeft.*
> He sang (such) as he has never sung before.

as

Zoals je weet, ga ik ook mee.
As you know, I'm going too.
Net zoals ik gezegd heb,...
Just as I said,...

'as, like'

Je moet doen zoals wij.
You should do as (like) we (do).
Hij heeft al zijn geld in de oorlog verloren zoals zoveel anderen.
He lost all his money in the war like so many others.

9   *Alsof* – as if

Very often the *als* is dropped and *of* maintains the full meaning of 'as if'. (see note p. 224)

Het ziet er naar uit of het gaat regenen.
It looks as if it is going to rain.

Somewhat less common is just *als* meaning *alsof* but in this case *als* acts as an adverbial conjunction.

Hij deed als hoorde hij het niet.
He pretended (acted as if) he didn't hear it.

Of as a subordinating conjunction can mean:

whether (note that 'or whether' is *of dat* to avoid a double *of*)

'as if', in which case it replaces *alsof* (see above)

It is often used superfluously after interrogative adverbs and pronouns in indirect questions (see p. 190) in much the same way as *dat* is sometimes used (see p. 183, 190). This practice should not be copied.

Ik weet niet wat of ze kan doen.
I don't know what she can do.

Note the following example which contains both a superfluous *of* and *dat*: *ik weet niet wie of dat er zal komen* – I don't know who will come.
For further uses of *of* see the footnote to *of* as a co-ordinating conjunction.

10   *Naar* is only found in higher style and usually in set expressions.

Naar ik meen.
As I believe.
Duidelijk is het, naar ik meen, dat het een mengtaal is.
It is clear, I believe, that it is a mixed language.
Naar men zegt.
It is said.
Naar verluidt.
It is rumoured.

12.3 Adverbial conjunctions

Grammatically speaking these words are adverbs but they often function as conjunctions introducing clauses. Their adverbial qualities are, however, obvious from the word order which follows, i.e. inversion of subject and verb so that the verb remains the second idea (the adverb being the first).

alleen [1]	only
dus [1]	thus, hence, for that reason
daarom	thus, hence, for that reason
vandaar	thus, hence, for that reason
daarvandaan	thus, hence, for that reason
toch	nevertheless, but, however
al [2]	even if
ook al	even if
als [3]	as if
anders	otherwise
desondanks	in spite of it/that
intussen	meantime, -while
inmiddels	meantime, -while
integendeel	on the contrary
dan [4]	then

Examples:

Al *had hij het gedaan, ik had er toch niets van gehoord.* (note the word order)
Hij zag eruit **als** *had hij dagenlang niet geslapen.*
Hij heeft het beloofd, **toch** *heeft hij het niet gedaan.* (compare p. 180)

Notes
1 *Alleen* and *dus* can also be co-ordinating (see p. 179)
2 *Al* in this sense is synonymous with *zelfs als* which is subordinating.
3 *Als* here is the same as *alsof* which is subordinating (see p. 185)
4 This *dan* is used after particular *als* clauses with the conditional tense. (see p. 183)

12.4 Correlative conjunctions

Correlative conjunctions are couplets of conjunctions that correlate two clauses of a sentence, i.e. each clause begins with a conjunction that forms a sense pair with the other. They can be classified as follows:

1 those that act as co-ordinating conjunctions in both parts if the sentence
2 those that act as adverbial conjunctions in both parts of the sentence
3 a few that don't fit into groups 1 or 2

12.4.1 CO-ORDINATING CORRELATIVE CONJUNCTIONS

hetzij... of	either... or
(óf)... óf	
(noch)... noch[1]	neither... nor
zowel... als (ook[2]*)*	both... and
(èn)... èn	both... and (less common)
niet alleen... maar ook[3]	not only... but also

Hij komt hetzij morgen of hij komt niet.
(Of) je doet het goed, óf je doet het helemaal niet.
Zowel de hoogleraar als(ook[2]*) de student heeft het boek gelezen.*
(En) de leraar èn de leerlingen mogen gratis naar binnen.
Niet alleen de leraar heeft het boek gelezen maar ook de student.[3]

Notes
1 *Noch...noch*

Noch mijn broer noch mijn vriend kon me helpen.
Ik heb noch gegeten noch gedronken.

When only one *noch* is used the verb is usually in the plural because it resembles *en* in meaning.

Mijn broer noch mijn vriend konden me helpen.

An English construction such as 'He may not stay here nor may he go home' is simplified in Dutch to *Hij mag niet hier blijven en hij mag ook niet naar huis.* (*ook niet* = not either)

2 Inclusion of *ook* is considered rather archaic these days.

3 See also p. 189.

Niet alleen heeft hij het boek al gelezen maar hij heeft het al teruggegeven.

12.4.2 ADVERBIAL CORRELATIVE CONJUNCTIONS

In this case the finite verb in each part of the sentence follows the conjunction.

nu...dan	one moment...the next
nu eens...dan weer	
de ene keer...de andere keer	
enerzijds...anderzijds	on the one hand...on the other
aan de ene kant...aan de andere kant	
deels...deels	partly...partly
ten dele...ten dele	
gedeeltelijk...gedeeltelijk	

Nu zie je het wel, dan zie je het niet.
Enerzijds wil hij werken, anderzijds wil hij nog blijven studeren.

12.4.3 There are four correlative conjunctions that are at odds with the patterns described in groups 1 and 2.

Notes
1 *nauwelijks...of*   scarcely/hardly...when

The first half acts as an adverb, the second as a co-ordinating conjunction. This rather idiomatic use of co-ordinating *of* has other parallels (see p. 180).

    Nauwelijks was ik thuis of mijn vader belde me op.

2 *niet alleen...maar ook*   not only...but

As with 1, the first half acts as an adverb, the second as a co-ordinating conjunction. There is, however, also a similar co-ordinating correlative conjunction (see p. 188).

    Niet alleen heeft hij het boek verloren maar hij heeft me er ook niet voor betaald.

3 *hoe...des te*   the...the
  hoe...hoe

Although synonymous, these two correlative couplets require a different word order:

hoe...des te (sub.conj. + adv.conj.)
hoe...hoe   (sub.conj. + sub.conj.)

    Hoe meer je studeert des te meer zul je weten.
    Hoe meer je studeert hoe meer je weten zult.

12.5 Conjunctions introducing infinitive clauses

Infinitive clauses contain no finite verb but rather an infinitive preceded by *te*; at the beginning of the clause stands one of the following conjunctions. Only the word *teneinde* is used exclusively as a conjunction in infinitive clauses; all the other words have other functions as well.

om[1]	in order to (see p. 148)
teneinde (lit.)	in order to
alvorens[2] (lit.)	before
na[2]	after
door[3]	by
in plaats van[4]	instead of
zonder	without
van	from

    Hij ging naar huis om zijn fiets te halen.
    He went home (in order) to fetch his bike.

Teneinde moeilijkheden te voorkomen wordt men vriendelijk verzocht dieren buiten te laten.
(In order) to avoid difficulties, you are kindly requested to leave animals outside.
Door dat te doen bereik je niets.
By doing that, you will accomplish nothing.
Na urenlang gewerkt te hebben, ben ik naar de bioscoop gegaan.
After having worked for hours I went to the cinema.
Men wordt vriendelijk verzocht zijn sigaret te doven alvorens de bioscoop in te gaan.
Your are kindly requested to extinguish your cigarette before entering the cinema.

Notes

For use of *te* with or without *om* see p. 145, 148.

2   *Alvorens* (also a very formal subordinating conjunction) and *na* + infinitive clause can always be replaced by *voordat* and *nadat* + subordinate clause, as in English.

Nadat ik urenlang gewerkt had, ging ik naar de bioscoop.
After I had worked for hours, I went to the cinema.

3   *Door* is replaced colloquially by *met.*

Met van een ladder te vallen, kun je je been breken.

4   *In plaats van* and *zonder* differ in usage from *in plaats van dat* and *zonder dat*: when the subject of both clauses is the same, the infinitive clause construction must be used; when the subjects are different, however, the appropriate subordinating conjunction must be used.

Hij ging weg zonder een woord te zeggen.
Hij kwam binnen zonder dat ik hem zag.

In plaats van op te staan, bleef hij zitten.
Ik moet het alleen doen in plaats van dat mijn broer me helpt.

12.6   Interrogative adverbs and pronouns introducing indirect questions

Although these words are not strictly speaking conjunctions, they function nevertheless as subordinating conjunctions (see p. 69, 103).

wat	what
wanneer	when
waarom	why
wie	who
welk(e)	which
hoe	how
hoeveel	how much
in hoever(re)	to what extent
waar	where

waar...heen	where...to
waar...vandaan	where...from
waar + prep.	(see Relative pronouns, p. 61)

Question: *Wat heeft hij in zijn hand?*
Answer: *Ik weet niet wat hij in zijn hand heeft.*
Question: *Waar komt ze vandaan?*
Answer: *Ik weet niet waar ze vandaan komt.*
Question: *Welke boeken hebben ze gelezen?*
Hij vroeg welke boeken ze gelezen hadden.
Ik weet niet in hoeverre dat mogelijk zal zijn.

Note: Often a superfluous subordinating *of* or *dat* is used after these words in colloquial speech. The practice should be avoided. (see also p. 183, 186)

Ik vroeg me af hoe of ze dat had kunnen doen.
Ik weet niet waar of ze de bruiloft willen houden.
Kun je me zeggen waar dat hij woont?

The same words are used as subordinating conjunctions in combination with *ook* to express 'whoever', 'wherever' etc. (see p. 67)

wie... ook	whoever
waar... ook	wherever
wat... ook	whatever
hoe... ook	however [1]
welk(e)... ook	whichever

Wie het ook gedaan heeft, het kan me niet schelen. (Note the word order in the second clause:)

Het zal hem goed gaan waar hij ook woont.
Welk boekje ook maar leest, is goed.

In addition to the above one will hear *wie dan ook, waar dan ook* etc. Such expressions must not be confused with the interrogative conjunctions. They are used as follows:

Hij kan het beter dan wie (dan) ook.
He can do it better than anyone.
Hoe dan ook ga ik er eentje vinden.
Somehow I am going to find one.
Hij moet ergens wonen, waar dan ook.
He has to live somewhere, anywhere.
(wherever it may be)

---

1 Note that the English adverb 'however' is *echter.*

Hij heeft het echter niet kunnen doen.
He wasn't able to do it, however.

13   Prepositions *(voorzetsels/preposities)*

Because prepositions are the most idiomatic part of speech, each with a vast number of meanings in many cases, the following list can only serve as a guide to the usage of Dutch prepositions. To have listed English prepositions with their various translations into Dutch would have been unwieldy and the student would have been prevented from getting a feeling for the nuances of Dutch prepositions. By doing the reverse it is hoped a certain pattern in the usage of individual Dutch prepositions will emerge and facilitate the learning of them. It will be noted that they are often used as adverbs too. Only the most usual of basic meanings of each preposition in English are given next to the Dutch form.

à – to, at

drie à vier weken	three to four weeks
à 5%	at five percent
à f. 10 per stuk	at ten guilders each

aan – on, at

This preposition is often confused by English speakers with *op*. In as far as its meaning can be defined at all, one can say that a vertical 'on' is rendered by *aan* (a horizontal 'on' by *op*, however) and 'on' or 'at' the edge of things is also *aan*.

het schilderij aan de muur	the picture on the wall
aan het plafond	on the ceiling
geen ster aan de hemel	no star in the sky
iemand aan de deur	somebody at the door
een klop aan (op) de deur	a knock at the door
aan de kust	on the coast
aan zee (compare *op*)	at the seaside
aan het strand (compare *op*)	at the beach
aan land gaan	to go on land
aan tafel (compare *op*)	at the table
aan de Rijn	on the Rhine
mijn huis staat aan (op) een gracht	my house is on a canal
aan de linkerkant	on the left-hand side
aan de telefoon	on the telephone
jij bent aan de beurt	it is your turn
aan het begin/einde	at the beginning/end
ik ben hard aan het werk	I am hard at work
aan de universiteit (compare *op*)	at the university (i.e. studying there)
wat had zij voor kleren aan?	what sort of clothes did she have on?

ik heb een gouden ring aan (see *om*)	I have a golden ring on
de lamp/het fornuis is aan	the light/stove is on
blind aan een oog	blind in one eye
doof aan een oor	deaf in one ear
een gebrek aan	a lack of
een behoefte aan	a need for
ze weten niet wat ze aan je hebben	they don't know what you're worth
hoeveel heb je aan belasting betaald?	what did you pay in tax?
f 2000 aan sieraden	f 2000 in jewels
ik herkende hem aan (door) zijn stem	I recognised him by his voice
verbeteringen aan het huis	improvements to the house
ik kan er niets aan doen	I can do nothing about it
ik heb er niets aan	it's useless to me
een bezoek aan Duitsland	a visit to Germany

achter – behind, after

achter het huis	behind the house
hij zit de hele dag achter zijn bureau	he sits at his desk all day
ik heb het volk achter me	I have the people behind me
de deur achter zich sluiten	to close the door behind one
mijn horloge loopt achter	my watch is slow
schrijf M.A. achter je naam	write M.A. after your name
tien achter elkaar	ten in a row

afgezien van – apart from, except for

afgezien daarvan	apart from that
afgezien van mijn broer	apart from my brother

aldus – according to (see *volgens*)

Found in journalese and formal style. It can only be followed by a noun or name; if a clause follows the noun, *volgens* is used.

..., aldus de minister-president	according to the prime-minister the prime minister said

als – as (see Conjunctions, p. 185)

Note that the indefinite article is often not used after *als*

als kind	as a child
ik wil het als asbak gebruiken	I want to use it as an ashtray
zich gedragen als een dame	to behave like a lady

behalve – except (for)

wie gaat behalve ik (subj. pronoun)	who is going apart from me
wie zag je behalve hem (obj. pron.)	whom did you see apart from him
behalve in de zomer	except (for) in summer
behalve mijn moeder gaat ook mijn oma	as well as my mother my grandma is going too

beneden – beneath, under

beneden mijn waardigheid	beneath my dignity
dat is beneden me	that is beneath me
beneden de Moerdijk	south of the Moerdijk
beneden de veertig	under forty

bij – by, near, at

Often preceded by *vlak/dicht* to render English 'near'. (see p. 89)

vlak bij het stadhuis	near the town hall
bij het postkantoor	near the post-office
ik woon bij (aan) het water	I live near the water
hij heeft geen geld bij zich	he has no money on him
ik woon bij mijn tante	I live at my aunt's/with my aunt
ik kom zo bij u	I'll be with you in a moment
wij horen bij elkaar	we are/belong together
iemand bij zijn naam roepen	to call someone by name
iemand bij de hand nemen	to take someone by the hand
bij de tandarts, groenteboer	at the dentist's, greengrocer's
ik heb het bij V en D gekocht	I bought it at V & D (a shop)
bij mooi weer	when the weather is nice
bij een oostelijke wind	when an easterly is blowing
bij honderden	by the hundreds
twee bij drie meter	two by three metres
de slag bij Waterloo	the Battle of Waterloo
bij het ontbijt	at breakfast
wenst u een koekje bij de koffie?	do you want a biscuit with your coffee?
doe een kaartje bij de bloemen	put a card in with the flowers
les nemen bij iemand	to have lessons from someone
bij uitstek	par excellence
examen doen bij iemand	to do an exam for someone (i.e. a particular teacher)
ik heb het bij Dickens gelezen	I read it in Dickens
ik ben bij Tiel-Utrecht verzekerd	I'm insured with Tiel-Utrecht
bij een firma werken	to work for a firm
bij een bezoek aan het museum	on a visit to the museum
bij nader inzien	on closer examination
bij zichzelf denken	to think to oneself
bij het raam/vuur zitten	to sit by the window/fire
bij de volgende halte uitstappen	to get at the next stop

binnen – within, in(side)

binnen het huis	inside the house
binnen een week	within a week
binnen het bestek van dit boek	within the scope of this book

boven – above, over

boven de waterspiegel	above water level
je vliegt urenlang boven Australië	you fly over Australia for hours
het ging boven mijn pet	it was above my head, beyond me
Zaandam ligt boven Amsterdam	Z'dam is north of A'dam
hij is boven de 50	he's over fifty
ik geef de voorkeur aan een VW boven alle andere auto's	I prefer a VW to all other cars

buiten – out of, beyond

buiten de stad	out of town
buiten gevaar	out of danger
buiten beschouwing laten	to leave out of consideration
buiten mijn competentie	beyond my competence
ik kan niet buiten hem (see *zonder*)	I can't do without him
buiten haar bestond er niets voor hem (see *behalve*)	apart from her nothing existed for him

dank zij – thanks to

dank zij jou	thanks to you
dank zij het mooie weer	thanks to the nice weather

door – through, by (see also p. 151)

door heel Nederland	throughout Holland
door de week	during the week
hij liep (dwars) door het bos	he walked (right) through the forest
door (een) rood licht (heen) rijden	to drive through a red light
het is door haar geschreven	it was written by her
ik heb hem door Anneke leren kennen	I got to know him through Anneke
door en door stom	very stupid
door en door een dame	a real lady

gedurende – during (see *tijdens*, a synonym)

gedurende het weekeinde	during the weekend
hij was gedurende 3 weken ziek (formal)	he was sick for 3 weeks

in – in, into

hij zit in zijn auto	he is in his car
ben je ooit in Engeland geweest?	have you ever been to England?
in het Nederlands etc.	in Dutch etc.
vertaal dit in het Frans	translate this into French
in het algemeen (see *over*)	in general, generally
5 meter in de breedte	five metres wide
in de bus, tram, trein	on the bus, tram, train

hij zit in een boek te lezen	he's reading a book
hij heeft zich in de vinger gesneden	he cut his finger
de slang heeft in zijn been gebeten	the snake bit his leg
in een boom klimmen	to climb a tree
in tweeën snijden	to cut into two
er gaan 16 ons in een Engels pond	there are 16 ounces to an English pound
hij is in de zestig	he's in his sixties
er waren in de 50 mensen	there were fifty odd people
in het weekend	at the weekend

jegens (lit.) – to(wards)

onze plicht jegens onze ouders	our duty to our parents
eerlijk zijn jegens mensen	to be honest with people

krachtens (lit.) – by virtue of

krachtens deze wet	under this law
krachtens mijn ambt	by virtue of my position/office

langs – along, past

langs het kanaal	along the canal
ik reed langs jouw huis	I drove past your house
langs een andere route/weg (see *via*)	via another route/road
kom een keer bij me langs	come and visit me some time

met – with

we waren met z'n tweeën	there were two of us
met de post	by mail
met de auto, tram etc.	by car, tram etc.
met dit weer	in this weather
met potlood schrijven	to write in pencil
met Pasen, Kerstmis	at Easter, Christmas time
ik ben met vakantie (see *op*)	I'm on holiday
een zak met geld	a bag of money
met of zonder (mayonaise)	with or without (mayonnaise – when buying chips/fries)
het steeg met 11%	it rose by 11%

When used with pronominal *er* (p. 178, 222) or as a prefix with separable verbs (p. 169) *met* becomes *mee*. In formal style it also occurs as *mede* in separable verbs, eg. *mededelen* = *meedelen* – to inform.

na – after

na het avondeten	after dinner
na achten	after eight
A. is de grootste stad na Londen	after London A. is the biggest city

op twee na de grootste stad	the third largest city
na ontvangst van	on receipt of
de een na de ander	one after another
regel na regel	rule after rule

naar – to (places), (see *aan*)

ik ga naar A'dam	I'm going to A'dam
ik ga naar huis	I'm going home
ik ga naar boven, beneden, binnen,	I'm going upstairs, downstairs, inside,
buiten	outside
naar bed	to bed
naar school (see *op*)	to school
naar Parijs vertrekken	to leave for Paris
een steen naar iemand/iets gooien	to throw a stone at s.o./s.t.
naar iets grijpen	to grab at s.t.
hij werd naar zijn vader genoemd	he was named after his father
naar mijn mening	in my opinion
een film naar een roman van Dickens	a film of a book by Dickens

naast – next to

hij woont naast mij	he lives next to me
naast borduren doet ze ook veel aan	apart from embroidery she also does a
haken	lot of crochet

namens – on behalf of

ik spreek namens alle aanwezigen	I speak on behalf of all those present

niettegenstaande – inspite of (see *ondanks*)

niettegenstaande het slechte weer	in spite of the bad weather

om – around, for

we zaten allemaal om de tafel	we all sat around the table
om de hoek	around the corner
de aarde draait om zijn as	the earth turns on its axis
ik kan de kinderen niet om me hebben	I can't have the kids around me
om zich heen kijken	to look around (oneself)
om tien uur	at ten o'clock
om die tijd van het jaar	at that time of (the) year
om de twee weken	every two weeks
om de andere boom	every other/second week
de tijd is om	time is up
ik heb een gordel/stropdas/halsketting om	I have a belt/tie/necklace on
oog om oog, tand om tand	an eye for an eye, a tooth for a tooth
om welke reden	for what reason

niet om mijzelf maar om jou	not for/because of myself but for/because of you
olifanten worden om hun ivoor gedood	elephants are killed for their ivory

ondanks – in spite of

ondanks zijn ziekte	in spite of his illness
desondanks	in spite of it/that

onder – under

onder het huis	under (neath) the house
bekend onder een andere naam	(well-)known under another name
onder Koning Willem I	under King William I
onder mijn voorganger	under my predecessor
onder de Duitse bezetting	during the German occupation
onder ons blijven	to remain between us
je bent onder vrienden	you're among friends
onder andere	among other things
onder het avondeten	during dinner
onder het lezen ontdekte hij...	while reading he discovered...
een dorpje onder A'dam	a village south of A'dam
hij is onder de 40	he is under forty
onder de 50 minuten	under 50 minutes

ongeacht – regardless of

ongeacht het land van oorsprong	regardless of one's land of origin

op – on

In its basic meaning of 'on' Dutch *op* designates a horizontal 'on' (see *aan* for vertical 'on'). Otherwise its meanings are too diverse to define.

op (de) tafel	on the table
op school	at school
op (het) kantoor	at the office
op zee	at sea
op het platteland	in the country
op de hoek	on the corner
op de universiteit (see *aan*)	at the university (i.e. the campus)
op de gang (also *in*)	in the hall
op de bank/markt	at the bank/market
op het postkantoor/station	at the post-office/station
op het stand (see *aan*)	on the beach
op de voor-, achtergrond	in the fore-, background
het op één na grootste schip ter wereld	the second largest ship in the world
op de foto	in the photo
op het spitsuur	at rush-hour
hij werkt op een fabriek	he's working in a factory

op een feest	at a party
op een eiland	on an island
op IJsland, Java, Kreta	in Iceland, Java, Crete (i.e. islands)
op het tweede plaatje	in the second picture
iemand op de koffie uitnodigen	to invite s.o. to coffee
iemand op een bruiloft uitnodigen	to invite s.o. to a wedding
iemand op een diner uitnodigen	to invite s.o. to dinner
hij had maar 5 cent op zak	he only had five cents on him
op vakantie (also *met*)	on holidays
op deze manier/wijze	in this way
op zoek naar	in search of
op afbetaling kopen	to hire-purchase
een aanval op	an attack on
een toast op de koningin	a toast to the queen
hij ligt op sterven	he is dying, about to die
op z'n Frans etc.	à la française etc.
op z'n vroegst	at the earliest/latest
op de maat van de muziek	in tune to the music
dat gebouw staat op instorten	that building is about to collapse
op dit uur	at this hour
de wet op het openbaar onderwijs	the public education bill/law
op een wenk van mij	at a sign from me
op de radio/t.v.	on the radio/T.V.
op één voorwaarde	on one condition
als kind heb ik op klompen gelopen	as a child I used to wear clogs
ze kookt op gas	she cooks with gas
op de fiets (also *met*)	by bike
op een hoogte van 2000 meter	at a height of 2000 metres
een op de 50 (mensen etc.)	one in every fifty (people etc.)
één telefoon op elke 50 inwoners	one phone to every 50 inhabitants
mijn auto rijdt een op 10	my car does 10 to the litre
op twintigjarige leeftijd	at the age of twenty
(op) de 23e	on the 23rd
mijn geld is op	my money has all gone
er is geen geld op de rekening	there is no money in the account

over – over, via, about

het vliegtuig vliegt over de stad (heen)	the plane is flying above the city (over)
tranen liepen over zijn wangen	tears ran down his cheeks
er waren over de 100 mensen	there were over 100 people
overdag	during the day
hij is over de 60	he's over 60
het is al over achten	it's already past eight o'clock
vrijdag over een week	a week from Friday
over 50 jaar	in fifty years' time
over het algemeen (also *in*)	in general, generally
een boek/film over iets	a book/film about something

dit boek gaat over de oorlog	this book is about the war
je moet er niet over praten	you mustn't talk about it
ik heb wat over	I have something left
De trein gaat over Leiden	The train goes via Leiden

per – by, per

per post/trein/tram etc. (see *met*)	by mail/train/tram etc.
5 keer per seconde/uur/jaar	five times a second/hour/year
ze worden per dozijn verkocht	they are sold by the dozen

qua – as, as far as…is concerned

hoe vind je dit boek qua presentatie	what do you think of this book as far as its presentation is concerned
qua aantal deelnemers was het een succes	as far as numbers go, it was a success

rond, rondom – around

rond het vuur	around the fire
hij liep rond het huis (heen)	he ran around the house
rondom de stad loopt een singel	a moat runs around the city

sedert* – since, for (see *sinds*)

sedert 12 mei	since the twelfth of May
sedert enige tijd	for some time

sinds* – since, for (see *sedert*)

sinds de oorlog	since the war
sinds lange tijd	for a long time

te – at, in (also *ter, ten* in set expressions, see p. 204)

For use with *om* before infinitives see p. 148.

te Amsterdam (lit.)	in Amsterdam
te paard	by horse, on horseback
te koop	for sale
je hebt f 10 te goed	you have f 10 to your credit
en terecht	and rightly so
een schip te water laten	to launch a ship
te voorschijn komen	to appear
te binnen schieten	to occur (to s.o.)

* *Sinds* is more common in speech than *sedert*

tegen – against

Ajax speelt tegen Feyenoord	A. is playing against F. (sport)
tegen de muur	against the wall
met mijn rug tegen de muur	with my back to the wall
tegen 8% rente	at 8% interest
tegen die prijs	at that price
het is duizend tegen één	a thousand to one (odds)
tegen acht uur	at about eight o'clock
hij is tegen de 50	he is about 50
ik kan er niet tegen	I can't stand it; it upsets me
ik heb er niets tegen	I don't object (to it)
iets tegen iemand zeggen	to say s.t. to s.o.

tegenover – opposite

hij woont tegenover een bank	he lives opposite a bank
recht/schuin tegenover	directly/diagonally opposite
er zijn er 900 overleden in 1977 tegenover 1200 in 1978	900 died in 1977 as against/opposed to 1200 in 1978
hij is verlegen tegenover dames	he is shy with ladies
dat kun je niet doen tegenover je ouders	you can't do that to your parents

tijdens – during (see *gedurende*, a synonym)

tot – until (see p. 178)

wij gaan tot Amsterdam	we are going as far as Amsterdam
tot nu toe, tot dusver	up till now
tot drie keer toe	up to three times
tot diep in de nacht	until late at night
ze werden tot de laatste man gedood	they were killed to the last man
tot ziens	good-bye (till we see each other again)
tot en met	up to and including
tot elke prijs	at any price
tot mijn verbazing/vreugde	to my amazement/joy
iemand overhalen tot stelen/meegaan	to talk s.o. into stealing/going along

tussen – between

tussen de twee bomen	between the two trees
tussen 3 en 4 uur	between 3 and 4 o'clock
dat blijft tussen ons	that must stay between you and me
je moet kiezen tussen...	you must choose between...

uit – out, out of, from

uit een glas drinken	to drink from a glass
hij komt uit Edam/België	he comes from Edam/Belgium
hij is uit het dorp verdwenen	he disappeared from the village

uit de 15e eeuw	from the fifteenth century
ik deed het uit liefdadigheid	I did it for the sake of charity
uit wraak/jaloezie/vrees	out of revenge/jealousy/fear
uit eigen ervaring	from one's own experience
uit het Nederlands vertalen	to translate from Dutch
we gaan een dagje uit	we are going out for a day
de verloving is uit	the engagement is over
de kachel/het licht is uit	the heater/light is off
heb je het boek al uit	have you finished the book

van – of, from, off

Usually written with a small letter in people's names, eg. *H. van den Berg*. (p. 15-16)

hij is net van A'dam gekomen	he has just come from A'dam
de auto van mijn oom	my uncle's car
een tante van mij	an aunt of mine
een vriend van mijn moeder	a friend of my mother's
van het dak vallen	to fall off the roof
van 1970 tot 1975	from 1970 to 1975
negen van de tien mensen	nine out of every ten people
van plan zijn	to intend
van nut zijn	to be of use
dit is van hout	this is made of wood
van brood leven	to live on bread
Nederlander van geboorte	a Dutchman by birth
iemand van naam kennen	to know somebody by name
ik rammel van de honger	I'm dying of hunger
een schat van een meid	a really nice girl
een kast van een huis	an enormous house
van ja/nee zeggen	to say yes/no
ik meen/denk/van wel/niet	I think so/not

Note: the preposition *van* is often used colloquially before direct objects where it assumes a sort of partitive function (compare the use of French *de* in such cases):

> *Ik hoef niet meer van die lange omwegen te maken.*
> *Ik heb van alles gezien.*

vanwege – because of, on account of (see *wegens*)

vanwege het weer	because of the weather
van overheidswege	from the government

via – via, from

hij gaat via Utrecht naar A'dam toe	he is going via Utrecht to A'dam
ik heb het via mijn zuster gehoord	I heard it indirectly from my sister
zij hoorde het via-via	she heard it on the grapevine

volgens – according to, in…('s) opinion

volgens mij	in my opinion
volgens de regels	according to the rules

voor – for

iets voor jou	something for you
voor de eerste keer	for the first time
voor alle zekerheid	for safety's sake
hij is voor zijn leven geborgen	he's fixed for life
woord voor woord	word for word
stuk voor stuk	piece by piece
één voor één	one by one
ik voor mij vond het lekker	I personally found it delicious
ik heb het voor het avondeten gemaakt	I made it for dinner

vóór - before, in front of

vóór het huis	in front of the house
ik heb veel werk vóór me	I have a lot of work ahead of me
het schip lag voor Tokio	the ship lay off Tokyo
vóór tien jaar	ten years ago
ik heb het vóór het avondeten gemaakt	I made it before dinner
een eiland voor de kust van	an island off the coast of

voorbij – past, beyond

hij woont voorbij de kerk	he lives past the church

wegens – because of, on account of (see *vanwege*)

zonder – without

een boek zonder kaft	a book without a cover
hij was zonder hoed	he didn't have a hat on
zonder u was het niet gelukt	but for you it wouldn't have succeeded
ik kan er niet zonder	I can't do without it

13.1   Prepositional phrases

The following phrases made up of usually two prepositions and a noun are in common use, although many will be found only in the written language. Those incorporating the preposition *te* usually have an enclitic form of *te* + *den* = *ten* or *te* + *der* = *ter*, these being the former definite articles in the dative case for masculine/neuter nouns and feminine nouns respectively (see p. 20*). Sometimes the noun also takes a dative *-e*. Many of these expressions are commonly abbreviated, eg. *i.p.v.* – *in plaats van*. (see p. 247).

aan de hand van	on the basis of, judging from
aan de voet van	at the foot of
aan deze/die kant van	on this/that side of
aan weerskanten, -zijden van	on both sides of, on either side of
als gevolg van	as a result of
door gebrek aan	through lack of
door middel van	by means of
in het midden van	in the middle of
in naam van	in the name of, on behalf of (also *namens*)
in oorlog met	at war with
in plaats van	instead of
in ruil voor	in exchange for
in strijd met	contrary to, in defiance of
in tegenstelling tot	as opposed to, as distinct from
in vergelijking met	in comparison with
in weerwil van	in spite of
met behulp van	with the help of, by means of
met betrekking tot	with reference to
met het oog op	in view/consideration of
met verwijzing naar	with reference to
naar aanleiding van	with reference to
onder auspiciën van	under the auspices of
onder invloed van	under the influence of
op grond van	on account of
op initiatief van	on the initiative of
op last van	by order of
per ingang van	as from (dates)
uit hoofde van	on account of, owing to
te midden van	in the midst of
ter ere van	in honour of
ter gelegenheid van	on the occasion of
ter wille van	for the sake of

---

* *Ter* as in *ter bevordering/verklaring van* etc. is still productive with feminine abstracts ending in *-ing*.

ten bate van	on behalf of, in aid of (charities)
ten bedrage van	to the amount of
ten behoeve van	on behalf of, in aid of
ten dienste van	for the use of
ten gevolge van	as a result of
ten gunste van	in favour of
ten huize van	at the home of
ten koste van	at the cost of
ten name van	in the name of
ten noorden van (or *benoorden*)	to the north of
ten oosten (of *beoosten*)	to the east of
ten opzichte van	with regard to
ten tijde van	at the time of
ten voordele van	to the advantage of
ten westen van (or *bewesten*)	to the west of
ten zuiden van (or *bezuiden*)	to the south of

13.2 Notes on prepositions

13.2.1 PREPOSITIONS FOLLOWING NOUNS (POSTPOSITIONS)

A number of common prepositions can follow the nouns to which they refer in which case the direction of the action is emphasised rather than the place of the action. When followed immediately by the verb in subordinate clauses or by past participles or infinitives in main clauses, they can be confused with separable prefixes (see p. 170).

zij gaat de stad in	she is going to town
hij liep de kamer uit	he walked out of the room
hij liep de kamer in/binnen	he went into the room
Roodkapje liep het bos helemaal door	Little Red Riding Hood walked right through the forest
de auto reed de hoek om	the car drove around the corner
gaat u de eerste brug rechts over	cross the first bridge on the right
we reden toen de hoofdweg op	we then drove up onto the main road
ze voeren de zeeën over	they sailed across the seas
we fietsten het kanaal langs	we cycled along the canal
de jongens roeiden de rivier af	the boys rowed down the river
hij gaat de berg op/af	he is going up/down the mountain
je moet die kant op/uit	you must go that way

For prepositions following ergens, *nergens* and *overal* see p. 69.

13.2.2 USE OF *HEEN* WITH PREPOSITIONS

Several prepositions are used together with *heen* (which follows the noun) to indicate direction. The meaning of a preposition + noun + *heen* is similar to that explained in 13.2.1 above; it can, however, have a figurative meaning, as some of the following examples illustrate

hij rende huilend door de menigte heen	he ran through the crowd crying
langs elkaar heen praten	to talk at cross purposes
we gaan er morgen heen	we are going there tomorrow
de kinderen renden om/rond het park heen	the kids ran around the park
hij keek om zich heen	he looked around (himself)
het vliegtuig vloog over de stad heen	the plane flew over the city
ik heb er overheen gelezen	it escaped me while reading

13.2.3 DOUBLE PREPOSITIONS

Many of the prepositions given above can be used together to further emphasis the position of direction of the action.

buiten mij om	without my knowledge
hij is aan promotie toe	he is due for a promotion
het water kwam tot aan zijn knieën	the water was up to his knees
achter in de tuin	at the bottom of the garden
hij is achter in de twintig	he is in his late twenties
hij reed achter uit de garage	he reversed out of the garage
binnen in de schuur	inside the shed
boven op de kast	(up) on top of the cupboard
dat gebeurde buiten mij om	it happened without my knowledge
midden in het bos	in the middle of the forest
je gaat onder de brug door	you go through under the bridge
hij kwam op me af	he came up to me
de op twee na grootste stad	the third largest city
op Dolf na	except for Dolf
hij is op winst uit	he is out for a profit
hij reed tegen een boom op	he drove into a tree
hij reed tegen een muur aan	he drove into a wall
hij reed tegen de wind in	he was driving against the wind
dat was tegen alle verwachtingen in	that was against all expectations
ze begeleidden hem tot aan de grens	they accompanied him up to the border
tot nog toe, tot nu toe	up till now
nou, tot over drie weken	well, till three weeks from now
tussen de huizen in staan bomen	there are trees in between the houses
vanaf volgende week	from next week
ik kon het vanuit het raam zien	I could see it from the window
ik kon het van het raam uit zien	
hij komt nu van Edam vandaan	he has just come from Edam

Note: Use of *vandaan* with verbs of motion is similar to that of *naartoe* (see above).

tegen de stroom op zwemmen	to swim against the current
voor in de auto	in the front of the car
hij zat voor zich uit te kijken	he was looking in front of him
ik heb iets voor bij de pudding	I have s.t. to have with (the) dessert
het is voor na het scheren	it is used after shaving

Note: Sentences such as *hij viel van de trap af, ze gingen met hem mee* seem to be utilising double prepositions as given here but are in fact separable verbs followed by a preposition, i.e. *afvallen van, meegaan met.*

Many of the above prepositional pairs can be written together and act as independent adverbs (see p. 102)

achterin	in the back
achterom	around the back
achteruit	backwards
binnenin	inside
bovenop	on top
middenin	in the middle
onderaan	down the bottom (of a page)
onderin	at the bottom (of a cupboard)
tussenin	in between
voorin	in the front

13.2.4   OMISSION OF ENGLISH 'OF'

It should be noted that the preposition 'of' is often left untranslated in Dutch:

een fles bier	a bottle of beer
een doosje lucifers	a box of matches
een kist appels	a box of apples
een krat bier	a crate of beer
duizenden mensen	thousands of people
een lijst namen	a list of names
een groep mensen	a group of people
de provincie Utrecht	the province of Utrecht
een soort (van) vaas	a sort of vase
de Republiek Suriname	the Republic of Surinam
het Koninkrijk België	the Kingdom of Belgium

14 Numerals *(telwoorden)*

14.1 Cardinal numbers *(hoofdtelwoorden)*

(on)even nummers – (un)even numbers (of houses or in a game)
(on)even getallen – (un) even numbers eg. *3 is een oneven getal*

0	*nul*	25	*vijfentwintig*
1	*een*[1]	26	*zesentwintig*
2	*twee*	27	*zevenentwintig*[2]
3	*drie*	28	*achtentwintig*
4	*vier*	29	*negenentwintig*
5	*vijf*	30	*dertig*
6	*zes*	40	*veertig*[3,5]
7	*zeven*[2]	50	*vijftig*[5]
8	*acht*	60	*zestig*[5]
9	*negen*	70	*zeventig*[5]
10	*tien*	80	*tachtig*[6]
11	*elf*	90	*negentig*
12	*twaalf*	100	*honderd*
13	*dertien*	101	*honderd een*[7,8]
14	*veertien*[3]	153	*honderd drieënvijftig*[7,8]
15	*vijftien*	266	*tweehonderd zesenzestig*[7,8]
16	*zestien*	1000	*duizend*
17	*zeventien*	1008	*duizend acht*[7,8]
18	*achttien*	5010	*vijfduizend tien*[7]
19	*negentien*	6788	*zesduizend zevenhonderd achtentachtig*[7]
20	*twintig*	200,000	*tweehonderdduizend*[7]
21	*eenentwintig*	1,000,000	*één miljoen*
22	*tweeëntwintig*[4]	2,000,000	*twee miljoen*
23	*drieëntwintig*[4]	one billion	*één miljard* (i.e. one thousand million)
24	*vierentwintig*		

Notes

1   The numeral *een* is written *één* in contexts where it could be read as the indefinite article or simply to emphasize it means one, eg. *Ik heb maar één broertje en dat is meer dan genoeg.* One must not conclude that whenever *een* means one it must bear acute accents – only when confusion could arise or emphasis is required, i.e. *een van de kopjes heeft geen oor* – here the word can only be read as one and the indefinite article would not make sense.

2 When pronouncing numbers deliberately as in giving telephone numbers, all derivatives of the word *zeven* are commonly pronounced *zeuven, zeuventien* etc. to avoid confusion with *negen*.

3 Note that *veertien* and *veertig* deviate in spelling and pronunciation from the basic cardinal *vier*.

4 In numerals combining *twee* and *drie* plus *en* a dieresis is required on the *en* to distinguish a separate syllable.

5 The initial letters of the numerals 40, 50, 60 and 70 are unvoiced for historical reasons, i.e. one says *feertig, fijftig, sestig, seventig*.

6 Note the initial *t* in *tachtig*. It has historical connections with point 5.

7 One will often find mistakes in Dutch texts with regard to the division of numerals over 100. The rule is that a space is left after the hundreds and/or thousands, but not between the multiples and the hundreds and/or thousands. To write them together as in German is considered unwieldy.

8 Note that no 'and' is inserted between *honderd/duizend* and the following figure. One does in fact hear *driehonderd en tien* but this is in more deliberate speech and is only used and found before low numerals and is never necessary. *En* is always used however, in standing expressions such as *Verhalen van duizend-en-één nacht* and *ze praatten over duizend en één dingen*. *Eén* is sometimes heard before *honderd* and *duizend* but is not common.

9 In the Netherlands, as in so many European countries, a seven is often written differently: 7 – seven.

10 Ten squared is *tien kwadraat* and ten to the power of seven etc. is *tien tot de zevende macht*.

Note: In Holland it is usual to count in hundreds up to 10,000 and only above that figure to count in thousands: 6,300 is read *drieënzestighonderd*. Even thousands are, however, said in thousands, i.e. 2000 is *tweeduizend* and not *twintighonderd*.
The Dutch use a full-stop when writing thousands, not a comma, but a comma is used where we use a full-stop, eg. 10.000 and 28.000,00

14.1.1 DERIVATIVES OF CARDINALS

Honderd, duizend and *miljoen* take an -*en* ending when one means 'hundreds of' etc., eg. *duizenden mensen gingen naar de kermis*.

Met ons/z'n tweeën, drieën, vieren, vijven, zessen etc. Such expressions are very common and mean two of us/them etc. Note that expressions with *ons* must have a *wij* as subject of the sentence whereas those with *hun/z'n* (never *zijn*) can have *wij* or *zij* as subject.

We gingen met ons/z'n vieren naar de bioscoop.
Zij hebben het met z'n tienen gedaan.

Theoretically any numeral can bear this ending, eg. *met z'n vijfenvijftigen* but it is only common among lower figures. It is in fact the only way the Dutchman has of expressing 'there were five of us.'
A more intimate and colloquial form of the above is *met z'n tweetjes, drietjes* etc. Also *in z'n eentje* = on his own. The *-en* ending is also found in expressions such as *een van ons tweeën* and in *in tweeën/drieën/vieren/vijven/zessen snijden* – to cut in two etc.; also in time (see Time below).
Another interesting derivative is *tweeling, drieling, vierling* etc. for twins, triplets, quadruplets etc. These words take a singular verb. eg. *Vandaag is er in Leiden een zesling geboren.* N.B. *Ik ben er een van een tweeling* – I am a twin.

een veertigtal etc. = about 40 altogether. *Het elftal* – (football) team

   Ik heb een vijftigtal studenten in de klas.

Note also *tientallen* – plural noun = tens of,

   tientallen mensen – tens of people

Enerlei, tweeërlei, drieërlei etc. mean 'of one/two/three kind(s)'. Also *allerlei* – all kinds of. Those formed from numerals are a little stilted, however.

Het dubbele, driedubbele, vierdubbele etc. render 'twice/three/four times as much'.

   Ik heb het vijfdubbele betaald.   I paid five times as much.

Note the verbs *verdubbelen* (to double), *verdrievoudigen/-dubbelen* (to treble).

Notes on cardinals

1
een goede veertig	a good forty, at least forty
een dikke honderd	a good hundred
een kleine zestig	no more than sixty
onder/over (boven) de zestig	under/over sixty
in de vijftig	about fifty
een twintig jaar geleden	about twenty years ago
een jaar of twintig geleden	about twenty years ago

The last expression is very common in all sorts of contexts: *een man of tien, een stuk of zes, een boek of twaalf.*

2   Telephone numbers:
When reading a telephone number aloud it is usual to divide the figure into couplets and read *tweeëndertig veertig eenenzestig* – 324061. It is, however, permissible to read the numbers out individually. Dutch phone numbers look as follows:
030-76 12 53: the first number is the *kengetal* or *netnummer* of the town concerned and the second is the *abonneenummer.*

3 One in every ten etc. is said *een op de tien (mensen)*. Nine out of every ten etc. is however, *negen van de tien (mensen)*.

4 The English word 'number' can be rendered in several ways in Dutch:

het telwoord	numeral as in *hoofdtelwoorden* (cardinals), *rangtelwoorden* (ordinals)
het nummer	number allotted to a person or place as in *telefoonnummer*, or *hij woont op nummer 5*,
het cijfer	a figure, cipher (also a mark at school)
het getal	arithmetical number, *getallen optellen* – to add up numbers
het aantal	quantity, i.e. *een aantal boeken* – a number of books
het tal	most common in the expression *tal van* eg. *tal van mensen zijn gekomen* = many people came, a number of

Note: *een aantal* + plural noun (a number of) requires a singular verb: *Een aantal mensen heeft het al gezien* (see note 9, p. 212).

14.2 Ordinal numbers *(rangtelwoorden)*

1st	*eerste*	22nd	*tweeëntwintigste*
2nd	*tweede*[1]	23rd	*drieëntwintigste*
3rd	*derde*	24th	*vierentwintigste*
4th	*vierde*	25th	*vijfentwintigste*
5th	*vijfde*[2]	26th	*zesentwintigste*
6th	*zesde*[2]	27th	*zevenentwintigste*
7th	*zevende*	28th	*achtentwintigste*
8th	*achtste*	29th	*negenentwintigste*
9th	*negende*	30th	*dertigste*
10th	*tiende*	40th	*veertigste*
11th	*elfde*[2]	50th	*vijftigste*
12th	*twaalfde*[2]	60th	*zestigste*
13th	*dertiende*	70th	*zeventigste*
14th	*veertiende*	80th	*tachtigste*
15th	*vijftiende*	90th	*negentigste*
16th	*zestiende*	100th	*honderdste*
17th	*zeventiende*	101st	*honderdeerste*[3]
18th	*achttiende*	121st	*honderdeenentwintigste*[3]
19th	*negentiende*	1000th	*duizendste*
20th	*twintigste*	8452nd	*achtduizendvierhonderdtweeënvijftigste*[3]
21st	*eenentwintigste*	1,000,000th	*miljoenste*

All ordinals after 20th end in *-ste* in Dutch. Ordinals can be used as nouns or as adjectives and always preserve the final *-e*, eg. *een tweede huis* (compare *een rood huis*).

Notes

1 *Tweede* actually contradicts the spelling rules of Dutch; in such an open syllable one would expect *twede*.

2 In these ordinals the f or s preceding the *-de* ending is voiced under influence of the following voiced sound, i.e. pronounced *zezde, elvde* etc. Compare p. 000.

3 Note the omission of 'and', i.e. one hundred and twenty-first.

Notes on ordinals

1 In certain standard expressions ordinals are found with the older case ending *-en*, eg. *ten eersten male, ten tweeden male*.

2 The ordinals are often used as follows when listing points, i.e. firstly, secondly, thirdly, finally – *ten eerste, ten tweede, ten derde, ten laatste*.

3 Expressions such as 'every tenth tree' can be translated literally as *elke/iedere tiende boom*, but are also commonly rendered as *om de tien bomen, om de drie weken*.

4 *Hoeveel* and *zoveel* can also take the ordinal ending *-ste*.

> *De hoeveelste bezoeker?* (see. 14.9)
> *Hij heeft me voor de zoveelste keer opgebeld* – the umpteenth time.

5 Foreign kings are always denoted by the ordinal as in English.

> *Karel de Vijfde, Elisabeth de Tweede* (note capital letter)

The Dutch kings, however, are usually referred to with the cardinal, i.e. *Koning Willem II* (pronounced *twee*).

6 The various English abbreviations st, nd, th etc. are all rendered in Dutch by *e*, eg. *1e, 122e* etc. One does occasionally find for 1st and 2nd. *1ste* and *2de*.

7 The Dutch have an unusual way of expressing 'the second largest', 'the fourth most important' etc.: *Het op één na grootste schip* – the second largest boat. *Op drie na de belangrijkste operazanger* – the fourth most important opera singer.

8 *andermaal* = second time; it is commonly used at auctions for 'going once, going twice' = *eenmaal, andermaal*.

9 Note the use of a singular verb after a fraction or a percentage followed by a plural noun, eg. *Ongeveer een derde/30% van de Nederlanders woont in een eigen huis*.

14.3 Fractions *(breukgetallen)*

$^1/_4$	*een kwart* [1]		
$^1/_2$	*een half* [2]		
$1^1/_2$	*anderhalf* [2] *(-ve)*		
$2^1/_2$	*twee-en-een-half* [2] *(-ve)*		
$^1/_8$	*een achtste (deel)*		
$^2/_3$	*twee derde* [3] *(van de mensen etc.)*		
$^3/_8$	*drie achtste*		
$^1/_{16}$	*een zestiende (deel)*		
0,5%	*nul* **komma** *vijf procent* [4]	= **point** five per cent	
1,8%	*één komma acht procent*	= one point eight per cent	

Notes

1 *een kwartier*(n)   1/4 of an hour (see Time)
   een kwartaal(n)   1/4 of a year, period of three months
   een kwartje(n)   25 cents Dutch currency

2 The English word *half* causes difficulties because the noun and the adjective in Dutch are different words unlike English, i.e. *de helft, half.*
The way the two are used is best illustrated by examples:

> *de helft van de mensen*   – half the people
>   (only possibility for people)
> *de helft van de fles*   – half the bottle
> *de halve fles*
> *Hij heeft de helft van de appel opgegeten.*
> *Hij heeft de halve appel opgegeten.*
> *Hij heeft de appel voor de helft opgegeten.*
> *Ik heb de helft van het boek al uit/Ik heb het halve boek al uit.*
> *Voor de halve prijs/Voor de helft van de prijs.*

'One and a half' retains an archaic form *anderhalf* which behaves like a normal adjective taking *-e* in cases where the adjective is normally inflected.

> *anderhalf uur, anderhalve meter.*

Notice that *anderhalf, twee-en-een-half(-ve)* etc. are always followed by a singular noun:

> *drie-en-een-halve week.*

In such expressions the *een* is usually swallowed in speech and hardly heard.

3 one tenth of a pound = *een tiende pond.*
Note the use of the singular in *twee derde van de bevolking is in de oorlog gestorven*; a plural of such fractions is possible if one refers to the parts as separate parts, eg. *twee derden van de taart moeten opgegeten worden.*

4 One can also say *percent* and the noun is *percentage* (n).

14.4 Arithmetic/calculation *(rekenen)*

to add	– *optellen*	*4 plus (en) 4 is 8*
to subtract from	– *aftrekken van*	*4 min 2 is 2*
to multiply by	– *vermenigvuldigen met*	*2 keer (maal) 3 is 6*
to divide by	– *delen door*	*10 gedeeld door 2 is 5*
to count to 10	– *tot 10 tellen*	

14.5 Temperature

$1°$ – *één graad*
$10°$ *C/F – tien graden Celsius/Fahrenheit*
$12°$ *beneden/onder nul*
Het heeft vannacht $12°$ (twaalf graden) gevroren – it was $12°$ below last night.
or   *We hebben vannacht $12°$ vorst gehad.*
De maximum-, minimimtemperatuur, de gemiddelde temperatuur.

14.6 Age

Hoe oud ben je (bent u)?	How old are you?
Ik ben pas tien (jaar oud).	I am only ten (years old).
*Wanneer **ben** je (bent u) geboren?*	When **were** you born?
*Ik **ben** (op) tien maart geboren.*	I **was** born on the tenth of March.
Ik ben twaalf augustus jarig.	My birthday is on August 12th.
Op 14-jarige leeftijd.	At the age of 14.
Op mijn (zijn etc.) veertiende jaar.	At the age of 14.
Tussen mijn twaalfde en mijn eenentwintigste	From the age of 12 to 21.
Tussen (de) 18 en (de) 20.	Between 18 and 20.
Hij is in de 60.	He is in his sixties.
Een man van begin 40.	A man in his early forties.
Een man van diep in de 60.	A man in his late sixties.
Een man van achter in de 60.	A man in his late sixties.
Hij is nog geen 60.	He is not yet 60.
Een man van boven/over de 50.	A man over fifty.
Een man van beneden/onder de 50.	A man under fifty.
Hij was ruim 40 (jaar oud).	He was a good 40 years old.
Hij is midden in de 40.	He is in his mid-forties.
Hij was een jaar of 40 (oud).	He was about 40.
De vijfenzestigplusser (65-plusser).	The pensioner.
De tiener.	The teenager.
De eenendertigjarige etc.	The 31-year-old etc.
De tachtigjarige.	The octogenarian.
(De) minderjarig(e), volwassene.	(The) minor, (the) adult.
Een man van middelbare leeftijd.	A middle-aged man.

14.7 Money

een cent, twee cent etc.
een stuiver (c) – *vijf cent*
een dubbeltje (n) – *tien cent*
een kwartje (c) – *vijfentwintig cent*
een gulden (c), *twee gulden etc.*
een rijksdaalder (c) – *twee gulden vijftig*
een tientje (n) – *tien gulden*

Notes on money

1 *cent/gulden* are always used in the singular when quoting prices. The plurals *centen/guldens* are used to refer to several one cent or one guilder coins.

> *Geef me twee guldens en twee kwartjes voor deze rijksdaalder.*

The same applies to foreign currencies: *tien, vijf frank* etc.

2 The abbreviation for guilder is *f*, eg. *f* 10. In banks one sometimes sees *Hfl.* = *Hollandse florijnen*, an old word for guilder.

3 Prices are written with commas, not decimal points: *f 12,50* – pronounced *twaalf (gulden) vijftig (cent);* the word *cent* is not necessary and not common, however.

Note: 5 guilders odd = *5 gulden zoveel.*

4 Colloquially the word *piek* is used for guilder, eg. *Het kostte 10 piek.* In a similar way the word *ton* is used for 100,000 guilders, eg. *een halve ton, vijf ton etc.* Also the word *mille* for thousands eg. *dat kostte twee mille.*

5 Expressions such as 'he earns f 250 a month, a week etc.' are *hij verdient f 250 in de maand (per maand), in de week (per week)* etc.

14.8 Time

Hoe laat is het?	What is the time?
Het is één uur.	It is one o'clock.
*Het is vijf **over** een.*	It is five past one.
*Het is **kwart** over één.*	It is **a quarter** past one.
*Het is **tien voor half** twee.*[1]	It is **twenty past** one.
*Het is **half** twee.*	It is **half past** one.
*Het is **vijf over half** twee.*	It is **twenty-five to** two.
*Het is **tien over half** twee.*[1]	It is **twenty to** two.

---

1 It is also possible to say *twintig over een* and *twintig voor twee*, but the practice is not common; *half twee* etc. is often also written as *halftwee.*

Het is kwart **voor** *twee.*　　　　　　It is a quarter **to** two.
Het is tien **voor** *twee.*　　　　　　It is ten **to** two.

Notes on time

1
at eight o'clock　　– *om acht uur*
　　　　　　　　　– *te acht uur* (lit.)
at exactly eight　　– *om acht uur stipt/precies/*
　o'clock　　　　　– *klokslag acht uur*
at about eight　　 – *om een uur of acht*
　o'clock　　　　　– *omstreeks acht uur*
　　　　　　　　　– *rond acht uur*
　　　　　　　　　– *tegen acht (uur)*
　　　　　　　　　– *tegen achten*
just after eight　　– *kort na achten*

2 There are also a number of expressions which add an *-en* ending to the numeral. They are frequently heard but can be avoided by using the alternatives already mentioned.
Het is al na/over drieën, vijven etc. – It is already past three, five etc.
Het was intussen bij zessen – It was six o'clock by then.

3 Remember that *kwartier* in itself means **a quarter of an hour.**

　I waited for a quarter of an hour.　　　*Ik heb een kwartier gewacht.*
　Three quarters of an hour.　　　　　　*Drie kwartier.*
　One and a quarter hours.　　　　　　 *Vijf kwartier.*
　　　　　　　　　　　　　　　　　　　(also: *een uur en een kwartier*)

4 A.m./p.m. are rendered by *v.m./n.m.*, abbreviations of *(des) voor-, namiddags.* They are too formal for the spoken language, however; in conversations one would say *om zes uur 's morgens ('s ochtends)/'s avonds, om een uur 's nachts (in de nacht).*

5 My watch is fast/slow/right – *Mijn horloge loopt voor/achter/goed.*
My watch says four o'clock. It's four by me – *Ik heb het vier uur.*

6 Note that *keer, kwartier, jaar* and *uur* are not used in the plural after numerals or after *een paar* (a few) and *hoeveel* (how many) although *jaren* and *uren* can be used to emphasise duration, eg.

　Ik heb drie uur zitten lezen. Ik ben er een paar keer geweest. Hij werkte drie lange jaren in die fabriek.

After indefinite numerals like *enkele* and *enige* they do appear in the plural, however,

　Ze hebben enkele uren rondgewandeld.

Minuut and *seconde* (common gender nouns) always occur in the plural after numerals,

　vijf minuten geleden; drie seconden later.

7	once an hour	*een keer in het uur, per uur; om het uur*
	three times a week	*drie keer in de week, per week*
	on the hour (half hour)	*op het hele (halve) uur*
	ten past the hour (the half hour)	*tien over het heel (half)*

14.9 Dates

zondag	*woensdag*	*zaterdag*
maandag	*donderdag*	
dinsdag	*vrijdag*	

januari (jan.)	*mei*	*september (sept.)*
februari (feb.)	*juni*	*oktober (okt.)*
maart (mrt.)	*juli*[2]	*november (nov.)*
april (apr.)	*augustus*[3] *(aug.)*	*december (dec.)*

Days of the week and months of the year are nowadays written with small letters but are still sometomes found in texts with capital letters.

begin april	at the beginning of April
half/midden/medio maart	halfway through March, mid-March
eind mei	at the end of May

Days of the week and months of the year are nowadays written with small letters but are still sometimes found in texts with capital letters.

It is important to note the following usage of cardinals and ordinals with regard to dates in Dutch:

Note: *De hoeveelste is het vandaag?* – What is the date today?

Het is **drie mei** – It is **the third of May.**
but
Het is **de derde** – It is **the third.**

When the month is mentioned the cardinal is usually used, when not, then the ordinal. It is, however, not incorrect to say *de derde mei.*

On Friday the twenty-second of April – *(Op) vrijdag tweeëntwintig april.*
The abbreviation at the top of a letter, for instance, is thus *vrijdag, 22 sept. 1977* – no *e* or . after 22.

---

2 At times confusion arises between *juni* and *juli* in which case they are pronounced slowly with the emphasis on the final syllable.
3 The stress is on the penultimate syllable: *augústus.*

The complete abbreviation is written 22-9-77.
22-10-77 is a *datum* (c)-date.
1977 is a *jaartal* (n)-date.
When reading *jaartallen* aloud it is not usual to insert the word *honderd: negentien (honderd) zevenenzeventig.*

In de zestiger jaren, in de jaren zestig – In the sixties.
In vijf jaar tijds – In five years' time. (i.e. in the course of five years)
Over vijf jaar – In five years' time. (i.e. from now)
Om de eeuwwisseling – At the turn of the century.

14.10   Weights

Het gram
Het ons
Het pond (i.e. *een halve kilo*; an English pound is 454 grams)
het kilo (but usually regarded as being of common gender, eg. *een halve kilo*)

These weights are always used in the singular after numerals (as are *kwartier, uur, jaar* and *keer*), eg. *vijf pond, twee ons* (200 grams).

Fractions of these weights are expressed as follows:
één tiende gram (one tenth of a gram)
anderhalf ons
twee-en-een half ons, 250 gram, een halfpond, een kwart kilo; een halve kilo, een pond, 500 gram;
driekwartkilo, anderhalf pond, 750 gram
Although officially disapproved of you will find the various expressions incorporating *pond* are the most common on the whole but prices of meat, cheese etc. are often given *per ons*.
Note also *een klein pondje* – a bit less than a pound.
One says *f 1,50 per pond, per kilo* etc. or *het pond, het kilo.* People always refer to their own weight in kilos, eg. *Ik weeg 70 kilo. Aangekomen* – to gain weight, *afvallen* – to lose weight: both are conjugated with *zijn* (see p. 133).

Ik ben dit jaar 10 kilo aangekomen/afgevallen

Bijkomen can be used instead of *aankomen.*

14.11   Measurements

1 Length, height

De lengte – length of objects or height of people.
The height of a tree etc. is *de hoogte.*
Hoe lang bent u? – How tall are you?
Ik ben 1,72 lang – pronounced *een meter tweeënzeventig.*

If quoting one's height in English measurements the words *voet* (feet) and occasionally *duim* (inches) are used.

Length up to one metre is said in centimetres (never decimetres).

Note: *de centimeter* – the tape measure.

de breedte	width
de grootte	size (i.e. largeness)
de maat	(shoe, shirt) size

2 Square and cubic measurements

vijf bij vijf (meter)	five by five (metres)
drie vierkante meter	three square metres
zes kubieke meter	six cubic metres

3 Distance

Distances are, of course, measured in kilometres in Holland and the word *kilometer*, like *centimeter* and *meter*, is never used in the plural after numerals,

We hebben vandaag 20 kilometer gereden.

Note: *honderden/duizenden kilometers.*

The English measure mile is *mijl* (c) and can be used (in the singular also) when talking of distances in Anglo-Saxon countries.
Petrol consumption of a car is rendered as follows:
Mijn auto rijdt één op vijftien (i.e. *één liter op vijftien kilometer*) – fifteen kilometres to the litre.
Speed is expressed as follows: *Hij reed tachtig kilometer per uur* – he was driving (at) 80 kilometres an hour. Compare: *Hij reed met tachtig kilometer per uur de rivier in* – he drove into the river at eighty kilometres an hour.

14.12 Playing cards

schoppen	spades
ruiten	diamonds
klaveren	clubs
harten	hearts

de schoppenaas, -heer, -vrouw, -boer, -negen – ace, king, queen, jack and nine of spades.
One can also say *twee harten, drie ruiten* etc.
de troefkaart – trump card

14.13   Marks

Marks (*cijfers*) at school and university in Holland are given out of ten, not as percentages. One expresses marks as follows:

Ik heb een zes voor wiskunde gekregen.
I got 60% for mathematics.

Een voldoende is 6-10 and *een onvoldoende* is 1-5

Ik heb een onvoldoende voor geschiedenis gekregen.
I failed history.

15 Er

Er has four functions in Dutch: repletive, partitive, pronominal and locative. The four are dealt with separately below. It is possible to have various combinations of these in one clause; the complications arising from such combinations are dealt with in the notes following the description of the four functions.

15.1 Repletive **er**

Indefinite subjects are very commonly placed after the verb in Dutch with *er* introducing the verb in much the same way as 'there' can be used in English.

> *Er loopt een man op straat* – There is a man walking in the street.
> *Er moeten nog veel meer mensen komen* – A lot more people should be coming.
> *Er bracht een juffrouw koffie rond* – A girl brought coffee around.
> *Toen kwam er een pastoor* – Then a priest arrived.
> *Wat is er gebeurd?* – What happened?
> *Wie is er vandaag jarig?* – Who has a birthday today?

On occasion, as in the last two examples, it can be omitted but the ear generally prefers it. To this category belong also *er is/zijn* – 'there is/are'.
It should be noted that *liggen, staan* and *zitten* (less commonly *hangen* and *lopen*) often replace 'to be' in Dutch and they then usually occur in *er* constructions.

> *Er zit een muis in de hoek.*
> There is a mouse in the corner.
> *Er staat een foto van haar in de krant.*
> There is a photo of her in the paper.
> *Er lagen vier boeken op tafel.*
> Four books were lying on the table.
> *Loopt er een gracht achter jullie huis?*
> Is there a canal behind your house?

Repletive *er* is frequently used in passive constructions (see p. 153) where there is no grammatical subject. There is a variety of ways to translate these constructions into English:

> *Er wordt (aan de deur) geklopt* – There's a knock at the door.
> *Er wordt te veel geroddeld* – There's too much malicious gossip going on.
> *Er werd heel weinig gedanst* – Not much dancing was done.

15.2 Partitive **er**

This *er* is used with numerals and adverbs of quantity, often corresponding to French 'en'. In English it means something like 'of them/it', but is usually not translated.

> *Hoeveel heb je er? Ik heb er drie.*
> How many do you have? I have three (of them).
> *Hij heeft er genoeg.*
> He has enough (of them/it).
> *Het aantal is toegenomen. Vijftien jaar geleden waren het er honderd.*
> The number has increased. Fifteen years ago there were one hundred (of them).
> *Hoeveel bomen staan er* (repletive) *in die straat?. Er* (repletive) *staan er* (partitive) *honderd.*
> How many trees are there in that street? There are one hundred (of them).

15.3 Pronominal **er**

This is the *er* which replaces the pronouns 'it' and 'them' (referring to things only) after prepositions, i.e. *op het, van het* etc. is an impossible combination in Dutch; this must be *erop, ervan* etc. *Op ze, van ze* etc. can only refer to people, never things – this would also be *erop, ervan* etc. (see p. 54)

> *De meeste ervan zijn te duur.*
> Most of them are too dear.
> *Ik heb het brood ermee gesneden/Ik heb er het brood mee gesneden.*
> I cut the bread with it (with them).
> *Ik kijk er vaak naar.*
> I often look at it.

It is more usual to place *er* immediately after the finite verb and the preposition at the end of the sentence, but before past participles and infinitives. Note, however, that pronominal objects go between the finite verb and *er* and that it **is** possible to put *er* after nominal objects (i.e. not after the finite verb) if there is another word or expression which can be inserted between *er* and the preposition dependent on it:

> *Ik heb er het brood toen mee gesneden.*
> *Ik heb het brood er toen mee gesneden.*
> I then cut the bread with it.
> *Ik heb het er toen mee gesneden.*
> I cut it with it then.
> *Ik heb me er zo aan geërgerd.*
> I was so irritated by it.

These constructions must not be confused with *waar... mee* etc. (see p. 61).

Note the following complicated usage of pronominal *er*: it is employed with verbs that are always followed by a set preposition i.e.: *overtuigen van* – to convince of, *denken aan* – to think of etc. (see 11.17.12 and 11.22).

Ik ben ervan overtuigd dat...
I am convinced that...
Ik had er nooit aan gedacht het zo te doen.
I would never have thought of doing it like that.
Hij verdenkt er zijn vriend van een overval op een bank te hebben gepleegd.
He suspects his friend of having raided a bank.
De administratie heeft erop gestaan dat...
The administration insisted that...
Also: *Ben je er zeker van dat we op de goede weg zitten.*
Are you sure that we are on the right road.

15.4   Locative **er**

This *er* replaces *daar* in unstressed positions.

Ik ben er nooit geweest.

Compare: *Daar ben ik nooit geweest.*

Zij heeft er tien jaar gewoond.
Je bent nog te jong om er in je eentje naar toe te gaan.
You are still too young to go there on your own.

Locative *er* is usually used with the verb *aankomen* (to arrive) when the place is not otherwise mentioned.

Hoe laat ben je er aangekomen?
What time did you arrive?

Notes on *er*

1 A repletive *er* and a pronominal *er* do not occur in the same clause – the pronominal *er* is usually deleted.

Er keken veel mensen naar het programma.
Er keken veel mensen naar.
Daar keken veel mensen naar.
Er werd niet veel over gesproken.
Dat artikel staat in de Volkskrant.
Dat artikel staat erin.
Er staat ook weinig sportnieuws in de Volkskrant.
Er staat ook weinig sportnieuws in.
Er lag een laagje zand op.

Note the emphatic forms:

Daar moet geld bij.
Hier staat geen prijs op.

2 When a clause begins with an adverbial expression of place, repletive *er* is usually dropped, eg.

> *Er staan veel auto's op de parkeerplaats.*
> *Op de parkeerplaats staan veel auto's.*

3 More than two *er's* in one clause is impossible. In a clause where the sense demands three, you either delete the third or rephrase:

Delition : *Er keken drie mensen naar het programma.*
Er keken er drie naar het programma.
Er keken er drie naar.
Rephrasing : *Er keken drie mensen naar het programma.*
Er waren er drie die naar het programma keken.
Er waren er drie die ernaar keken.

4 The verb *uitzien* always requires *er* and should be learnt as *eruitzien*. This is an unusual idiomatic usage of the particle.

> *Hij ziet er ziek uit.*

eruitzien translates 'to look' in the sense of 'to appear' or 'to look as if':

> *Hij ziet eruit alsof hij ziek gaat worden.*

In such a construction *er* and *uit* are usually joined.

Note: *Het ziet ernaaruit alsof/dat het gaat regenen.*
Naar is used with this verb in impersonal constructions with *het*.

5 It is common when using a split pronominal *er* construction in a sentence in the perfect tense for the writer to join the preposition (which is actually dependent on the *er*) to the following past participle, treating the two as a separable verb,

> *Zie je die koffer? Ik heb er mijn sokken in gedaan.*
> *Zie je die koffer? Ik heb er mijn sokken ingedaan.*

(see also p. 170)

16 Negation *(ontkenning)*

16.1 Position of *niet/nooit*

The negative follows:

1 Adjuncts of time

Ik kom morgen niet,

but for emphasis it could on occasion precede *morgen.*

We willen het dit jaar niet doen,

but for emphasis:

We willen het niet dit jaar doen (maar volgend jaar).

Note: *Niet* always precedes *altijd:*

Zij verhalen worden niet altijd geloofd.

2 The object (definite)

The negative follows the direct object as long as it is definite, i.e. preceded by *de/het/deze/ dit/die/dat*, possessives or is a pronoun.

	Hij heeft het boek nooit gelezen.
Compare:	*Hij heeft nooit een boek gelezen.* (indefinite)
	Ik kan de sleutel niet vinden.
Compare:	*Ik heb nooit een sleutel kunnen vinden.* (indefinite)
	Hij leest het boek niet. Leest hij het boek niet?
	Jij kent hem niet. Ken je hem niet?

It does, of course, precede infinitives, past participles and separable prepositions in such sentences:

Ik heb het hem niet gegeven
but
Ik heb het niet aan hem gegeven. (see prepositional objects)
Heeft zij het boek nooit gelezen?
Ik heb er mijn sokken niet in gedaan.

The negative either precedes or follows:

Complements of the verb *zijn*

>*Dat is niet de bedoeling.*
>*Dat is de bedoeling niet.*
>*Hij is niet mijn vader.*
>*Hij is mijn vader niet.*

The negative precedes:

1 The object (indefinite)

The negative precedes the direct object as long as it is indefinite, i.e. a noun preceded by *een, zo'n, veel* or indefinite pronouns like *iets, iemand* etc.

>*Hij heeft nooit een auto gehad.*
>*We zullen niet veel (dingen) kunnen kopen.*
>*Heb je er nooit iets over gehoord?*

For *niet een* see Notes on negatives.

2 Adjuncts of manner

>*Ik ga niet met de auto.*
>*Ik reis niet per vliegtuig.*
>*De dokter zei dat mijn tante niet te hard moet werken.*

In this example there is only one position possible. The doctor had not prescribed that she must not work, merely that she must not work too hard.

3 Adjuncts of place

>*Ik woon niet op de achtste etage.*
>*Hij is nooit in Engeland geweest.*

However, the negative can precede or follow *daar* or *hier*.

>*Hij is nooit daar geweest.*
>*Hij is daar nooit geweest.*
>(Also: *Daar is hij nooit geweest.*)
>**but only:**
>*Hij is er nooit geweest.*

As *er* is an unemphatic *daar*, it cannot be stressed by putting *niet/nooit* before it.

>*Ik heb niet in de tuin gewerkt*
>**but**
>*Ik heb in de tuin niet gewerkt (maar gespeeld).*
>*Hij werkt niet in Amsterdam.*

4 **Prepositional objects**

Ik had nooit aan een dergelijke oplossing gedacht.
Ze heeft niet naar zijn onzin geluisterd.
Ik heb het niet aan hem gegeven.

5 **Predicative adjectives**

Het boek is niet groen.
Ik ben niet rijk.

Notes on negatives

1 'Not...a/any' of 'no + noun' are always translated by *geen*:

I don't have a car.
I have no car.   *Ik heb geen auto.*

He doesn't spend any money.
He spends no money.   *Hij geeft geen geld uit.*

Note: the combination *niet...een* **is** possible when a contrast is being made.

Ik heb niet in een hotel gelogeerd maar in een huis.

In such cases it cannot be replaced by 'no' in English.

2 'Not one' is *niet een* or *geen een.*

Niet een van mijn vrienden kwam me bezoeken.
Geen een van mijn vrienden kwam me bezoeken.
also
Geen van mijn vrienden – None of my friends.

3 In colloquial Dutch 'never...a/any' is often expressed by *nooit...geen*, a grammatically
incorrect double negative.

Zij hebben nooit geen auto gehad.
They have never had a car.

It should be:

Zij hebben nooit een auto gehad.

4 Further uses of *geen*:

The following examples show how *geen* sometimes renders a simple English 'not'.

Geese don't eat bananas.
Ganzen eten geen bananen.
also
Bananen eten ganzen niet.

They were not ordinary cats.
Het waren geen gewone katten.
He didn't know Dutch.
Hij kende geen Nederlands.

Also the expressions: *dienst hebben* (to be on duty), *dorst hebben* (to be thirsty), *haast hebben* (to be in a hurry), *honger hebben* (to be hungry), *slaap hebben* (to be sleepy) are negated by the use of *geen*, not by *niet* as in English.

Hij had geen haast.
He wasn't in a hurry.
Ze heeft geen slaap.
She isn't sleepy.

5 'No(t)…at all' is translated by *helemaal niet/geen*.

I didn't think of it at all.
Ik heb er helemaal niet aan gedacht.
I haven't got a car at all.
Ik heb helemaal geen auto.
He has no money at all.
Hij heeft helemaal geen geld.

6 'Not…until' is translated by *pas* (never *niet…tot*); in literary style *eerst* is found.

He's not coming until tomorrow.
Hij komt pas morgen.
They are not coming till next Monday.
Zij komen pas aanstaande maandag.
Not till then will it happen.
Eerst dan zal het geschieden.

7 'Not…either' is translated simply by *ook niet/geen*.

I'm not going either.
Ik ga ook niet.
She hasn't got one either.
Zij heeft er ook geen.

8 'Not yet' is translated by *nog niet*:

They aren't home yet.
Zij zijn nog niet thuis.

9 Note the following affirmative/negative couplets:

iets	– something	*iemand*	– someone, -body
niets	– nothing	*niemand*	– no-one, -body
ergens	– somewhere	*ooit*[1]	– ever
nergens	– nowhere	*(nog) nooit*	– never
wel			
niet	see 11.15		

Note: *nooit eerder* – never before. (see p. 99)

10 'Even' is usually translated by *zelfs*, while 'not even' is normally translated by *niet eens*; nevertheless, *zelfs niet* does exist as an expression and seems to be used after a list of negative things, eg.

He can't even read – *Hij kan niet eens/zelfs niet lezen.*
His name wasn't even (not so much as) mentioned – *Zijn naam werd niet eens/zelfs niet genoemd.*

11 'Not very' is rendered by *niet erg* (see p. 90)

1 *Ooit* also frequently renders 'once', eg.

A factory once stood here - *Hier stond ooit een fabriek.*

Appendix 1: Letter writing

The envelope

The titles

Dhr. L. Smit	– Mr.	*Prof. H. Segers*	– Prof.
Mevr. ,,	– Mrs.	*Ds. ,,*	– Rev.
Mej. ,,	– Miss	*Drs. ,,*	– (Dutch graduate title)
Mw. ,,	– Ms. (pron. *mevrouw*)	*Dr. ,,*	– Dr.

The address

> *Gildstraat 149*
> *7762 AD HEESWIJK*

Note that the number follows the name of the street. The town or city is in the upper case when type-written. If it is a letter for abroad the country is given in capitals, not the town. In 1978 postcodes were introduced in the Netherlands; they consist of four numbers followed by two capital letters and are placed before the name of the town, as illustrated.

Back of envelope

> *afz. B. de Bruin*
> *Hoogstraat 10*
> *2509 BA 's-GRAVENHAGE*

The Dutch always put the address of the sender on the back of the envelope. The abbreviation *afz.* stands for *afzender*. Note too that Dutch names in *de, den* or *van* are capitalised only when initials are not mentioned (see p. 15). In telephone books etc. too such names are found under the noun, not the preposition or article.

The letter

Address and date

The date is placed at the top right hand corner under the sender's address (but this is not always included in less formal letters as it is always written on the back of the envelope):

> *10 september 1977*

There is no dot after the numeral, nor is there a small *e* (abbreviation for ordinals) because in such expressions the cardinal numeral is used in Dutch (see p. 220). The months are always written with small letters nowadays.

Modes of address in opening a letter

1 When writing to a firm

Mijne heren,
Geachte heren,
Geachte heer/mevrouw,

2 When writing to an individual one doesn't know

Zeer geachte heer B.,
Geachte mevrouw B.,
Geachte mejuffrouw B.,

The *zeer* need only be used when one is being hyper-polite or writing to people in high positions, i.e. professors, politicians etc.

3 When writing to acquaintances and friends

Beste heer Meijer,
Beste mevrouw M.,
Beste mejuffrouw M.,
Beste Joop,

Particularly close friends, girl and boy friends and relatives are addressed as follows

Lieve Anneke,

Endings

1 When writing to a firm or stranger

Met de meeste hoogachting,
Hoogachtend,

If one has been in touch with the individual previously, one can replace the above with:

Met vriendelijke groet(en),

2 To acquaintances and friends one writes

Vriendelijke/Hartelijke groeten,

This may be followed by or simply replaced by

(Uw) Je
Otto

In very informal letters one can end simply with

Groetjes,
Wim

Expressions used in formal letter writing

lectori salutem (l.s.)	to whom it may concern
Uw kenmerk/referentie	your reference
ter kennisneming + name	cc + name (put at top of letter)
met verwijzing naar	with reference to
naar aanleiding van	with reference to
Met verwijzing naar uw brief	With reference to your letter of...
van...moge ik	I would like
Hartelijk (Vriendelijk) dank	Many thanks for your letter of the 22 nd inst.
voor uw brief van 22 dezer	
op de 28ste dezer	on the 28th of this month
28 okt. j.l. (jongstleden)	28th October last
per 26 dec. a.s. (aanstaande)	as from 26th December next
Uw brief d.d. 15 mei (= de dato)	your letter of the 15th of May
Wilt u zo vriendelijk zijn...	Please
Gelieve mij...te sturen	Please send me...
Wilt u mij nadere gegevens/	Please supply further details
inlichtingen verstrekken	
iets per omgaande sturen	to send something by return mail
het verschuldigde bedrag	the amount owed
Ik sluit...hierbij in	I hereby enclose
Hierbij ingesloten vindt u...	
ondergetekende	the undersigned
U bij voorbaat (voor uw moeite)	thanking you in anticipation
dankend,	(for your trouble)
Uw spoedig antwoord tegemoetziende	Looking forward to a prompt reply
Met belangstelling zie ik uw	I anxiously await a reply from you
antwoord tegemoet	
Uw antwoord zie ik te zijner tijd	Looking forward to hearing from you
gaarne tegemoet	

U/Uw are still commonly written with capital letters in very formal style but this convention is fast losing ground.

Many married women in Holland sign and have letters addressed to them as follows: *Mrs. A Smit*, whose maiden name was *Scherpenzeel*, would be addressed as *mevr. A. Smit-Scherpenzeel*. A married woman never adopts the initial of her husband as is sometimes done in Anglo-Saxon countries.

Appendix 2: Proper nouns

1 Countries, inhabitants, nationalities, adjectives, languages

Country	Man (+ plural)	Woman	Adjective (language)	
Europa	*Europeaan, Europeanen*	*Europese*	*Europees*	Europe
Albanië	*Albanees, Albanezen*	*Albanese*	*Albanees*	Albania
België	*Belg, Belgen*	*Belgische*	*Belgisch*	Belgium
Vlaanderen	*Vlaming, Vlamingen*	*Vlaamse*	*Vlaams*	Flanders
Wallonië	*Waal, Walen*	*Waalse*	*Waals*	Wallonia
Bulgarije	*Bulgaar, Bulgaren*	*Bulgaarse*	*Bulgaars*	Bulgaria
Ceylon	*Ceylonees, Ceylonezen*	*Ceylonese*	*Ceylonees*	Ceylon
Cyprus	*Cyprioot, Cyprioten*	*Cypriotische*	*Cypriotisch*	Cyprus
Denemarken	*Deen, Denen*	*Deense*	*Deens*	Denmark
Duitsland	*Duitser, Duitsers*	*Duitse*	*Duits*	Germany
Bondsrepubliek			*Westduits*	Federal Republic
Duitsland (BRD)				of Germany
de Duitse			*Oostduits*	German Democratic
Democratische				Republic
Republiek (DDR)				
Engeland	*Engelsman, Engelsen*	*Engelse*	*Engels*	England
het Verenigd Konink-	*Brit, Britten*	*Britse*	*Brits*	United Kingdom
rijk, Groot-Brittannië				Great Britain
Estland	*Estlander, Estlanders*	*Estlandse*	*Estlands*	Estonia
Finland	*Fin, Finnen*	*Finse*	*Fins*	Finland
Frankrijk	*Fransman, Fransen*	*Fran(çaise*	*Frans*	France

Griekenland	Griek, Grieken	Griekse	Grieks	Greece
Hongarije	Hongaar, Hongaren	Hongaarse	Hongaars	Hungary
Ierland	Ier, Ieren	Ierse	Iers	Ireland
IJsland[1]	IJslander, IJslanders	IJslandse	IJslands	Iceland
Italië	Italiaan, Italianen	Italiaanse	Italiaans	Italy
Joego-Slavië	Joegoslaaf, Joegoslaven	Joegoslavische	Joegoslavisch	Yugoslavia
Lapland	Lap, Lappen	Lapse	Laps	Lappland
Letland	Let, Letten	Lettische	Lettisch	Latvia
Litouwen	Litouwer, Litouwers	Litouwse	Litouws	Lithuania
Malta[1]	Maltezer, Maltezers	Maltese	Maltees	Malta
Nederland	Nederlander, Nederlanders	Nederlandse	Nederlands	Netherlands
Holland	Hollander, Hollanders	Hollandse	Hollands	Holland
Noorwegen	Noor, Noren[2]	Noorse	Noors	Norway
Oostenrijk	Oostenrijker, Oostenrijkers	Oostenrijkse	Oostenrijks	Austria
Polen	Pool, Polen	Poolse	Pools	Poland
Portugal	Portugees, Portugezen	Portugese	Portugees	Portugal
Roemenië	Roemeen, Roemenen	Roemeense	Roemeens[3]	Rumania
Rusland	Rus, Russen	Russische, Russin	Russische	Russia
Sovjet-Unie				Soviet Union
Oekraïne	Oekraïner, Oekraïners	Oekraïnse	Oekraïnisch	Ukraine
Schotland	Schot, Schotten	Schotse	Schots	Scotland
Spanje	Spanjaard, Spanjaarden	Spaanse	Spaans	Spain
Tsjecho-Slowakije	Tsjech(oslowaak), Tsjechen	Tsjechische	Tsjechisch	Czechoslovakia
Turkije	Turk, Turken	Turkse	Turks	Turkey
Wales				Wales

1 One says op IJsland/Malta where in English we say 'in'.
2 een Noor = a Norwegian; Noorman = Viking; Normandiër = Norman; Oudnoors = Old Norse
3 Roemeens = Rumanian; Romeins = Roman; Romaans = Romance

Country	Man (+ plural)	Woman	Adjective (language)	
Zweden	Zweed, Zweden	Zweedse	Zweeds	Sweden
Zwitserland	Zwitser, Zwitsers	Zwitserse	Zwitsers	Switzerland
Afrika	Afrikaan, Afrikanen	Afrikaanse	Afrikaans	Africa
Algerije	Algerijn, Algerijnen	Algerijnse	Algerijns	Algeria
Angola	Angolees, Angolezen	Angolese	Angolees	Angola
Egypte	Egyptenaar, Egyptenaren	Egyptische	Egyptisch	Egypt
Ethiopië	Ethiopiër, Ethiopiërs	Ethiopische	Ethiopisch	Ethiopia
Ghana	Ghanees, Ghanezen	Ghanese	Ghanees	Ghana
Guinea, Guinee	Guinees, Guinezen	Guinese	Guinees	Guinea
Ivoorkust	Ivoorkuster, Ivoorkusters	Ivoorkustse	Ivoorkusts	Ivory Coast
Kenia	Keniër, Keniërs	Keniase	Keniaa(n)s	Kenya
Liberië	Liberiaan, Liberianen	Liberiaanse	Liberiaans	Liberia
Libië	Libiër, Libiërs	Libische	Libisch	Libya
Marokko	Marokkaan, Marokkanen	Marokkaanse	Marokkaans	Morocco
Mozambique	Mozambikaan, Mozambikanen	Mozambikaanse	Mozambikaans	Mozambique
Nigerië	Nigeriaan, Nigerianen	Nigeriaanse	Nigeriaans	Nigeria
Oeganda	Oegandees, Oegandezen	Oegandese	Oegandees	Uganda
Rhodesia	Rhodesiër, Rhodesiërs	Rhodesische	Rhodesisch	Rhodesia
Zimbabwe	Zimbabw(e)aan, -anen	Zimbabw(e)aanse	Zimbabw(e)aans	Zimbabwe
Soedan	Soedanees, Soedanezen	Soedanese	Soedanees	Sudan
Somalië	Somaliër, Somaliërs	Somalische	Somalisch	Somalia
Tanzania*	Tanzaniër*, Tanzaniërs	Tanzaniaanse	Tanzaniaans	Tanzania
Tunesië	Tunees, Tuneziër	Tunese	Tunees	Tunesia
Zaïre	Zaïrees, Zaïrezen	Zaïrese	Zaïrees	Zaïre
Belgisch-Kongo	Kongolees, Kongolezen	Kongolese	Kongolees	Belgian Congo
Zambia	Zambiër, Zambiërs	Zambiaanse	Zambiaans	Zambia
Zuid-Afrika	Zuidafrikaan, -afrikanen or Zuidafrikaner, -afrikaners	Zuidafrikaanse	Zuidafrikaans	South Africa

Azië	*Aziaat, Aziaten*	*Aziatisch*	Asia
Arabië (Saoedi-A.)	*Arabier, Arabiers (Bedoeïnen)*	*Arabisch*	Arabia
	Mohammedaan,	*Mohammedaans*	Muslim
	Mohammedanen		
	Moslim, Moslims		
Armenië	*Armeniër*	*Armenisch*	Armenia
Irak	*Irakees, Irakezen*	*Iraaks, Irakees*	Iraq
Israël	*Israëli, Israëli's*	*Israëlisch*	Israel
	Israëliër, Israëliërs		
Jordanië	*Jordaniër, Jordaniërs*	*Jordaans*	Jordan
Jemen	*Jemeniet, Jemenieten*	*Jemenietisch*	Yemen
(de) Libanon	*Libanees, Libanezen*	*Libanees*	Lebanon
Palestina	*Palestijn, Palestijnen*	*Palestijns*	Palestine
Perzië	*Pers, Perzen*	*Perzisch*	Persia
Iran	*Iraniër, Iraniërs*	*Iraans*	Iran
Syrië	*Syriër, Syriërs*	*Syrisch*	Syria
Afghanistan	*Afghaan, Afghanen*	*Afghaanse*	Afghanistan
Birma	*Birmaan, Birmanen*	*Birmaans, Birmees*	Burma
Cambodja	*Cambodjaan, Cambodjanen*	*Cambodjaans*	Cambodia
China	*Chinees, Chinezen*	*Chinees*	China
de Chinese			People's Republic
Volksrepubliek			of China
de Filippijnen	*Filippijn, Filippijnen*	*Filippijns*	Philippines

* the accents are only to show the stress

Country	Man (+ plural)	Woman	Adjective (language)	
India	*Indiër, Indiërs*	*Indiase*	*Indiaas[3]*	India
Indonesië	*Indonesiër, Indonesiërs*	*Indonesische*	*Indonesisch*	Indonesia
Nederlands-Indië	*Inlander, Inlanders* (pej.)	*Indische*	*Indisch[3]*	Dutch East Indies
Java	*Javaan, Javanen*	*Javaanse*	*Javaans*	Java
Ambon	*Ambonnees, Ambonnezen*	*Ambonnese*	*Ambonnees*	Ambon
Zuid-Molukken	*Zuidmolukker, -molukkers*	*Zuidmolukse*	*Zuidmoluks*	South Moluccas
Japan	*Japanner, Japanners*	*Japanse*	*Japans*	Japan
Korea	*Koreaan, Koreanen*	*Koreaanse*	*Koreaans*	Korea
Laos	*Laotiaan, Laotianen*	*Laotiaanse*	*Laotiaans*	Laos
Maleisië	*Maleisiër*	*Maleisische*	*Maleisisch*	Malaysia
Malaja	*Maleier*	*Maleise*	*Maleis*	Malaya
Mongolië	*Mongool, Mongolen*	*Mongoolse*	*Mongools*	Mongolia
Nepal	*Nepalees, Nepalezen*	*Nepalese*	*Nepalees*	Nepal
Pakistan	*Pakistaan, (-ani),* *Pakistanen, (-ani's)*	*Pakistaanse*	*Pakistaans*	Pakistan
Sri Lanka	*Srilankaan, Srilankanen*	*Srilankaanse*	*Srilankaans*	Sri Lanka[5]
Taiwan	*Taiwanees, Taiwanezen*	*Taiwanese*	*Taiwanees*	Taiwan
Thailand	*Thailander, Thailanders*	*Thailandse, Thaise*	*Thailands, Thais*	Thailand
Tibet	*Tibetaan, Tibetanen*	*Tibetaanse*	*Tibetaans*	Tibet
Viëtnam	*Viëtnamees, Viëtnamezen*	*Viëtnamese*	*Viëtnamees*	Vietnam
Australië	*Australiër, Australiërs*	*Australische*	*Australisch*	Australia
Nieuw-Zeeland	*Nieuwzeelander, -zeelanders[4]*	*Nieuwzeelandse*	*Nieuwzeelands*	New Zealand
Nieuw-Guinea	*Papoea, Papoea's*		*Nieuwguinees*	New Guinea
de Fidji-eilanden				Fiji

Amerika *de Verenigde Staten (de USA, VS)*	*Amerikaan, Amerikanen*	*Amerikaanse*	*Amerikaans*	America the United States
Argentinië	*Argentijn, Argentijnen*	*Argentijnse*	*Argentijns*	Argentina
Bolivië	*Boliviaan, Bolivianen*	*Boliviaanse*	*Boliviaans*	Bolivia
Brazilië	*Braziliaan, Brazilianen*	*Braziliaanse*	*Braziliaans*	Brazil
Canada	*Canadees, Canadezen*	*Canadese*	*Canadees*	Canada
Chili	*Chileen, Chilenen*	*Chileense*	*Chileens*	Chile
Columbia	*Columbiaan, Columbianen*	*Columbiaanse*	*Columbiaans*	Columbia
Cuba	*Cubaans, Cubanen*	*Cubaanse*	*Cubaans*	Cuba
de Dominicaanse Republiek				Dominican Republic
Groenland	*Groenlander, -landers*	*Groenlandse*	*Groenlands*	Greenland
Jamaica				Jamaica
Mexico	*Mexicaan, Mexicanen*	*Mexicaanse*	*Mexicaans*	Mexico
	Azteek, Azteken	*Azteekse*	*Azteeks*	Aztec
de Nederlandse Antillen	*Antilliaan, -anen*	*Antilliaanse*	*Antilliaans*	Netherlands Antilles
Aruba	*Arubaan, Arubanen*	*Arubaanse*	*Arubaans*	Aruba
Panama	*Panamees, Panamezen*	*Panamese*	*Panamees*	Panama
Paraguay	*Paraguaan, Paraguanen*	*Paraguaanse*	*Paraguaans*	Paraguay
Peru	*Peruaan, Peruanen*	*Peruaanse*	*Peruaans*	Peru
Porto-Rico	*Portoricaan, Portoricanen*	*Portoricaanse*	*Portoricaans*	Puerto Rico
El Salvador	*Salvador(i)aan, Salvador(i)anen*	*Salvador(i)aanse*	*Salvador(i)aans*	El Salvador
Suriname	*Surinamer, Surinamers*	*Surinaamse*	*Surinaams*	Surinam
Uruguay	*Uruguaan, Uruguanen*	*Uruguaanse*	*Uruguaans*	Uruguay
Venezuela	*Venezolaan, Venezolanen*	*Venezolaanse*	*Venezolaans*	Venezuela

3   *Indiaan/Indiaans* – American Indian
    Indisch = Indonesisch prior to 1950 and is still used in literature and by ex-colonials.
4   An inhabitant of the Dutch province of *Zeeland* is a *Zeeuw* (see p. 240).
5   Note the forms *Ceylonees* (Ceylonese). *Singalees* (Singhalese) and *Tamil* (pl. *s*).

Notes on nationalities

a   The names of female inhabitants are not ever used in the plural with very few exceptions, eg. *Engelsen, Françaises, Russinnen*; otherwise the plural is avoided by paraphrasing, eg. *Die meisjes komen uit Australië* or *Die meisjes zijn Australisch.*
b   Nowadays one sees in progressive publications the ending *-isch* spelt *-ies*. This is not an official alternative, however.
c   When saying 'I am a Palestinian' etc. the indefinite article is often omitted in more formal style, i.e. *Ik ben Palestijn* (see p. 21).
d   Note that words ending in *-ees* go *-ese* in the feminine or when the adjective is inflected, but the plural of the masculine is always *-ezen.*
e   Countries for which there is no special word for the inhabitant or that have no particular adjectival form, usually paraphrase, i.e. *Hij komt uit Trinidad, deze rum is van Jamaica, olie uit Koeweit.*
f   Countries ending in *-ije* take the stress on the *-ij*.
g   Several countries have a different stress from English, e.g. *Hongarije, Oekraïne.*
h   Although *Noord, Zuid, Oost* and *West* are hyphenated in the names of provinces, countries etc., the corresponding adjectives and names of inhabitants are written as one word, eg. *Zuid-Afrika, Zuidafrikaans, Zuidafrikaan(se).*
i   The *Lijst van Landennamen* (Staatsuitgeverij, The Hague, 1980) recommends small letters for inhabitants and adjectives/languages but this is as yet at odds with common practice although small letters in such cases are not infrequent in modern texts. The *Algemene Nederlandse Spraakkunst* (Wolters-Noordhoff, Groningen, 1984), which gives a far fuller list than I do here and includes the derivatives of many Dutch and Belgian towns (pp. 1214-1246), prescribes capital letters for all such derivatives.

2   Geographical names

Dutch provinces	Inhabitant (female)	Adjective
Noord-Holland	*(Noord)Hollander (Hollandse)*	*Noordhollands*
Zuid-Holland	*(Zuid)Hollander (Hollandse)*	*Zuidhollands*
Zeeland	*Zeeuw (Zeeuwse)*	*Zeeuws*
Noord-Brabant	*(Noord-)Brabander (Brabantse)*	*Brabants*
Limburg	*Limburger (Limburgse)*	*Limburgs*
Gelderland	*Gelderlander (Gelderse)*	*Gelders*
Utrecht	*Utrechtenaar*[1] *(Utrechtse)*	*Utrechts*
Overijssel	*Overijsselaar (Overijsselse)*	*Overijssels*
Drent(h)e	*Drent (Drentse)*	*Drents*
Groningen	*Groninger (Groningse)*	*Gronings*
Friesland	*Fries (Friezin)*	*Fries*[2]

---

1   The inhabitants of *Utrecht* are also known as *Utrechters.*
2   *De Friese taal* **but** *de Friezen* (compare *Chinees, Portugees etc.*).

Provincial capitals	Adjective	Inhabitant
Haarlem	Haarlems [3]	Haarlemmer
's-Gravenhage, Den Haag	Haags	Hagenaar
Middelburg	Middelburgs	Middelburger
's-Hertogenbosch	Bosch (Bossche)	Bosschenaar
Den Bosch		
Maastricht	Maastrichts	Maastrichtenaar
Arnhem	Arnhems	Arnhemmer
Utrecht	Utrechts	Utrechtenaar [1]
Zwolle	Zwols	Zwollenaar
Assen	Assens	Assenaar
Groningen	Gronings [3]	Groninger
Leeuwarden	Leeuwardens	Leeuwarder

Note: The towns *Leiden* and *Gouda* and the region *Twente* have their own irregular adjectival forms: *Leids, Gouds, Twents.*
Towns ending in *-dam* take the stress on *-dam*, eg. *Amsterdàm, Edàm* etc. The inhabitant is an *Amsterdammer* etc.

Belgian provinces	Inhabitant (female)	Adjective
West-Vlaanderen (W. Flanders)	(West) Vlaming (Vlaamse)	Westvlaams
Oost-Vlaanderen	(Oost)Vlaming (Vlaamse)	Oostvlaams
Antwerpen (Antwerp)	Antwerpenaar (Antwerpse)	Antwerps
Brabant	Brabander (Brabantse)	Brabants
Limburg	Limburger (Limburgse)	Limburgs
Luik (Liège) [4]		Luiks
Namen (Namur) [4]		Naams
Luxemburg [4]	Luxemburger (Luxemburgse)	Luxemburgs
Henegouwen (Hainaut) [4]	Henegouwer (Henegouwse)	Henegouws

Provincial capitals		Adjective	Inhabitant
Brugge	– Bruges [5]	Brugs	Bruggeling
Gent	– Ghent	Gents	Gentenaar
Antwerpen	– Antwerp	Antwerps	Antwerpenaar
Brussel	– Brussels	Brussels	Brusselaar
Hasselt		Hasselts	
Luik	– Liège	Luiks	Luikenaar
Namen	– Namur	Naams	
Aarlen	– Arlon	Aarlens	
Bergen	– Mons		

3 In some standard contexts an adjectival form in *-er* is heard, eg. *Groninger koek, Haarlemmer olie.*
4 All French-speaking provinces.
5 In English we usually refer to these cities by their French names if there is not a specifically English form as in the case of Ghent and Brussels for example.

Other important Belgian cities with two names (i.e. Dutch, French)

Doornik	Tournai
Kortrijk	Courtrai
Leuven	Louvain
Mechelen	Malines
Oosténde	Ostend

Other cities with different names in Dutch from English
(corresponding adjectives given in brackets)

Aken	Aix-La-Chapelle, Aachen
Athene	Athens
Berlijn	Berlin
Bèlgrado	Belgrade
Boedapest	Budapest
Boekarest	Bucharest
Duinkerke	Dunkirk
Florence[6] *(Florentijns)*	Florence
Frankfort	Frankfurt
Genève (Geneefs)	Geneva
Gotenburg	Gothenburg
Hannover	Hanover
Caïro	Cairo
Keulen (Keuls)	Cologne
Kopenhagen	Copenhagen
Leiden	Leyden
Lissabon	Lisbon
Londen	London
München	Munich
Milaan (Milanees)	Milan
Moskou	Moscow
Napels (Napolitaans)	Naples
Neurenberg	Nuremberg
Parijs (inh. Parijzenaar)	Paris
Praag	Prague
Rome (Romeins)	Rome
Rijs(s)el	Lille
Straatsburg	Strasbourg
Tanger	Tangier
Teheran	Tehran
Tokio	Tokyo
Turijn	Turin
Venetië	Venice
Warschau (pron. sh)	Warsaw
Wenen (Weens)	Vienna

6 Pronounced as in French.

If there is not a specifically Dutch name for a town, the Dutch usually attempt to pronounce the name as in the language of the country concerned. In some cases they adapt the spelling to the sounds of Dutch; this is particularly the case with African and Asian names, eg. *Beiroet, Kinsjasa, Loesaka, Mekka, Addis Abéba.*

European rivers with different names in Dutch from English

de Donau	Danube
de Maas	Meuse
de Moezel	Moselle
de Rijn	Rhine
de Roer	Ruhr
de Schelde	Scheldt
de Theems	Thames

Provinces and regions of other European countries
(corresponding inhabitant and adjective given in brackets)

de Balkan, -staten	Balkans
Baskenland (Bask, Baskisch)	Basque country
Beieren (Beier, Beiers)	Bavaria
Bohemen (Bohemer, Boheems)	Bohemia
Bretagne (Bretons)	Brittany
Canarische Eilanden	Canary Islands
Elzas (Elzasser, Elzassisch)	Alsace
Gallië (Galliër, Gallisch)	Gaul
Kaukasus (Kaukasisch)	Caucasus
Kreta (Kretenzer, Kretenzisch)	Crete
Kroatië (Kroaat, Kroatisch)	Croatia
Lombardije (Lombardisch)	Lombardy
Lotharingen	Lorraine
Normandië (Normandiër, Normandisch)	Normandy
Picárdië	Picardy
Pommeren	Pomerania
Pruisen (Pruis, Pruisisch)	Prussia
Rhodos	Rhodes
Saksen (Saks, Saksisch)	Saxony
Sardinië	Sardinia
Servië (Serviër, Servisch)	Serbia
Siberië	Siberia
Sicilië (Siciliaan, Siciliaans)	Sicily
Silezië (Silezisch)	Silesia
Sleeswijk	Schleswig
Stiermarken	Styria
Tirol (Tilorer, Tirools)	Tyrol
Toscane (Toscaans)	Tuscany
Zwaben (Zwaab, Zwaabs)	Swabia

Other geographical areas

de Alpen	Alps
de Apennijnen	Apeninnes
de Atlantische Oceaan[7]	Atlantic Ocean
Bengalen	Bengal
de Bodensee	Lake Constance
het Caribische Gebied	Caribbean
de Caribische Zee	Caribbean Sea
de Golf van Biscaje	Bay of Biscay
De Golf van Bengalen	Bay of Bengal
de Indische Oceaan[7]	Indian Ocean
Kaap de Goede Hoop	Cape of Good Hope
Het Kanaal	English Channel
De Kaspische Zee	Caspian Sea
Klein-Azië .	Asia Minor
de Krim	Crimea
Latijns-Amerika	Latin America
de Maagdeneilanden	Virgin Islands
Mantsjoerije	Manchuria
de Middellandse Zee	Mediterranean Sea
Midden-Europa	Central Europe
het Midden-Oosten	Middle East
het Nabije Oosten	Near East
de Noordpool	North Pole
de Noordzee	North Sea
de Oeral	Urals
de Oostbloklanden	Iron Curtain Countries
de Oostzee	Baltic Sea
het Paaseiland	Easter Island
de Perzische Golf	Persian Gulf
het Roergebied	Ruhr
de Stille/Grote Oceaan[7]	Pacific Ocean
het Vaticaan	Vatican
het Verre Oosten	Far East
de Vogezen	Vosges
Vuurland	Tierra del Fuego
de Zuidpool	South Pole
de Zuidzee	South Seas
de Zwarte Zee	Black Sea
het Zwarte Woud	Black Forest

7   Note the stress *oceáán*.

3 Historical personages

When referring to well-known people who have names normally written in an alphabet other than the Latin alphabet, the names are usually transcribed according to Dutch phonetics,

> *Chroetsjev, Kaoenda, Tsjechow* etc. Also *de Likoed* (Israeli political party)

Kings of England, France, Germany etc. as well as popes are also given Dutch names where such exist (see also p. 212):

> *Karel* (Charles), *Jacobus* (James), *Lodewijk* (Louis, Ludwig), *Boudewijn* (Baudouin, Baldwin), *Hendrik* (Henry, Heinrich), *Jan* (John, Johann).

Karel de Grote	Charlemagne
Lodewijk Napoleon	Louis Napoleon
Jacobus de Tweede	James II
Johannes Paulus II	John Paul II

Note: *Calvijn* – Calvin, *Galilei* – Galileo. The names of many biblical personages are somewhat different in Dutch, eg. *Noach* (Noah), *Sálomo* (Solomon). The ending *-iaans* is often added to male surnames to create adjectives, eg. *Breugeliaans, Freudiaans* (stress on final syllable).

Appendix 3: Common Dutch abbreviations (afkortingen)

Abbreviations can be of three kinds:

1 those that are simply a form of short-hand and which are read aloud as the words they represent, eg. f = gulden, bv. = bijvoorbeeld.

2 those that are regarded as words in themselves and may (and usually are) pronounced using the letters, eg. KLM pronounced KA-EL-EM. Such abbreviations are designated by an asterisk in the list below.

3 a few abbreviations are read as words in themselves, not as letters. These acronyms are designated by +.

Many abbreviations can take an article which agrees in gender with the final noun in the name, eg. het KNMI because instituut is neuter. Sometimes other words are formed from these abbreviations, eg. de A.O.W. = de Algemene Ouderdomswet, hence een AOW'er = a pensioner; NSB = de Nationaal-Socialistische Beweging hence een NSB'er = a Dutch Nazi.

(het) ABN*	Algemeen Beschaafd Nederlands	Standard Dutch
(de) ABN*	Algemene Bank Nederland	a Dutch bank
(het) ANP*	Algemeen Nederlands Persbureau	Dutch News Agency
(de) ANWB*	Algemene Nederlandse Wielrijdersbond	Dutch AA or R.A.C.
(de) AOW('er)*	Algemene Ouderdomswet	pension(-er)
a.s.	aanstaande	next
a.u.b.	alstublieft	please
aug.	augustus	August
(de) AVRO+	Algemene Vereniging Radio Omroep	a broadcasting association
(de) AWW*	Algemene Weduwen- en Wezenwet	Widows' pension
bl., blz.	bladzij(de)	page
(de) BRD	Bondsrepubliek Duitsland	German Federal Republic
(de) BTW*	Belasting Toegevoegde Waarde	Value Added Tax
(de) B.V.*	besloten vennootschap	Pty. Ltd.
bv	bijvoorbeeld	for example, eg.
(het) CDA*	Christen-Democratisch Appèl	Dutch political party
Cie	compagnie	company
(de) CP*	Centrumpartij	Dutch political party
(de) C.P.N.*	Communistische Partij van Nederland	communist party

C.S. *	*centraal station*	main station
dec.	*december*	December
derg. dgl.	*dergelijke*	and such
dhr.	*de heer*	Mr.
d.i.	*dat is*	i.e.
d.m.v.	*door middel van*	by means of
dr.	*dokter, doctor*	Doctor
drs.	*doctorandus*	a Dutch academic title (M.A.)
ds.	*dominee*	Reverend
d.w.z.	*dat wil zeggen*	i.e.
e.d.	*en dergelijke*	and such
(de) EEG *, *EG* *	*Europese (Economische) Gemeenschap*	(European) Common Market
EHBO *	*Eerste Hulp bij Ongelukken*	First Aid
enz.	*enzovoort(s)*	etcetera
(de) EO *	*Evangelische Omroep*	a broadcasting association
excl.	*exclusief*	excluding
f.	*florijn (= gulden)*	guilder
febr.	*februari*	February
fr.	*frank (eg. 50 fr.)*	franc
Frl.	*Friesland*	Friesland
geb.	*geboren*	born
(de) gebrs.	*gebroeders*	brothers
Gld.	*Gelderland*	Gelderland
Gr.	*Groningen*	Groningen
(de) H.A.V.O. +	*hoger algemeen voortgezet onderwijs (school)*	a form of secondary school
(de) H.B.S. *	*hogere burgerschool*	,,
H.fl.	*Hollandse florijnen (= gulden)*	guilders
H.K.H.	*Hare Koninklijke Hoogheid*	Her Royal Highness
H.M.	*Hare Majesteit*	Her majesty
(het) H.O.	*Hoger Onderwijs*	tertiary education
hs. (hss.)	*handschrift (handschriften)*	manuscript(s)
incl.	*inclusief*	including
i.p.v.	*in plaats van*	instead of
ir.	*ingenieur*	engineer (academic title)
i.v.m.	*in verband met*	in connection with
jan.	*januari*	January
jg.	*jaargang*	volume, series
Jhr.	*Jonkheer*	aristocratic title (Lord)
Jkvr.	*Jonkvrouw*	aristocratic title (Lady)
jl.	*jongstleden*	last, past
(de) KLM *	*Koninklijke Luchtvaartmaatschappij*	Royal Dutch Airlines
(het) KNMI *	*Koninklijk Nederlands Meteorologisch Instituut*	Dutch weather bureau

(de) KRO *	*Katholieke Radio-Omroep*	a broadcasting association
l.g.	*laatstgenoemde*	the latter, last mentioned
lic.	*licentiaat, licentie*	Belgian University degree (M.A.)
m.	*mannelijk*	masculine
(de) M.A.V.O.+	*middelbaar algemeen voortgezet onderwijs (school)*	a form of secondary school
Mej.	*Mejuffrouw*	Miss
Mevr.	*mevrouw*	Mrs.
m.i.	*mijns inziens*	in my opinion
Mij.	*maatschappij*	company
(de) MO *	*Middelbaar-Onderwijsakte*	secondary teaching diploma
Mr.	*Meester (in de rechten)*	Dutch academic title
mrt.	*maart*	March
ms. (mss.)	*manuscript(-en)*	manuscript(-s)
(de) M.U.L.O.+	*Meer Uitgebreid Lager Onderwijs (school)*	a form of secondary school
m.v.	*meervoud*	plural
Mw.	*Mevrouw/Mejuffrouw*	Ms.
n.a.v.	*naar aanleiding van*	with reference to
(de) NAVO+	*Noordatlantische Verdragsorganisatie*	NATO
N-B	*Noord-Brabant*	North Brabant
n. C(hr)	*na Christus*	A.D.
(de) NCRV *	*Nederlandse Christelijke Radio-Vereniging*	a broadcasting organisation
Ndl./Ned.	*Nederlands*	Dutch
N-H	*Noord-Holland*	North Holland
nl.	*namelijk*	namely
n.m.	*namiddags*	p.m.
(de) NOS+	*Nederlandse Omroep Stichting*	a broadcasting organisation
nov.	*november*	November
nr.	*nummer*	number
de N.S. *	*Nederlandse Spoorwegen*	Dutch Railways
(de) NSB('er) *	*Nationaal-Socialistische Beweging*	Dutch Nazi Party (Dutch Nazi)
(de) N.V. *	*naamloze vennootschap*	Pty. Ltd.
o.	*onzijdig*	neuter
o.a.	*onder andere(n)*	among others
okt.	*oktober*	October
O.L.V.	*Onze-Lieve-Vrouw*	Our Lady
o.l.v.	*onder leiding van*	under direction of
o.m.	*onder meer*	among other things
p., pag.	*pagina*	page
p.a.	*per adres*	c/o

pct.	*procent*	percent
p.k.	*paardekracht*	horse power
prk.	*post(giro)rekening*	postal account (giro)
*(de) PTT('er)**	*Posterijen, Telegrafie en Telefonie*	PMG (PMG employee)
*(de) PvdA**	*Partij van de Arbeid*	Dutch political party
R'dam	*Rotterdam*	Rotterdam
resp.	*respectievelijk*	respectively
R-K, r-k	*Rooms-Katholiek*	Roman Catholic
sept.	*september*	September
(de) SNV	*Stichting Nederlandse Vrijwilligers*	Volunteers Abroad
str.	*straat*	street
s.v.p.	*s'il vous plaît (= a.u.b.)*	please
t.a.v.	*ten aanzien van*	with regard to
	ter attentie van	att.
*t.b.c.**	*tuberculose*	t.b.
t.b.v.	*ten bate van*	in aid of
	ten behoeve van	on behalf of
*(de) TEE**	*Trans Europa Express*	international express train
tel.	*telefoonnummer*	telephone number
*(de) TH**	*Technische Hogeschool*	technical college
t/m	*tot en met*	up to and including
t.n.v.	*ten name van*	in the name of
t.o.v.	*ten opzichte van*	with relation to
(de) TROS+	*Televisie- en radio-omroep- stichting*	a broadcasting association
Ts.	*Tijdschrift*	periodical, magazine
t.u.	*te uwent*	at your place
t.w.	*te weten (= nl., d.i.)*	i.e., to wit
t.z.t.	*te zijner tijd*	in due course
u.	*uur (om 5 u.)*	o'clock
*(de) U.B.**	*de Universiteitsbibliotheek*	University Library
v.	*van*	of (in people's names too)
v., vr.	*vrouwelijk*	feminine
v.a.	*vanaf*	from
(de) VARA+	*Vereniging van Arbeiders- Radio-Amateurs*	a broadcasting association
v. C(hr.)	*voor Christus*	B.C.
v.d.	*van den/der/de*	of the (in people's names too)
vgl.	*(men) vergelijk(e)*	compare
vh.	*voorheen*	formerly
v.m.	*voormiddag*	a.m.
*(de) V.N.**	*Verenigde Naties*	United Nations
*(de) V.O.C.**	*Verenigde Oost-Indische Compagnie*	Dutch East India Co.
*(de) VPRO**	*Vrijzinnig Protestantse Radio-Omroep*	a broadcasting association

(de) VS *	*Verenigde Staten*	United States
(de) V.U. $^+$	*Vrije Universiteit te Amsterdam*	Free University of Amsterdam
(de) VUT $^+$	*Vervroegde Uittreding*	early retirement
(de) VVD *	*Volkspartij voor Vrijheid en Democratie*	Dutch political party
(de) VVV *	*Vereniging voor Vreemdelingen- verkeer*	Tourist bureau
(de) W.W. *[1]	*Werkloosheidwet*	unemployment benefits
(de) W.A. *	*Wettelijke aansprakelijkheid*	third party insurance
(de) W.A.O. *	*Wet op de arbeidsongeschiktheid*	invalid pension
zg. zgn.	*zogenaamd, zogenoemd*	so-called
Z-H	*Zuid-Holland*	South Holland
z.i.	*zijns inziens*	in his opinion
Z.K.H.	*Zijne Koninklijke Hoogheid*	His Royal Highness
Z.M.	*Zijne Majesteit*	His Majesty
z.o.z.	*zie ommezijde*	p.t.o.

---

1   *In de W.W. lopen* – to be on unemployment benefits

Index

The numbers given are page numbers. In many instances relevant information is also to be found on the pages immediately following the page indicated here.

Recommended texts for future reference

Apeldoorn, C.G.L.   *Afkortingslexicon*
Spectrum, Utrecht, 2nd ed. 1976

Coninck, R.H.B. de   *Groot Uitspraakwoordenboek van de Nederlandse Taal*
De Nederlandse Boekhandel, Antwerp 1970

Van Dale Groot Woordenboek der Nederlandse Taal,
Van Dale Lexicografie, Utrecht, 11th ed. 1984

Geerts, G, W. Haeseryn,   *Algemene Nederlandse Spraakkunst*
J. de Rooij, M.C. van der   Wolters-Noordhoff, Groningen, 1984
Toorn (ed.)

Hermkens, H.M.   *Spelling en Interpunctie*
Malmberg, Den Bosch

Hertog, C.H. den   *Nederlandse Spraakkunst* – bewerkt door H. Hulshof
Versluys, Amsterdam, 1973

Rijpma, E. and   *Nederlandse Spraakkunst*
Schuringa, F.G.   Wolters-Noordhoff, Groningen, 1969

Shetter, W.Z.   *Introduction to Dutch*
Martinus Nijhoff, The Hague, 5th ed., 1984

Smit, J. and Meijer, R.   *Dutch Grammar and Reader*
Stanley Thornes, London, 1976
Tacx, J.P.M.
Nederlandse Spraakkunst voor Iedereen
Spectrum, Utrecht, 10th ed. 1978

Toorn, M.C. van den   *Nederlandse Grammatica*
Tjeenk Willink, Groningen, 1976

Vooys, C.G.N. de   *Nederlandse Spraakkunst*
Wolters-Noordhoff, Groningen, 7th ed. 1967

Woordenlijst van de Nederlandse Taal
Staatsuitgeverij, The Hague, 1954